Essential Guide to Lt. General Herbert (H.R.) McMaster, National Security Advisor: Thinking and War Scholarship, Moral and Ethical Soldiers, War on Terrorism, Paper on Future Wars and Technology

* * * * * * * * * * *

U.S. Government, U.S. Military, Department of Defense (DoD), Lt. Gen. Herbert (H.R.) McMaster

* * * * * * * * * * *

Progressive Management

Questions? Suggestions? Comments? Concerns? Please contact the publisher directly at

bookcustomerservice@gmail.com

Remember, the book retailer can't answer your questions, but we can!

* * * * * * * * * * *

* * * * * * * * * * *

CONTENTS

* * * * * * * * * * *

2

Crack in the Foundation: Defense Transformation and the Underlying Assumption of Dominant Knowledge in Future War

Lieutenant Colonel Herbert R. McMaster

United States Army

USAWC STRATEGY RESEARCH PROJECT

Professor Stephen Biddle * Project Advisor

* * * * * * * * * * *

U.S. Army War College Carlisle Barracks, Pennsylvania 17013

* * * * * * * * * * *

07 April 2003

This paper examines and evaluates the basic assumption that underpins much of the defense transformation initiative. The intellectual foundation for building tomorrow's military force rests on the unfounded assumption that technologies emerging from the "information revolution" will lift the fog of war and permit U.S. forces to achieve a very high degree of certainty in future military operations. The assumption of dominant knowledge in future war threatens to undermine the best efforts of senior military and civilian officials and create vulnerabilities in future American forces. The paper examines the origin and growth of the assumption and demonstrates how it has pervaded and corrupted joint and service visions of future war and is already having a negative effect on doctrine and organization. The paper exposes the fallacy of near-certainty in future war using logic and military history including analysis of recent conflicts. Desert Storm, Somalia, Kosovo, and Operations Enduring Freedom and Iraqi Freedom receive particular attention. The paper also evaluates Joint experimentation and concept development and makes recommendations concerning the next steps to take in defense transformation. The paper concludes that an embrace of the uncertainty of war, balanced Joint Forces, effective joint integration, and adaptive leadership will prove critical to future national security.

* * * * * * * * * * *

* * * * * * * * * * * *

ACKNOWLEDGEMENTS

This study has benefited from the guidance of many officers, civilian defense officials, and professors. Colonel James Harris, USA, of the National Defense University and CAPT Scott Jasper of the Naval Postgraduate School helped direct my reading and thinking on defense transformation. The guidance of General John Shalikashvili and Secretary William Perry at the outset of the project proved invaluable. Professor Williamson Murray, Colonel Robert Cone and the rest of the team at the Joint Advanced Warfighting Project provided early direction and advice. I am indebted to the officers and Department of Defense Civilians of J7 and J8 on the Joint Staff as well as J9 and the Joint Futures Lab of Joint Forces Command for the time they took to explain the processes of concept development and experimentation. Officers at the Objective Force Task Force and Mounted Maneuver Battle Lab at Fort Knox, Kentucky helped illuminate Objective Force organization and doctrine. Professors James Wirtz and Douglas Porch of the Naval Postgraduate School as well as Dr. Conrad Crane of the U.S. Army War College Military History Institute gave me the benefit of their ideas and analysis of defense transformation. Dr. Stephen Biddle of the Strategic Studies Institute provided invaluable guidance. The environment of the Hoover Institution at Stanford University proved ideal for research, thought, and writing. Access to top scholars in all relevant disciplines informed my thinking and sharpened the analysis. Insights from Dr. Mark Peattie, Dr. Tom Henriksen, and Dr. Tom Metzger were particularly valuable. My colleagues in the National Security Fellows Program, Colonel Rocky Morrison USMC, Colonel Don Halpin USAF, and CAPT Bruce Fecht USN helped me gain access to service perspectives on transformation. I received valuable criticism and assistance from Professors Fred and Kim Kagan and Lieutenant Colonel Barrye Price. This effort would have been far narrower in scope and shallower in analysis had it not been for the invaluable assistance and insights of Ms. Sharmeen Obaid. The subject of this paper has been and is likely to remain contentious. Any errors or shortcomings are mine alone.

CRACK IN THE FOUNDATION

From Plato to NATO, the history of command in war consists of an endless quest for certainty.

— Martin Van Creveld

A failure to examine critically the fundamental assumption that underpins much of the defense transformation initiative threatens to undermine the best efforts of senior military and civilian officials and create vulnerabilities in future American forces. While this failure may not affect initiatives connected with homeland security, the ballistic missile defense program, or business practice reforms, it has permitted the development of an unrealistic vision of future conventional war. The intellectual foundation for building tomorrow's military force rests on the unfounded assumption that technologies emerging from the "information revolution" will lift the fog of war and permit U.S. forces to achieve a very high degree of certainty in future military operations.

Concepts for future war assume the ability to achieve "information superiority." Information superiority is defined variously as "the capability to collect, process, and disseminate an uninterrupted flow of information while exploiting an adversary's ability to do the same" or "an imbalance in one's favor in the information domain with respect to an adversary" or "that degree of dominance in the information domain which permits the conduct of operations without effective opposition." It is further assumed that information superiority will permit "dominant battlespace knowledge" or "the comprehensive awareness of all the decision-relevant elements within a defined battlespace, and the ability to predict, with a very high degree of confidence, nearterm enemy actions and combat outcomes." Another definition of dominant battlespace knowledge (DBK) is similar: "DBK involves everything from automated target recognition to knowledge of an opponent's operational scheme and the networks relied on to pursue that scheme. The result will be an increasing gap between U.S. military forces and any opponent in awareness and understanding of everything of military significance in any area in which we may be engaged." In addition to these terms, various others such as information dominance, dominant awareness, knowledge superiority, situational understanding, robust intelligence, and predictive intelligence represent a similar message: sensors, communications, computers, and information technologies will provide near-certainty in future war and permit the United States to overmatch future enemies.[1]

All descriptions of how near certainty is to be achieved are based primarily on emerging technologies. A Global Information Grid of "persistent surveillance" will gather information and share that information in a networked "collaborative information environment." Automated systems will fuse that intelligence and make possible "virtual collaboration among geographically dispersed" analysts who will generate intelligence and, ultimately, knowledge. Some even assume that this "robust intelligence" will deliver not only a clear appreciation for the current situation, but also generate "predictive intelligence" that will allow US forces to "anticipate the unexpected."[2] Despite its enthusiastic embrace, the assumption of near-certainty in future war is a dangerous fallacy.

This is not to say that the Department of Defense should pursue transformation with diminished vigor; many changes and initiatives are long overdue and the possibilities associated with emerging technologies are significant. Indeed, initiatives to develop and field new sensor, communications, and information management capabilities hold great promise for increasing the effectiveness of our military forces. The dramatic advances in command and control technologies, especially abilities to gain real-time access to imagery and maintain a clear picture of friendly forces, vastly improved the agility and interoperability of units during Operation Iraqi Freedom. The ability to translate intelligence into action was clearly evident in attacks on the Iraqi leadership as well as the flexibility to modify plans for the air campaign. Flawed assumptions about the nature of future war, however, are impeding effective change and preventing our forces from taking full advantage of emerging capabilities. What is required is a focused effort to define the nature of future conventional war at the operational and tactical levels as a basis for transformation efforts. The first step is to abandon explicitly the assumptions that future war will lie mainly in the realm of certainty and that American forces will be able to achieve and maintain information dominance during combat operations. If we fail to do so, transformation efforts based on that assumption would disadvantage rather than advantage our forces and create vulnerability rather than build strength.

MANDATE FOR CHANGE

I have an uneasy feeling that in engineering, as in other parts of our education and perhaps in many other parts of our experience, we are getting out of touch with the single, limiting circumstance, the resistant, intractable material, the hard particular that gets snowed by the general theoretical proposition.

—Elting Morison

For over a decade, the issue of defense reform generated numerous studies, a vast amount of literature, considerable debate, and disappointing results? Recognizing the lack of progress, President George W. Bush pledged "new thinking and hard choices" in defense. However, the time needed to make a comprehensive assessment as well as bureaucratic inertia slowed the Administration's efforts. Responses to the September 11, 2001 terrorist attacks including military operations in Afghanistan and the Philippines, homeland security initiatives, intelligence reforms, the build-up in the Persian Gulf region and Operation Iraqi Freedom caused further delay. Despite these obstacles and competing priorities, the Bush Administration remained committed to defense transformation. Indeed, only three months after the ill fated flight in that remote field in Pennsylvania and the murderous attacks on New York and Washington, D.C., President Bush renewed his commitment to reform defense citing a "sense of urgency" based on "the need to build this future force while fighting a present war." It would not be easy; he likened the effort to "overhauling an engine while you're going at eighty miles an hour." He insisted, however, that America had "no other choice.'4 In September 2002, Secretary of Defense Donald Rumsfeld told senior defense officials that the war on terrorism was not an excuse to delay defense transformation any further. He urged the Department to "accelerate our organizational, operational, business, and process reforms."5

According to the 2001 Quadrennial Defense Review (QDR), the purpose of defense transformation "is to maintain or improve US Military pre-eminence" through "the evolution and deployment of combat capabilities that provide revolutionary or asymmetric advantages to US Forces." Although transformation is often described as a continuous process rather than a destination, the QDR stated that current transformation efforts would have succeeded when "we divest ourselves of legacy forces and they move off the stage and resources move into new concepts, capabilities and organizations that maximize our warfighting effectiveness and the combat potential of our men and women in uniform." Successful transformation would allow the United States to "dominate future military competitions."6

The Department of Defense worked to impose direction and unity of effort on defense transformation.7 Under President George W. Bush, the Department has made progress in many areas including business practices, acquisition, and joint interoperability (the ability of the services and other agencies to plan and operate together synergistically). The Pentagon developed a new process for determining defense requirements to help ensure the relevancy of equipment and compatibility among all of the services. A "Joint Capability Integration and Development System" now prioritizes service requirements based on their contribution to "joint warfighting capabilities." The initiative holds promise for solving long-term problems like communications incompatibilities between the services. The Joint Requirements Oversight Council (JROC) increased its influence over the procurement process. "Evolutionary Acquisition and Spiral Development" processes aimed to accelerate the delivery of advanced capabilities.8 Efforts to improve the interoperability of the services included standardized communications, standard tactical procedures for operations such as close air support and urban combat, realistic joint training at all appropriate levels of command, and the establishment of Standing Joint Task Force Headquarters for each of the Regional Combatant Commands. The Department undertook a study to determine how to build on the successes of the Goldwater-Nichols Act of 1986 and advance joint professional military education. Inter-agency training and standardization of procedures to harmonize all elements of national power also received attention. The Office of Force Transformation now evaluates each of the service's transformation activities to recommend ways to integrate them into broader Defense Department efforts.9 The most significant initiative, however, received little public attention -the development of "Joint Operations Concepts" that articulate how American forces intend to fight the wars of the future.

The intellectual component of transformation will have a profound and lasting influence on future defense organization, education, training, and even institutional culture. President Bush pledged in February 2001, that "our defense vision" would "drive our defense budget, not the other way around."10 In August 2002, Secretary Rumsfeld directed the Chairman of the Joint Chiefs of Staff, General Richard Myers, to develop Joint Operations Concepts based on the Defense Planning Guidance. Secretary Rumsfeld intended to use the document to "test proposals from the various services" and determine whether they match the joint vision of future war. 11 The Joint Staff and Joint Forces Command, with assistance of the services, developed the concepts to describe "how the Joint Force intends to operate" and "provide the foundation for the development and acquisition of new capabilities." Their work will have broad implications; it is also intended to shape "development and acquisition of future capabilities across doctrine, organization, training, materiel, leadership and education, personnel, and facilities.12 In fact, the Department of Defense is already basing resource decisions on its idealized view of future military operations.13 As Vice Chairman of the Joint Chiefs of Staff General Peter Pace observed, there are high hopes that this "validated war-fighting concept that the services have all worked on together" will also increase joint interoperability.14 As the 2001 Quadrennial Defense Review stated, "choices made today may constrain or enhance options tomorrow."15 It is important to get the conception of future combat operations right.

Many of the ideas set out in the Joint Operations Concepts are fundamentally sound and propose using new technologies to operate effectively in emerging strategic and operational environments.16 Operation Iraqi Freedom exposed many of these capabilities to the American public. Proposals to use advances in communications and information technologies to permit collaborative planning and allow decentralized operations based on mission-oriented orders are particularly promising. The concept also identifies the need to keep forces dispersed, then concentrate rapidly as future adversaries develop many of the long-range surveillance and precision fires capabilities that America currently possesses. It is difficult to argue with the call for powerful joint forces capable of unprecedented strategic, operational, and tactical mobility -these seem precisely the capabilities that America needs to counter attempts to deny entry into a theater of operations and accelerate the deployment of Army units in particular. If resourced, the stated priority of developing an enhanced strategic lift capability will achieve a high degree of responsiveness and strategic agility. Perhaps most important, emphasis on joint integration and the "networking" of the force takes head on a pressing lesson from Desert Storm, operations in Afghanistan, and Operation Iraqi Freedom - that the services need a joint command and control architecture and a common understanding of how they operate together. The emphasis on Joint Forces that train together habitually will also generate vast improvements in combat capability.17 While technology is certain to improve the quality and timeliness of intelligence, the assumption that emerging technologies will lead to near-certainty undermines many of the positive aspects of defense transformation.

The new joint concept envisions "Full Spectrum Dominance Through Joint Integration." The concept promises to "defeat any adversary or control any situation across the full range of military operations" based on the capability to "sense, understand, decide, and act faster than any adversary in any situation." Commanders will receive "precise, fused intelligence at all levels of war" to facilitate "decision superiority," or the ability to make decisions faster than the enemy. Additionally, the high degree of certainty in future war will permit commanders to employ "tailored" joint forces in "globally and operationally distributed operations."18.

Joint Operations Concepts contains weaknesses and contradictions, all of which derive from the assumption of near certainty in future war. Contradictions arise mainly from the tension between that assumption and realities associated with the strategic environment and likely characteristics of future enemies. Overall the strategic environment is "dynamic, uncertain, and complex."19 Similarly, the paper describes potential adversaries as complex, adaptive, and capable of determined action with destructive technologies. Readers are warned that unique cultural, political, and geographical factors might enhance enemy capabilities and make enemy behavior difficult to predict. Likely enemy actions such as blurring the distinction between combatants and non-combatants or operating from ungoverned territories and urban areas will challenge US forces further. Because of American technological advantages, enemies will 20 disguise their behavior and "avoid US strengths and exploit our perceived weaknesses." Without explanation, what the paper portrayed as immanent uncertainties associated with an adaptive enemy operating in a complex environment succumb to the network and "robust intelligence." The enemy is reduced to "a system of nodes and linkages." Without addressing how specific obstacles to certainty might be overcome, the paper asserts that the "Joint Force must gain and maintain information superiority." A new definition of information superiority acknowledges a two-way fight for intelligence, but then assumes that US forces and commanders will win that fight:

The power of superiority in the information domain mandates that we fight for it as a first priority even before hostilities begin. This requires that we develop doctrine, TTPs, organizational relationships and technologies to win this two-sided fight. The quality of our information position depends upon the accuracy, timeliness and relevance of information from all sources. A priority responsibility of command is to ensure access to all relevant information sources within and among all DoD organizations, and in coalition operations with our mission partners. The continuous sharing of information from a variety of sources enables the fully networked Joint Force to achieve the shared situational awareness necessary for decision superiority. 21

The contradiction between the assumption of information superiority in future war and the "dynamic, uncertain, and complex" security environment undermines the intellectual foundation for defense transformation. The cause of that contradiction is the assumption that US forces will be able to achieve information superiority and dominant battlespace knowledge in future war.

Officers who worked on Joint Operations Concepts were skeptical about those assumptions and sought to suppress what they viewed as an unrealistic vision of war. Although they were successful in editing out the most extreme assertions such as claims that "robust intelligence" would permit commanders "not only to understand the adversary's current situation, but also to anticipate the unexpected," they were unable to eliminate the basic assumption of information superiority.22

Although the lack of evidence associated with the assumption of near-certainty in future war and its fundamental incompatibility with realities of the strategic environment seem sufficient to abandon the idea, the belief in information superiority and dominant knowledge in future war proved surprisingly resilient. Although, many questioned these assumptions, there was no official debate or deliberate effort to scrutinize them.23

When faced with criticism of dominant knowledge and its companion concepts, proponents avoided tough questions with increasingly ambiguous language and the argument that technology was still forthcoming. New terminology was in a perpetual state of reinvention. Adjectives such as dominant, seamless, precision, adapted, networked, integrated, tailorable, scalable, transparent, focused, robust, and full dimensional appeared with increasing frequency and were often linked together to multiply ambiguity. The difficulty of confronting directly the assumption of certainty in future war grew more remote as the confusing imprecise lexicon of transformation expanded. Additionally, qualifiers softened initial claims of perfect intelligence, but documents contained otherwise undiminished support for certainty in future war. "Perfect" became "near-perfect," but the meaning and consequences of the assumption remained unchanged.24

A combination of advocacy and passivity has also prevented exposure of flawed concepts and the assumptions that underpin them. Concept authors take ownership of their work and resolve to defend it rather than abandon bad ideas and go back to the drawing board. In briefings and working sessions, the language of transformation, when combined with PowerPoint slides, seems to lull what otherwise might be critical audiences into passivity. PowerPoint's "bulletizing" of ideas leads to shallow analysis. Color graphics and contrived charts substitute for thought and logic, yet create a facade of analytic credibility. The briefing dynamic often betrays an unspoken agreement between presenter and audience to give a higher priority to getting through the slides than examining the ideas and proposals that those slides represent.

While, it is clear that significant changes in the services and Department of Defense are necessary and are long overdue in some cases, it is dangerous to regard change as a virtue in itself. Change has become a mantra and the general need to adapt to new realities in defense gave "out of the box" ideas special status, often regardless of quality or degree of development. The Department of Defense and each of the services have held conferences on how to effect change. The services portrayed themselves in the midst of radical transformation and all adopted the language of transformation even as some of the best-developed concepts for change were disregarded. 25 There are clear incentives to support the flawed vision of future war. In addition to the possibility of being labeled as an unimaginative Luddite, those who are not seen as sufficiently visionary stand to lose the confidence of senior leadership. Indeed, retired Vice Admiral Arthur Cebrowski, the head of the Department of Defense's Office of Force Transformation, stated that the "future elite must recognize disruptive technologies or processes, and the associated opportunities they present, as they emerge."26 A failure to support new concepts might also result in a loss of resources for one's service or program. New "metrics" that grade how "transformative" programs are serve as a basis for funding decisions.27

The underlying assumption about future war generated contradictions in Joint Operations Concepts and is undermining the vitally important enterprise of defense transformation. There is an obvious contradiction between acknowledging the uncertainty of contemporary strategic and operational environments and asserting that war in those environments will be nearly certain, low cost, low risk, and efficient. Acceptance of a flawed vision of future war persists despite an utter lack of evidence and recent combat experience that runs directly counter to it. Understanding the origin of the idea of near-certainty in future war and how it gained official sanction will prove helpful in repairing the intellectual foundation of defense transformation.

MISUNDERSTOOD VICTORY AND THE ALLURE OF SIMPLE TRUTH

What I want to suggest here is the persistent human temptation to make life more explicable by making it more calculable; to put experience into some logical scheme that by its order and niceness will make what happens seem more understandable, analysis more bearable, decision simpler—. And this seems to have been the human tendency from the time of Plato's quantification of the Guardian's role right on down.

—Elting Morison

The years 1989 through 1991 marked a watershed in American national security policy. Events forced America away from the familiar dangers of the Cold War and the structures designed to control those dangers. Dramatic geopolitical changes including the emancipation of Eastern Europe, the breakup of the Soviet Empire, and the concomitant end of the Cold War moved American national security interests away from containing and deterring the Soviet Union toward other priorities such as the promotion of regional stability and prevention of nuclear proliferation. The changes were welcome, but brought with them a high degree of uncertainty. Ebullient optimism about a "New World Order" followed the triumph of capitalism and democracy over communism and totalitarianism, but was short lived. Indeed, the post-Cold War world emerged as anything but "orderly;" conflicts engulfed Southwest Asia, the Balkans, and portions of Africa. Scholars began to describe the world of the 1990s as chaotic and increasingly prone to devastating conflict. 28.

By the middle 1990s, dialectic was apparent between profound uncertainty concerning the strategic environment and the belief that future war will lie squarely in the realm of certainty. Confidence in American power grew out of victory in the Cold War and the impressive performance of the US military in the 1991 Gulf War. The causes of overwhelming victory in the Gulf War, however, were misunderstood and that misunderstanding generated flawed assumptions about the nature of future war. Flushed with victory and impressed with American technological superiority, many believed that new technologies in the areas of surveillance, communications, long-range precision weaponry, and stealth made possible a new way of waging war. An emerging thesis of future war depended on an unfounded yet widely accepted belief that sensors, communications, and information technologies would generate near-certainty in armed conflict. → Gulf War

By the mid-1990s, many observers concluded that the overwhelming military victory in Desert Storm provided not only a demonstration of American military prowess, but also revealed a solution to post-Cold War national security problems. In 1994, defense analyst Andrew Krepinevich suggested that America might be on the verge of a military revolution. He argued that such a revolution: "occurs when the application of new technologies into a significant number of military systems combines with innovative operational concepts and organizational adaptations in a way that fundamentally alters the character and conduct of conflict." 29 The prevailing explanation for victory in the Gulf War - technological superiority - led many to believe that America had already generated or now had the opportunity to craft a "revolution in military affairs" or RMA. A National Defense University study that consulted major commanders from the Gulf War, for example, suggested that if America invested its defense dollars mainly to develop new technologies, it could create capabilities that would "shock and awe" potential adversaries and thereby compel behavior consistent with US interests. In short, the technology would not only provide a capability, it would also provide a strategy. The argument relied on the ability to achieve a high degree of certainty in future war.

While there is much talk about "military revolutions" and winning the "information war," what is generally meant in this lexicon and discussion is translated into defense programs that relate to accessing and "fusing" information across command, control, intelligence, surveillance, target identification, and precision strike technologies. What is most exciting among these revolutions is the potential to achieve "dominant battlefield awareness," that is, achieving the capability to have near-perfect knowledge and information of the battlefield while depriving the adversary of that capacity and producing "systems of systems" for this purpose. 30

Despite the focus of Krepinevich and others on the organizational and conceptual components of military revolutions, emphasis remained on technology. The belief in near-certainty in future war led many to conclude that a strategy of "shock and awe," the term popularized seven years later during Operation Iraqi Freedom, was the answer to the problem of future war.

Some advocates were particularly enthusiastic about the RMA. Immediately following the 1991 Gulf War, Colonel John Warden, the lead planner for the Desert Storm air campaign announced "a new kind of war had its birth in Mesopotamia." He asserted that America's technological capabilities including the ability to identify, target, and hit critical nodes with precision strikes rendered the Iraqi cause hopeless after the first week of bombing. The fact that the Iraqi Army was not removed from Kuwait until after four additional weeks of bombing and a large ground offensive seemed not to matter. Warden declared the Gulf

shock & awe
Napolean — calvary.
infantry

War as the first in a new era of "hyper-war" in which American forces would have the unprecedented ability to "find the enemy 24 hours a day and strike—with precision means."31

The belief that industrial age warfare had been supplanted by yet-to-be-defined information age warfare gained wide acceptance. Adherents to the technological superiority explanation for overwhelming victory in the Gulf not only advocated the aggressive pursuit of new technologies such as sensors and precision weapons, they also argued that the capabilities associated with these technologies would be decisive in future war. New concepts for the employment of these technologies, many believed, could bias future military operations dramatically in favor of the U.S. for the foreseeable future.32

When evidence from the Gulf War became accessible, however, studies revealed that the technological superiority explanation for overwhelming victory was simplistic. Dr. Stephen Biddle, one of the first analysts to gain access to detailed data on the ground war, concluded that it was a combination of Iraqi errors, American technological superiority, and a dramatic skill imbalance between Iraqi and coalition forces that produced powerful, "nonlinear" results.33

Indeed, Desert Storm was a far less "precise" war than many believed in the immediate aftermath of victory. American forces encountered significant difficulties and experienced a high degree of uncertainty.34 The air forces were unable to target the Iraqi nuclear program due to a lack of intelligence. Air crews fought through inadequate intelligence, equipment malfunctions, and poor weather. The ground offensive permitted some Iraqi units to escape, in part, due to imprecise communications and differences in perspectives between theater, army, and corps commanders. Confusion and incomplete information characterized ground operations at the Corps level and below. 35 Additionally, imprecise coordination measures between Air Force and Army units created gaps in responsibility that permitted Iraqi armored forces to move unimpeded by air power. 36 Perhaps the most significant consequence of uncertainty was the decision in Washington to implement a cease fire after one hundred hours of ground combat, a decision that permitted much of the Iraqi Republican Guard to withdraw with equipment, repress incipient uprisings, and bolster the regime of Saddam Hussein.37

The effects of air power were impressive, but were also exaggerated. The Gulf War Air Power Study concluded that the air war revealed "no fundamental breaks with the past." Numbers of enemy vehicles destroyed in the air campaign were inflated, due, in part, to successful Iraqi deception operations. After the air campaign, the Iraqi Army retained a large force of over 1750 tanks, 900 armored personnel carriers, and 1450 artillery pieces. Despite claims that the Iraqis were incapable of communicating with or repositioning forces, large Republican Guard units reoriented to the West in an attempt to block the coalition enveloping attack. Republican Guard forces were well supplied and morale was high; units fought with determination. 38

Air power did, however, disrupt Iraqi command of control, constrain Iraqi logistics, dismantle the air defense system, cause significant attrition on enemy ground forces, decrease enemy morale (and in the case of some conscript units break their will to fight), bolster the confidence of friendly troops, and ensure freedom of action of U.S. and coalition units with absolute air supremacy. Those accomplishments were critical to achieving the overwhelming victory. 39 They did not, however, signal revolutionary change in the nature of war.

Others argued that generalizing about the nature of future war based on the experience of Desert Storm was inherently unwise. Historian Martin van Creveld noted the myriad weaknesses of the Iraqi military and observed that the war occurred almost exclusively on coalition terms and lacked "the interplay between opposing forces that an alert opponent would have created."40 The Gulf War Air Power Study warned explicitly against basing conclusions about the nature of future war on Operation Desert Storm because of political, geographic, and military factors unique to that experience. The study concluded that the Gulf War presented ideal conditions for an air campaign (i.e. air supremacy, desert terrain, and a mechanized conventional enemy); it would be unrealistic thinking to hope for similar conditions in future conflict.41 The survey identified two major factors that limited the effectiveness of air power despite those ideal conditions: "the inherent uncertainties in the information on which action in war must inevitably be based; and the often unseen or unpredictable consequences of those actions." 42 Yet, the technological explanation for victory grew and contributed to the belief that a revolution in military affairs might soon produce near-perfect intelligence that, when combined with precision weaponry, would constitute the key to future victories.43

Misperceptions persisted despite evidence and analysis to the contrary, in part, because popular images from the Gulf War portrayed impressive technologies and flawless operations that went exactly according to plan. In contrast to media coverage of Operation Iraqi Freedom, reporters did not witness close combat on the ground and the public was left with only videos of precision strikes against fixed targets and hapless Iraqi conscripts surrendering in droves without a fight. By the time that mistaken claims of technological success such as the destruction of mobile SCUD missile launchers in Iraq's western desert or the defeat of the Iraqi spoiling attack at Khafji by air power were corrected, the public's attention had turned away from the war. Misunderstood success created the idea that America was in the midst of a revolution in military affairs.44 Only one obstacle remained for those who advocated pursing the dream of the RMA - what the Gulf War Air Power Study had called "the inherent uncertainties" of war and "unseen or unpredictable consequences" of actions in combat.45 With precision intelligence, precision weapons could become the decisive instruments of war.

Disconnecting armed conflict from ambiguity and uncertainty, however, meant overturning Carl von Clausewitz's theory of war. The theory contained in Clausewitz's On War had a profound influence on American military thought, especially after the Vietnam War. On War provided much of the intellectual foundation for the post-Vietnam renaissance in doctrine, education, and training -- reforms that produced the forces of Operation Desert Storm.46 Military officers embraced Clausewitz's description of war as complex and unpredictable. Air and ground training centers tried to replicate the conditions of battle with live exercises against capable, thinking enemies. The prevailing conception of war as unpredictable and chaotic shaped service cultures; the Army and Marine Corps encouraged mission orders, initiative at all levels of leadership, and decentralization.

While Clausewitz did not treat uncertainty in war in an organized manner, he identified several factors that cause it: the "politics" of war, the human dimension of war, the complexity of war, and the interaction or non-linearity of war.47 Those factors are not susceptible to elimination with technology.

A fundamental source of uncertainty is the political nature and context of war. Writing in the wake of Prussia's defeat in the Napoleonic Wars of the early nineteenth century, Clausewitz witnessed the French Revolution unleash powerful social and political dynamics that changed the nature of war. War was an extension of politics by other means; war's conduct depended in large measure on subjective factors such as the will of the people, the wisdom of political objectives, and consistency between those objectives and military strategy. Other factors, such as the culture, political identity and interests of the people who are the object of military operations or populate the battleground increase complexity and influence the course of events. Because the political determinants of war rarely exhibit homogeneity, constancy, or certainty, political tensions and ambiguities carry over into military strategy and operations. Because war is indeed an extension of politics, it is impossible to have uncertain, unpredictable strategic and operational environments, yet enjoy certainty in military operations. 48

Because so many factors interact to determine the conditions of war, it is impossible to achieve certainty or guarantee outcomes. Because of war's complexity, Clausewitz stressed the pervasiveness of chance and the need for a commander to use intuition, look for opportunities, and turn the unpredictability of war to advantage.49

One such struggle or interaction takes place in the psychological and emotional realms and effects fighting power on both sides. War is a unique human activity that involves killing and the prospect of death. Uncertainty both derives from and reinforces the strains of war in ways that defy prediction. In his classic study of battles spanning six centuries, historian John Keegan found that this dimension of war provided continuity in the experience of combat despite dramatic social, organizational, and technological change. He observed that: W" hat battles have in common is human: the behavior of men struggling to reconcile their instinct for self-preservation, their sense of honor and the achievement of some aim over which other men are ready to kill them."50 Similarly, Clausewitz observed that danger, "is part of the friction of war."51 Indeed, what some refer to as the moral domain of war involves psychological and emotional dynamics that defy quantification or prediction.

Even if sensors were able to identify all enemy positions, the human and psychological dimensions of war would preserve uncertainty. Clausewitz was sensitive to the qualitative and moral sources of fighting ability. Clausewitz provided an example of how the human and psychological dimension of war preserves uncertainty. In the following passage, Clausewitz observed that prior to direct contact with the enemy it is impossible to know "whether the first shock of battle will steel the enemy's resolve and stiffen his resistance, or whether, like a Bologna flask, it will shatter as soon as its surface is scratched." Even with near-perfect information on the enemy one still has to "guess the extent of debilitation and paralysis that the drying up of particular sources of supply and the severing of certain lines of communication will cause in the enemy; guess whether the burning pain of the injury he has been dealt with make the enemy collapse with exhaustion or, like a wounded bull, arouse his rage; guess whether the other powers will be frightened or indignant, and whether and which political alliances will be dissolved or formed."52 Additionally, the enemy commander's intentions remain unclear until he is forced to reveal them.

Clausewitz observed that war is not "directed at inanimate matter." It is directed at an "animate object that reacts." 53

Several scholars have compared Clausewitz's observation concerning war as an "interaction of opposites" with contemporary non-linearity and chaos theories. In addition to psychological and emotional interactions, war at its fundamental level entails interaction between the combatant forces. Clausewitz also observed that various factors that influence war also interact with one another and make linear progression toward goals and objectives impossible. Clausewitz suggested that the theory of war be considered as "an object suspended between three magnets" of the "blind natural force of violence, hatred, and enmity—, chance and probability—, and war's rational subordination to the policy of government." Consistent with Chaos theory, these countless and continuous interactions in an unstable environment generate innumerable possibilities that defy prediction.54

Clausewitz observed that uncertainty and the factors that preserve it generate a friction that makes "action in war like movement in a resistant element."55 Friction is both a product and a cause of uncertainty. Friction, however, is not immutable and technology can greatly reduce it. There is no doubt that technology has ameliorated sources of uncertainty since Clausewitz observed that three quarters of the factors on which action in war is based are wrapped in the "fog" of war. 56 Digital communications and the ability to see all friendly forces and much of the enemy on a digital maps, has reduced the fog of war greatly. During Iraqi Freedom, images of American forces using global positioning systems to move rapidly despite blinding desert sandstorms illustrated come of the power associated with these technologies. Equipment that permits staffs to develop orders and graphics rapidly and burst them across the battle area so all participants have a common operating picture and understanding of the plan has also reduced friction and increased speed of action. Routine training at the joint level and standardized tactics will reduce further the friction and uncertainty of war. While it is vitally important to take all possible measures to reduce uncertainty and friction, it is equally important to recognize those factors that preserve uncertainty as a basic feature of war.

As technology advances, new sources of uncertainty emerge. Precision weapons, for example, demand better intelligence. The speed, precision, lethality, and range of weapon systems have compressed events in time such that commanders must make decisions faster and therefore have less time to process and evaluate intelligence. The sheer volume of information available and the fact that much of it is conflicting or irrelevant "noise" confuses situations further.

The technology-based assumption of dominant battlespace knowledge gained acceptance even though technology could not remove the causes of uncertainty that Clausewitz identified. In January of 1995, Admiral William Owens, the Vice Chairman of the Joint Chiefs of Staff, suggested that it would soon be possible to "see and understand everything on the battlefield." Just seven months later he declared that new technologies "will allow us to dominate battlefield awareness for years to come—. And while some people say there will always be a 'fog of war,' I know quite a lot about these programs."57 Whether one accepts certainty or uncertainty as the dominant condition of war is important because the type of force one designs, the training that force conducts, the education of officers, and military culture will differ greatly based on that fundamental belief.

Admiral Owens' assertion of certainty in future wars appealed to Americans' faith in technological solutions to complex problems as well as a more general cultural belief in progress through applied science and engineering. 58

It was also a case of wishful thinking—a definition of war as one would like war to be. Admiral Owens was not alone in overlooking the human and psychological dimensions of war. Many other military theorists have simply ignored those factors that could not be quantified.59 Clausewitz's criticism of his contemporaries who posed simple, prescriptive solutions to the problem of war remains appropriate today: "They aim at fixed values; but in war everything is uncertain—. They direct inquiry exclusively toward physical quantities, whereas all military action is entwined with psychological forces and effects. They consider only unilateral action, whereas war consists of continuous interactions of opposites."60 Clausewitz used words like uncertain, dangerous, primordial violence, hatred, and destruction to describe the physical and emotional milieu of war.61 Admiral Owens' image of war permitted a "system of systems" approach that promised to "dissipate the fog of war" and permit the use of force "without the same risks as before."62 As Alan Beyerchen has observed, this sort of reduction is natural among people who are educated to understand linear systems and are thereby conditioned to believe that "truth" lies in simplicity rather than complexity.63

The new theories of war took on names that evoked a sense of control and swept the imagination off the battlefield and into the computer room and command center: cyber war, third wave warfare, information age war, and later, network-centric warfare. Each version of an evolving theory of war was grounded in the assumption that technology would provide certainty. Under these constructs, wars would be efficient and even more humane. Near-perfect information would make possible precise application of force from great distances which would, in turn, reduce the risk to US forces, minimize "collateral damage," and even make the battlefield a safer place for the enemy; US forces would use the exact amount of force necessary to achieve desired effects.

Although it became fashionable to include selective, usually flawed historical examples to justify new theories of war, there was a sense among true believers that emerging technologies were so revolutionary that historical experience no longer applied. Paradoxically, the future appeared much clearer to them than the past or present. Because of misunderstood victory in the Gulf War, American faith in technological solutions, a simplistic understanding of the nature of war, and a desire to make war easier and even humane, faith in certainty continued to gather adherents. Even contrary combat experience could not overcome its appeal and growing acceptance.

The American experience in Somalia between December 1992 and early 1994 might have exposed the folly of assuming information superiority. The United States military intended Operation Restore Hope to be what it was then calling an "operation other than war." The mission was to impose enough stability for the United Nations to first stop mass starvation, then facilitate long-term political and economic reforms. The complex operational environment included the lack of central government, the absence of law and order, and a complex web of competing clans. Ultimately, the complexity of the social-political situation in Somalia interacted with UN initiatives to create a chaotic, unpredictable situation that undermined the plans of the United Nations and the United States.

Technological sources of intelligence were of little value in Somalia. Commanders relied on human intelligence as the primary source of information. As General Anthony Zinni, then Director of Operations at United Nations Task Force Somalia recalled, he had access to very good technical intelligence, but sensors could not: "penetrate the faction leaders and truly understand what they were up to. Or maybe understand the culture, the clan association affiliation, the power of the faction leaders, and maybe understanding some of the infrastructure too."64 The experience in Somalia demonstrated the folly of assuming that military certainty can derive from sensors and other technical means of gathering and assessing information.

Ambiguities in American policy objectives contributed to uncertainty, especially as operations shifted from humanitarian assistance to capturing a powerful clan leader, General Mohammed Farah Aidid. To protect his base of power Aidid undermined the United Nations' effort. After militiamen loyal to General Aidid ambushed two Pakistani units on 5 June 1993 a battalion of US Army Rangers and Special Operations Forces received the mission to hunt down and capture the warlord. That fundamental change in American military operations was authorized under a previous United Nations resolution, but the significance of the decision was lost on the five-month-old administration of President Bill Clinton.65 Even as Task Force Ranger arrived and combat operations such as raids were intensifying, the Administration endeavored to portray a small and decreasing commitment to the mission. After the administration denied military commanders' requests for armored vehicles; the lack of those capabilities increased both risk and uncertainty in operations. U.S. forces became reliant on allies, many of whom did not share U.S. priorities or sense of urgency and were not subordinate to American command66 Uncertainty in Somalia stemmed from politics in Washington as well as the confusing political situation within the country.

Strategic and operational uncertainties were amplified at the tactical level. Soldiers and marines operated in a populous, congested urban area in which almost everyone was armed; it was difficult to distinguish between friendly forces, neutrals, and those opposed to the humanitarian effort. For marines and soldiers, the complex social, political, and geographical environment blurred distinctions between peacekeeping operations and combat operations. Confiscation of weapons, for example, was often contested and could lead to firefights with clans unwilling to give up arms or even submit to inspections. Blurred distinctions between peacekeeping and combat operations led Major General Tom Montgomery to remark, "If this isn't combat, then I'm sure having a helluva nightmare." 67

Convoluted command channels and disagreements between the participating nations added to the uncertainty of the situation. The Pakistanis, stung by the horrible ambushes of 5 June were reluctant to take unnecessary risks. Italians were generally sympathetic to General Aidid and were widely believed to be one of the General's intelligence sources. The resultant reluctance to share intelligence created greater uncertainty. Because it was a strategic asset, Task Force Ranger complicated matters further. Although the force was under "tactical control" of US Forces Somalia, it also remained under the "operational control" of U.S. Central Command, headquartered in Tampa, Florida. Its orders and reports flowed from and to Central Command without going through U.S. or UN headquarters in Somalia. A study of lessons learned in Somalia concluded that the complex command relationship "effectively created a condition that allowed no one to set clear unambiguous priorities."68

 The inherent uncertainties of the Somalia operation were revealed and amplified on October 3, 1993 as U.S. Army Rangers began what they thought would be a mission of short duration to apprehend two of General Aidid's principal deputies. Despite initially confusing reports, intelligence sources located the "targets" near the Olympic Hotel in Mogadishu. Despite American technological superiority, a Somali warlord was able to achieve information superiority over Task Force Ranger during the raid. Spies working for Aidid were in all American troop locations. They provided intelligence and early warning to the rogue warlord and his deputies. They watched American forces conduct previous operations, identified patterns, and planned to attack vulnerabilities.69 The result was tactical surprise over Task Force Ranger and a desperate fourteen-hour fight in a densely populated, hostile urban environment.

The interactions that occurred between Somali militia and the Rangers defied situational understanding: the shoot-down of two helicopters, heroic actions by isolated teams of American soldiers against armed mobs, repeated attacks by armed Somalis who used women and children as shields, application of tremendous firepower from American helicopters and the dispatch of wheeled convoys, multiple Somali ambushes against those convoys, and the commitment of an armored reaction force including Pakistani and Malay forces. It is difficult to imagine a more confusing fight from the vantage points both of the command post and the soldiers and leaders engaged in action. 70

As a close observer of urban combat noted, "the realities of urban warfare mean that the fog of war remains to a considerable degree impenetrable even to the latest technology." Although the soldiers of Task Force Ranger won a fight in which they were grossly outnumbered, the Battle of Mogadishu highlighted many of the inherent limits of technology and revealed the absurdity of basing military doctrine and organization on the assumption of information superiority.71

Growing confidence in technology as the answer to the problem of future war, however, overwhelmed the lessons of Somalia. Despite the inescapable conclusion that the technologies that were supposed to provide certainty in future war could not even influence the causes of uncertainty in Somalia, the growing effort to use the assumption of information superiority as the basis for conceptualizing future war continued. RMA advocates argued that it was unnecessary for theories to be grounded in current realities because even better technology was on the way.72 A belief in insurmountable American military supremacy developed among senior military and civilian officials that manifested itself in the often-heard declaration that the United States would have "no peer competitor until [at least] 2020.73 Because of American technological predominance, some assumed that America enjoyed a period of easy security during which emphasis ought to be placed on futuristic concepts and the development of "leap ahead" technologies. The absence of any perceived threat led many to argue that historical or recent experience was irrelevant and confining. Grounding change in reality would result in unimaginative solutions to the problem of future war. It was important, they argued, not to miss an opportunity to "skip a generation" to extend American dominance well into the twenty-first century. Those who saw revolutionary promise in new technologies seemed to regard the lack of evidence for their claims as an indicator of their powers of imagination rather than a deficiency.

Millenialism, may have reinforced this tendency. Some declared that the end of the millenium coincided with a "new epoch of conflict" with "no good old-fashioned wars in sight.74 Although most qualified their description of this new epoch with statements that technology "can never eliminate completely the fog" of war, they assumed a level of certainty that redefined the nature of war. By 1996, the language of defense transformation began to exhibit a remarkable degree of confidence, promising "full spectrum dominance," essentially the capability to defeat decisively any adversary or control any situation.

Paradoxically, these declarations of American dominance grew as the readiness of America's military dropped. As the Department of Defense spoke of revolutionary technologies, shortages in repair parts, lack of training funds, turbulence associated with force reductions, and a dramatic increase in overseas deployments placed great strains on the military. Even a partial list of missions that the Department of Defense conducted during the eight years of the Clinton administration indicates how stretched forces were: operations in Somalia, air campaigns in Bosnia and Kosovo and against Serbia and Iraq, peacekeeping deployments to Bosnia, Haiti, Rwanda, and Kosovo, support for Haitian refugees in Guantanamo Bay, continuous operations in Iraq and deployments to Southwest Asia in response to Saddam Hussein's intransigence, and strikes in Afghanistan and Sudan.75 The lack of a sound strategy to transition from a Cold War to a post-Cold War defense organization was taking its toll. Formal defense planning efforts such as the 1993 Bottom-Up Review and the 1997 Quadrennial Defense Review exhibited inconsistencies between strategy, force structure, and resources.76 Critics characterized the 1990s as a period of "paralysis" in connection with Defense reform.77

While military and civilian leaders of the services and Department of Defense coped with the consequences of over-commitment and lack of direction, significant shifts in the intellectual basis for transformation occurred. Revolutionary concepts of future war might have provided a welcome escape from readiness crises and increasing demands on the force. An overworked officer corps contracted out many of the intellectual functions of the military. Based on a flawed understanding of victory in the Gulf war and bolstered by dreams of American technological dominance of any opponent, the assumption of certainty in future war received official sanction in a document published by the Chairman of the Joint Chiefs of Staff in 1996.

General John Shalikashvili intended Joint Vision 2010 to serve as the "conceptual template for how America's Armed Forces will channel the vitality and innovation of our people and leverage technological opportunities to achieve new levels of effectiveness in warfighting." 78

Information technology and assumptions about how that technology would change war formed the basis for the concepts contained in JV2010. Improvements in information and systems integration technologies will also significantly impact future military operations by providing decision makers with accurate information in a timely manner. Information technology will improve the ability to see, prioritize, assign, and assess information. The fusion of all source intelligence with the fluid integration of sensors, platforms, command organizations, and logistic support centers will allow a greater number of operational tasks to be accomplished faster. Advances in computer processing, precise global positioning, and telecommunications will provide the capability to determine accurate locations of friendly and enemy forces, as well as to collect, process, and distribute relevant data to thousands of locations. Forces harnessing the capabilities potentially available from this system of systems will gain dominant battlespace awareness, an interactive "picture" which will yield much more accurate assessments of friendly and enemy operations within the area of interest.

JV2010 stated that technological advances would "not eliminate the fog of war," but asserted that dominant battlespace awareness would "make the battlespace considerably more transparent." 79

Despite the qualifiers, the Department of Defense and each of the services embraced certainty as a condition of future war and the basis for transformation efforts. In his cover letter to the 1997 Quadrennial Defense Review Report to Congress, Secretary of Defense William Perry placed information superiority at "the heart" of defense transformation and identified the "key to success" in future war as "an integrated system of systems that would give [forces] superior battlespace awareness permitting them to dramatically reduce the fog of war." 80

The assumption of near-certainty in future war exerted an immediate influence on the American armed forces. What was supposed to be a vision of the future became an organizing imperative for the current force. The Army, for example, accepted uncritically the promised reduction in the uncertainty of war. Based on that acceptance, the Army reorganized the division in a way that cut twenty-five percent of its heavy close combat formations, centralized logistical assets, and preserved command and staff overhead. In constructive computer simulation exercises designed to "validate" the new design, near perfect intelligence permitted centralized targeting of large conventional forces such that long-range rocket artillery, Apache helicopters, and other fires compensated for the division's reduction in combat power. The new division was "smaller" yet "more lethal" because the assumption of dominant knowledge gave the unit "situational understanding."81

Acceptance of the assumption of certainty in future war was illogical because the claimed source of certainty - technology - was unable to remove or even reduce significantly principal sources of uncertainty in war. Indeed, the idea that future war would be near-certain failed to account for enemy actions, reduced the complexity of warfare to identifying and targeting things, and ignored the human and psychological dimensions of war. After it received official endorsement in JV2010, however, the assumption of near-certainty in future war continued to gain wide acceptance in the Department of Defense and within the services.

Ignorance of history, a misunderstanding of the Gulf War, and a failure to learn from even contemporary combat experiences such as the battle of Mogadishu permitted a fundamentally flawed assumption to become orthodoxy. While officers were reminded of the old quotation that the only thing harder than getting a new idea into the military mind is to get an old one out, the real problem was a lack of skepticism and critical inquiry.

Historian Williamson Murray found that the familiar contention that military institutions fail in war because they focus too closely on the last war is incorrect. In the often-cited case of German military triumph and French defeat in 1940, for example, the Germans benefited from a detailed study of World War I to determine what really happened and identify implications for future war. Meanwhile, the French studied their last war only superficially and used selective observations to justify existing organizations and doctrinal trends. The French avoided meaningful debate and designed wargames and exercises to ensure results that reinforced flawed assumptions. As historian Eugenia Kiesling observed, "hard truths were blurred both by optimistic language and by refusal to ask questions whose answers might have proved unsettling."82 Because flawed assumptions escaped exposure, French military doctrine and institutional culture developed in a way that was incongruous with the conditions of war in 1940. When the Germans invaded, the French, who had assumed they would be able to conduct "methodical battle," maintain communications, prevent surprise, and control operations very closely were paralyzed and unable to contend with the actual conditions of war. 83

Operation Iraqi Freedom and other recent conflicts represent opportunities to learn from contemporary experience, repair the intellectual foundation of defense transformation, and build a capable force for the future. Understanding how deeply flawed assumptions about the nature of future war have penetrated the Department of Defense and each of the Services is a necessary first step in setting a new course.

THEORY OVER PRACTICE

Theory cannot be accepted as conclusive when practice points the other way.

—Charles E. Callwell

After the 1991 Gulf war, the Air Force embraced the concepts of information superiority and dominant battlespace knowledge enthusiastically. Certainty in war, when combined with increased accuracy of weapons would permit the Air Force finally to achieve decisive, fast, efficient, and low-cost victory in war through air power; it was a vision that airmen had pursued since 1918.84 As the precision of weapons increased, target identification and target location remained limiting factors in the application of air power. 85

Precision weapons demand precision intelligence and thereby generate demands for even more accurate information. In late 1996, Air Force Chief of Staff General Ronald Fogleman, referring to the idea of dominant battlespace awareness in JV2010, declared that "in the first quarter of the twenty-first century, it will be possible to find, fix or track, and target anything that moves on the surface of the earth." He declared the Air Force "capable of dominating enemy operations in all dimensions of warfare: land, sea, air, and, in the future, space across a spectrum of time and conflict."86 General Fogleman's assertions were consistent with the Air Force's faith in technology and confidence gained while operating in the most transparent of the "dimensions" he mentioned.

The pursuit of dominance from the air required more resources. As General Fogleman predicted dominant awareness in future war, the Air Force was in the midst of a budget battle over funding its new fighter aircraft, the F-22. In this context, the Air Force marketed a new concept called the "Halt Phase Strategy." The Halt concept assumed that "superior knowledge" was already attainable and would permit the Air Force to dominate future battlefields, especially early in a conflict. The Halt strategy, however, suffered from obvious limits in its applicability. The enemy it portrayed, a large invading mechanized ground force, was a mirror image of US heavy forces. The strategy failed to consider countermeasures to American technologies such as dispersion, concealment, deception, and intermingling with civilian populations. 87

21

The Halt strategy met skepticism because of the difficulty of identifying and targeting an enemy determined to foil American technological capabilities.88 In 2002, the Air Force Transformation Flight Plan announced a remedy for that difficulty: "decisive awareness." Close in meaning to the term dominant battlespace awareness, decisive awareness would permit the Air Force to achieve near-certainty in future war through: "Machine to machine interface of C4ISR [Command Control Communications Computers Information Surveillance Reconnaissance] systems through the horizontal integration of manned, unmanned, air, surface, information, and space systems to provide executable, decision-quality knowledge to the commander in near-real time from anywhere."

The degree of certainty the Air Force required included not only near-perfect knowledge of the current situation, but also knowledge of enemy intentions. When confronted with that limitation, the proponents of certainty assumed predictive abilities. "Predictive battlespace awareness" debuted as a component of decisive awareness; it would "anticipate our adversary's next move before he makes it" and "eliminate surprise." Predictive intelligence depended on automated decision aids to magnify the intellects of talented analysts who would have continuous access to near-perfect intelligence on the current situation. Those analysts would collaborate with one another on a network to identify trends and penetrate the minds of enemy commanders. They will also assess accurately other factors such as cultural predilections, morale, skill level and leaders' competence.89

Those fantastic claims allow the application of the logical test of reductio ad absurdum to the belief in certainty in future war. Under reductio reasoning a premise is taken to its logical conclusion and thereby reveals its fatal flaws. The Air Force clung to the assumption of certainty in war even as "dominant awareness" required clairvoyance under conditions of combat.

The Navy joined and might have even surpassed the Air Force in its advocacy of certainty in future war. Senior naval officers were among the most enthusiastic about the promise associated with information age technologies. Admiral Bill Owens, as Vice Chairman of the Joint Chiefs of Staff, helped develop the concept of "dominant battlespace knowledge." In his influential book, Lifting the Fog of War, the retired Admiral who is co-CEO of a satellite communications company, asserted that future commanders would "be able to see everything of military significance in the combat zone" and also gain a "deeper comprehension of the enemy's intentions, planned actions, and capabilities and limitations." Dominant battlespace knowledge would permit US commanders to launch strikes that "paralyze the enemy force."90 With the publication of Sea Power XXI in September 2002, the Navy embraced Admiral Owens' ideas and made information superiority the basis for future naval operations.

Sea Power XXI organized the Navy's vision of future war around three concepts: Sea Strike, Sea Shield, and Sea Basing. Sea Strike is the ability to project precise and persistent offensive power from the sea; Sea Shield extends defensive assurance throughout the world; and Sea Basing enhances operational independence and support for the joint force. All three concepts depended on ForceNet, the Navy's emerging system for command and control, intelligence, and communications.91

Officers charged with developing ForceNet were confident in the ability to deliver "superior knowledge." After years of concept development work, the Chief of Naval Operations'

Strategic Studies Group in Newport, Rhode Island finalized the definition of ForceNet as: "the operational construct and architectural framework for naval warfare in the information age that integrates warriors, sensors, networks, command and control, platforms, and weapons into a networked, distributed combat force that is scalable across all levels of conflict from seabed to space and sea to land." ForceNet was designed to implement "the theory of network-centric warfare" and "draw on vast amounts of information and share the resultant understanding." Although the authors acknowledged the danger of information overload as volume of information increased and time to make decisions decreased, they were confident in ForceNet's ability to deliver "immediate and detailed information." ForceNet would "develop and deploy next-generation systems and analytical processes that provide broad situational awareness by harnessing the torrent of data flowing through military, interagency, and public channels." The result would be "expansive visibility and understanding, arming the joint force with knowledge dominance." The language of ForceNet revealed an engineering approach to war. The ForceNet concept was based on the belief that war would succumb to information age engineering just as nature succumbed to industrial age engineering. ForceNet appeared as the Hoover Dam and information as the wild waters of the Colorado River; the information age engineers of ForceNet would "harness" a "torrent of data" and "stream of information" to produce "power." That the human, psychological, and moral elements they sought to control might prove indomitable seemed not to dissuade them. Besides, the blueprints and work plans were finished and ground was already broken.

The architects of ForceNet do acknowledge that "military actions must be informed by political, economic, and cultural understanding" and that action in war can generate disproportionate reaction such that "a single shot can have global ramifications." It is assumed, however, that these sources of uncertainty will succumb to the power of "broadened knowledge" and shared "databases."

Integral to this effort will be employment of knowledge enhancement centers within which intelligent computer agents help elite analysts search, filter, and classify information to produce a comprehensive understanding of the environment as quickly as possible—. Automated tools will be developed to continuously map and analyze critical variables in the operational environment, adversary forces, and friendly assets. Such tools will keep U.S. and allied commanders updated on the status of increasingly fluid operational environments. Our asymmetric advantages in information collection and processing technologies are ideally suited to such tasks, involving data-intensive functions for which computer capabilities vastly exceed those of human planners.

Sea Power XXI will create "decisive advantage conferred by superior information management and knowledge dominance."92

The enemy is generally absent from these descriptions of future war. When the enemy does appear, he is quickly overwhelmed by American strength and the interaction between forces is limited to the application of U.S. military power followed closely by enemy capitulation. Enemy countermeasures are not fully considered. Indeed, Sea Power XXI dismissed the enemy explicitly, extolling "strengths that are powerful and uniquely ours" such as "the expanding power of computing, systems integration, a thriving industrial base, and the extraordinary capabilities of our people—." The strengths of Sea Power 21 promise to make the enemy irrelevant to the outcome as "information technology will empower us to dominate timelines, foreclose adversary options, and deny enemy sanctuary." 93

Like the Air Force, the Navy plans to: "predict what will happen next, so that an adversary's actions can be preempted. By drawing on superior information and understanding, ForceNet will allow joint force commanders to foresee potential enemy actions days or weeks in advance. This will empower our commanders to decisively alter conditions and dominate opponents—."94 Linear thinking and the absence of the enemy ensure dominance, at least in theory.

In addition to the absence of the enemy, the orthodoxy of knowledge dominance survives because it is assumed that technological advantage at sea and in the air applies absolutely to operations on land. Since the end of the Cold War, the Navy's and the Air Force's uncontested mastery of sea and sky have bolstered claims of certainty in future war. It is easiest for the Air Force and Navy to assume certainty in future war because they operate in similar, relatively transparent media. After earning vast superiority over all potential adversaries in their domains, both services appropriately focused greater attention on the ability to influence operations on land, the only medium in which American power is currently contested. Innovations in tactics and capabilities have increased air-to-land and sea-to-land capabilities tremendously, but claims concerning what naval and air forces can achieve on land do not consider the fundamental differences between air, land, and sea environments.

Important efforts to enhance joint interoperability began to describe the air, ground, and sea environments as a "singular" or "unified" battlespace. While encouraging a holistic view and recognizing the need for improved integration of air, sea, and land operations was a positive development, those terms obscured critical differences. Joint concept developers operate at a high level of generality and base their efforts mainly on emerging technological capabilities and the operational level of war. They fail to consider tactical combat and most are not predisposed by either experience or education to recognize the unique complexity of operations on land.95 Some military analysts tend to consider the media of air, sea, and land equivalent in complexity and transparency. Analysts Daniel Goure and Stephen Cambone asserted in 1997, for example, "air and space power provides the ability to see the entire theater/battlespace in three dimensions." They went on to argue that air forces could "use the information gained to develop an appreciation for how an adversary performs as a complex system." That knowledge would then permit air and space power alone "to achieve strategic results.96

As the American combat actions in Desert Storm, Somalia, Afghanistan and Operation Iraqi Freedom indicated, the factors that preserve uncertainty in war despite technological superiority are mainly land-based. Because people live there, land is where political, social and cultural, factors interact with complex geography to generate uncertainties that can alter the best-laid plans. As C. Kenneth Allard observed, the numbers of "targets" on land are far greater than on sea or in the air. He noted that "many of these potential targets resist that characterization by becoming extremely adept at using terrain, vegetation, and similar features of an environment that is far more "cluttered" and "dirty" that either the sea or aerospace- and therefore much less susceptible to electronic or other forms of penetration." Operations on land, he observed, provide challenges "for which technology at best provides only incomplete answers." 97

24

The air and sea domains share many of the same characteristics and are transparent and uniform relative to land. Both are unforgiving environments. Air and sea forces reduce friction in very complex operations through centralized planning and control.98 The speed of air and naval strikes make the contested portion of missions and the actual interaction with the land domain often-high risk, but short in duration. It is difficult for many who conduct or witness impressive strikes from sea and air to understand how superior technology and highly developed skills that earned dominance in those domains do not transfer directly to land. It is especially confounding given the tremendous destructive power that air and naval forces can now deliver precisely on target. That precision strikes might be ineffective or even counterproductive because of political factors, enemy strategy, or tactical countermeasures requires them to transcend personal experience and balance enthusiasm for their technological capabilities with an appreciation of limitations.

Air and sea are not without their own frictions, uncertainties, and challenges that draw into question the assumption of dominant knowledge even in fluid environments. Indeed, the professionalism and high degree of skill in American air and naval forces conceal the complexity and danger associated with them. Air forces' duel with air defense systems is a tactical and technological game of cat-and-mouse. Air space management for rotary wing, fixed wing, unmanned aerial vehicles, and air defense assets can create dangerous uncertainties even without enemy action. Long bombing missions push human endurance to the limit. The vulnerability of ships and aircraft increase as they approach land because proximity to land reduces warning time and maneuver space and subjects forces to the uncertainty that land harbors. The naval environment increases in complexity as ships enter shallow or confined waters. Submarines, mines, and land-based conventional threats such as missiles, underwater demolition teams, and high-speed boats blend into the clutter of inhabited areas and busy commercial shipping routes. The October 12, 2000 terrorist attack on the USS Cole demonstrated that vulnerabilities persist despite vast technological superiority.99 Because gaining access to land from sea and air is a critical capability for US forces and because missiles that can target sea and air platforms continue to increase in range and capability, naval and air forces will continue to operate in uncertain, dangerous environments and dominance of the air and sea domains enjoyed in recent conflicts through Operation Iraqi freedom will not go unchallenged in the future.

The Marine Corps, a service that operates in the air, on the sea, and on land understands the unique complexity of the ground environment and has rejected the prevailing assumptions about future war. In its "capstone concept," the Marine Corps emphasized "timeless realities of human conflict" over technological change. It eschewed attempts "to redefine war on more humane or less risky terms." It defined the nature of war as Clausewitz did: "A violent struggle between hostile, independent, irreconcilable wills characterized by chaos, friction, and uncertainty - will remain unchanged as it transcends advancements in technology."100 Other services might adopt the Marine Corps definition rather than impose onto land a vision of war consistent only with operations in the air or at sea under conditions of unchallenged technological supremacy.

Hubris is an ancient Greek term defined as extreme pride that leads to overconfidence and often results in misfortune. In Greek tragedies, the hero vainly attempts to transcend human limits and often ignores warnings that portend a disastrous fate. The idea of dominant knowledge in war and the related overconfidence in so called 'shock and awe' precision strikes transcends the limits of the nature of war and, in particular, war's human dimension. Hubris permeates the language of defense transformation and is particularly evident in the reductive fallacies of information superiority, dominant battlespace knowledge, and their various companion terms. Warnings were ignored.

The experience in Somalia from 1992-1994 might have served as a corrective to overconfidence in American military technological superiority. Ironically, Somalia instead reinforced faith in technology as a solution to complex national security problems. Painful images of the aftermath of Task Force Ranger's fight in Mogadishu provided incentive to expect even more from sensors, missiles, and airplanes. President William Clinton resolved to substitute missiles and bombs for ground forces as a method for avoiding another Mogadishu. Engagement from a safe distance offered the comfort of action without risk of irreversible commitment.101 The Balkans became a testing ground for a strategy based on American military technology.

In July 1995, the horror of Srebrenica, including the humiliating surrender of Dutch peacekeepers to the Bosnian Serb war criminal Ratko Mladic, and the subsequent murder of seven thousand Muslim men, finally overcame American and European reticence to use force against the Bosnian Serbs. To many, Mladic's Serbs had seemed a formidable opponent; estimates of the number of ground troops needed to intervene in Bosnia were high. Bosnian Serb brutality against defenseless civilians, however, masked weakness. In early August, Croat and Muslim forces that America trained and equipped attacked and began to rout the Bosnian Serbs. Finally, in response to a brutal and senseless mortar attack on the Sarajevo marketplace that killed thirty-eight people and wounded eighty-five others, NATO air power struck Serbian forces in Bosnia hard. During the first twenty-four hours of Operation Deliberate Force, 300 strike sorties attacked Serb forces. It was a sharp contrast with the previous two years of irresolute and ineffective air strikes that NATO carried out in Bosnia under Operation Deny Flight. Deliberate Force complimented the Croat and Muslim ground offensives. For example, as Croat forces advanced across the Krajna River, any Serb unit that concentrated to stop them was subjected to devastating attacks from the air. The eleven day, 3,515-sortie air campaign was a success. Deliberate Force contributed significantly to the signing of the Dayton Accord in November after which NATO troops occupied the war-stricken province to enforce the peace. 102

Deliberate Force demonstrated air power's ability to achieve strategic effects as part of a broad strategy and in conjunction with a complementary ground offensive. In 1999, however, when the Clinton administration confronted Serbian brutality in Kosovo the emphasis was on precision air power as the solution to that problem. Missile strikes and bombing, made increasingly effective by technological advances, appeared very attractive to an administration that wanted to use force, but also wanted to minimize risk and avoid public or congressional opposition. Between March 24 and June 7, 1999, the United States and its NATO allies conducted an air campaign against Yugoslavia to end human rights abuses against the ethnic Albanian, Muslim population in the province of Kosovo.

Operation Allied Force was planned as a five-day air campaign to coerce Yugoslavian President Slobodan Milosevic to "withdraw his forces and cease hostilities" against the ethnic Albanian population in the province of Kosovo. 103

There was a high degree of confidence at the outset of the war. Rump Yugoslavia was a weak state unable to threaten NATO bases of operation or lines of communication. American military technology had continued to improve since the Gulf War. It was less than three years since the publication of Joint Vision 2010, but information superiority seemed within grasp. Unmanned aerial vehicles would provide greater fidelity of the battlefield in real-time. Joint STARS radar systems had an improved ability to track ground targets. Precision munitions including laser-guided bombs, cruise missiles, the new Joint Direct Attack Munition (JDAM), and Stand Off Weapon (JSOW) were available in great quantities. As the campaign began, American Secretary of State Madeline Albright declared on national television, "I think this is achievable in a very short period of time."[104]

Confidence, however, did not equate to certainty, even at the outset of the war. Political factors both within the United States and between the United States and its allies generated ambiguities and tensions that complicated military planning. The adversary was a sovereign nation with historical, cultural, and religious ties to Russia and much of Europe. As a result, the resolve of NATO allies was uneven despite the record of Serbian brutality in Bosnia-Herzegovina and Kosovo.[105] Macedonia provided a base of operations, but the situation there was unstable; the majority of its populace was sympathetic to the Serbs and feared an uprising by their own ethnic Albanian population. Protests in Greece, a NATO member, threatened to shut down critical supply lines. The French and Italians were unenthusiastic about an intensive air campaign against Serbia and favored measured attacks to communicate resolve. Despite working on war plans from May of 1998 to March of 1999, differences among NATO members kept those plans in flux. As in Somalia, it proved difficult to operate as part of a broad coalition even under the rubric of the NATO Alliance.[106]

Ambiguities in US policy and strained relationships between top civilian and military officials created more uncertainty and friction. President Clinton kept his policy deliberately ambiguous to forestall debate in the US Congress. The President's announcement that he had no intention of using ground forces removed an important capability and dimmed the prospect of coercing Milosevic. The administration was determined to minimize the risk of casualties even if achieving that goal placed the achievement of strategic objectives in jeopardy. "Force protection" became part of the mission. Emphasis on minimizing collateral damage and the desire to maintain consensus among allies led to disagreements between top civilian and military officers; military officers regarded constraints on the use of force excessive. Strained relationships between top military officials over these and other issues added even more friction and impeded effective communication. [107]

Even before it began, Operation Allied Force demonstrated how political considerations are connected inexorably to the conduct of war and that intractable uncertainty in war derives, in part, from the interaction of military means with political ends and factors that impede congruence between them. [108]

Assumptions of near-certainty in war are both a product of and encouraged by linear thinking. Once the psychological dynamic of war was unleashed, the future course of events depended not only (or even primarily) on NATO's bombing plan. It depended also on Yugoslav reactions and initiatives that proved impossible to predict. Without the necessary force to impose NATO's will on Yugoslavia and having based initial actions on unrealistically sanguine assumptions about the coercive power of air strikes, Yugoslavia seized the initiative soon after the war began.

Despite considerable preparation time and a weak enemy, NATO failed to achieve information superiority. Much was known about the enemy, but intelligence was not detailed enough to keep track of the Serbian Army.109 Poor weather, heavy cloud cover, and mountainous, forested terrain degraded satellites, UAVs, and radars. Serbian decisions surprised NATO despite numerous personal interactions with Yugoslavian leader Slobodan Milosevic over the previous four years and the opportunity to develop detailed intelligence estimates.

Milosevic anticipated NATO's actions and countered them. He moved troops to the border of Kosovo weeks prior to the initiation of air and missile attacks. When the campaign started, those forces threw the Albanian population into the street, stripped them of their identification, looted their possessions, burned their houses, and drove them like cattle toward the Macedonian and Albanian borders. NATO was surprised and unprepared. The air campaign had the unintended consequence of actually accelerating the brutal ethnic cleansing operations it was intended to stop. A few weeks after the start of Allied Force, three-fourths of the ethnic Albanian population were refugees. Eight hundred thousand people crammed into camps outside Kosovo's borders. Five hundred thousand more hid in the hills inside the province. Milosevic was not as easy to coerce as had been assumed. What was supposed to be a five-day air campaign drug into weeks, then months. The British government estimated that Serbs murdered ten thousand ethnic Albanians during the course of Operation Allied Force. 110 The experience revealed the dangers of linear thinking and being unprepared for the interaction that occurs with one's enemy once war begins.

Interaction with the enemy created considerable friction, complicated the conduct of the air campaign, and generated uncertainty. On the air campaign's seventh day, General Wesley Clark observed that NATO was facing "an intelligent and capable adversary who is trying to offset all our strategies." Even though Serbian air defenses were antiquated, they forced NATO aircraft to altitudes above fifteen thousand feet which made target identification difficult. They also used innovative methods to keep their radars active, yet prevent them from being hit. The Serbs used low-technology tactics and improvisation to down an F-117 Stealth Fighter. Those tactics forced thirty-five percent of combat sorties to be allocated against air defense.111

The Serbians learned to deceive and manipulate American intelligence. Serb forces allowed reconnaissance aircraft to identify actual targets then replaced them with decoys. Approximately five hundred of the three thousand precision munitions used struck those decoys. The Serbs learned the times when JSTARS conducted reconnaissance flights and had their forces halt on the sides of the road so the system would not detect "moving target indicators." After NATO began employing successfully a forward air controller in an A-10, Yugoslav forces sought concealment immediately upon hearing the aircraft.112

The Serbs' ability to obtain considerable intelligence on allied operations despite their technological inferiority draws into question the denial component of "information superiority" against even a foe that has very basic capabilities. The Serbs evacuated certain targets soon after they appeared on target lists. It is likely that the Yugoslav government had access to plans through spies at NATO headquarters. Additionally, spies stationed outside Aviano Airbase provided early warning when aircraft departed on missions.113

Perhaps most important, the instruments of Milosevic's ethnic cleansing campaign, small mobile groups of paramilitary and police, were intermingled with the innocent civilian objects of their terror and were, therefore, unidentifiable and immune to NATO air power. Intelligence analysts often had clear pictures of Albanian refugees cowering in the hills, but could not locate the Serbs who were terrorizing them. Aircraft looked for targets in vain, sometimes refueling four times without dropping a bomb. Because aircraft could not land with bombs, millions of dollars of ordinance landed in the Adriatic Ocean or on the vacant countryside. Serbian Army tanks and other vehicles dispersed and hid. Even when Serbian tanks and artillery pieces were located, bombing might have provided an emotional catharsis, but the activity was irrelevant to stopping the Serbian ethnic cleansing campaign. It was not until peacekeepers moved into Kosovo that NATO discovered the full extent of Serbian atrocities committed against Kosovar Albanians.114

Evidence that uncertainty remained the dominant feature of war was also found in the confusion over results of the bombing campaign. NATO greatly exaggerated losses inflicted on the Serbian military. Initial reports estimated that the bombing destroyed over 450 artillery pieces, 120 tanks and self-propelled artillery vehicles, and 220 armored personnel carriers. Nothing close to those numbers, however, were counted physically. The Allied Force Munitions Effectiveness Assessment Team later reported the following numbers of destroyed equipment: 14 tanks, 18 armored personnel carriers, and 20 artillery pieces. Those numbers suggested that less than five percent of the Serbian combat systems had been destroyed during the seventy-eight day campaign. NATO's effort to attack enemy ground units failed. The extent of that failure became apparent only after the air war was over.115

Because of ambiguities in target selection and identification, many targets were hit unintentionally. Mistakes occurred not because of a lack of information; the sheer volume of data and the difficulty in separating good from bad information presented difficulties. As Secretary of Defense William Cohen attested after the war, "our vast intelligence system can create such a haystack of data that finding the one needle that will pinpoint a target in the right time frame is difficult, indeed."116 The best-known intelligence failure was the bombing of the Chinese Embassy in Belgrade. At the time of the bombing, planners were under pressure to find two thousand targets in Serbia because targets for the five-day air campaign were exhausted. Human errors, including the use of an old map and a failure to update a no-strike list caused the error. 117 There were at least twenty other incidents of "collateral damage" including bombs that fell in Bulgaria and struck trains, convoys, a school, and hospitals. 118

These mistakes occurred despite great discipline on the part of the pilots. After an incident in which eighty Albanian refugees were reported killed in what was mistaken for a military convoy, Brigadier General Leaf, commander of the unit who conducted that attack, observed that it was "a very complicated scenario and we will never be able to establish all the details."119

Collateral damage concerns and unrealistic expectations created additional friction and uncertainty as the air campaign continued; commanders and planners were determined to avoid another disastrous error that might unhinge already decreasing political support for the effort. Benjamin Lambeth, an expert on the air campaign, observed that: "Thanks to unrealistic efforts to treat the normal friction of war as avoidable human error, every occurrence of unintended collateral damage became overinflated as front-page news and treated as a blemish on air power's presumed ability to be consistently precise." 120

Many targets hit in Serbia were selected due to distance from the civilian populace rather than for their military value and thus contributed little to the objective of coercing Milosevic. Even very careful targeting procedures, however, could not prevent inadvertent damage. After the two-week moratorium on bombing Belgrade that followed the Chinese embassy incident, the first night of renewed bombing damaged the residences of the Swedish, Spanish, and Norwegian ambassadors as well as the Libyan embassy and a hospital. 121

The Kosovo experience demonstrated that even extreme technological superiority does not lead to information superiority or remove uncertainty and friction. The Serbs were no "peer competitor." NATO enjoyed air supremacy and faced antiquated, minimal air defenses. The Serbs had no ability to disrupt NATO communications or information systems. Kosovo demonstrated that the causes of uncertainty in the conduct of war lie mainly outside technology's reach: war's political nature, its human dimension, its complexity, and interaction with the enemy. Military organizations should, of course, take all possible action to minimize uncertainty and friction, but they must be prepared to win in an uncertain environment. In Kosovo, NATO has assumed certainty and was unprepared.

The assumption that the war in Kosovo would lie in the realm of certainty undermined NATO's ability to meet objectives and prevent suffering. Near-certainty combined with long range precision fires was supposed to vitiate the need for ground forces and a make possible a fast, low-cost, low-casualty war. The campaign was supposed to last five days; ti lasted eleven weeks and ended after 40,000 aircraft sorties and the threat of a ground invasion. The way in which the war was conducted increased the suffering of both Kosovar Albanians and Serbian civilians and made air power much less effective than it would have been if it had been employed as part of air-land operations. NATO achieved dominance of the air, but that achievement did not translate into dominance on the ground. The absence of a ground force to compel the Serbs to desist from their campaign of terror and to render ineffective the countermeasures taken against air forces allowed Serbia to terrorize the ethnic Albanians and work to turn world public opinion against NATO. The mismatch between stated objectives and military strategy made it a war of paradoxes. It was a war waged with one sided casualties, but one that generated ambiguous results. It was also a war waged under the auspices of compassion, but conducted in a way that increased, or at least permitted the suffering of those on whose behalf it was initiated. 122

Those who conducted Operation Allied Force deserve great credit for laboring under constraints and overcoming considerable uncertainty and friction. The failures of Operation Allied Force were not failures of air power; they were failures based on unrealistic expectations that elevated a military capability to the level of strategy. The U.S. experience during Operation Allied Force exposed the ideas of information superiority and dominant battlespace knowledge as fundamentally unsound. Once the effects of Operation Allied Force were combined with other elements such as increased diplomatic pressure (especially from Russia), a Kosovo Liberation Army offensive, and the threat of a NATO ground offensive, NATO succeeded and Milosevic acquiesced. 123

Even if the war had been waged with technology anticipated in the year 2020, those capabilities would not have reduced significantly the uncertainty and friction. In 2020, enemy in forests and villages would have remained undetected and supply of Serbian forces could not have been interdicted because Serbs used small civilian trucks to get supplies to their units. Perhaps most important to the outcome in Kosovo, technology of the future will remain unable to distinguish the small forces that carried out the ethnic cleansing from innocent civilians.124 Even if one assumes near-perfect information, that information is only relevant if it can be translated into near-perfect military operations in the context of a sound strategy that supports policy goals. Information, in other words, is not an end in and of itself. Kosovo, however, like Somalia, did not provide a corrective to flawed assumptions concerning future war.

As one book on the subject of Kosovo observes, NATO "won ugly," but won nevertheless and even a modest success can emasculate lessons. Senior administration officials declared Operation Allied Force "history's most successful air campaign." 125

The Defense Department's Kosovo After Action Report stated that Operation Allied Force "provided a real-world test of information superiority concepts outlined in Joint Vision 2010." The report noted that: "U.S. intelligence, surveillance, and reconnaissance capabilities provided unprecedented levels of support to NATO warfighters. The supporting intelligence architecture included a worldwide network of processing centers and high-speed data communications, all operating in direct support of combat operations in Kosovo. " Those observations were true, but they appeared without qualifications concerning the limitations of technologies.

The intelligence section of the report recognized that precision munitions require precision intelligence and cited obstacles intelligence collection such as "adverse weather, nighttime, concealment and deception techniques, or rapid movement," but suggested that these difficulties would succumb to the "modernization path." Defense procurement programs would generate an improved "sensor mix" that when combined with processes such as "dynamic collection management, common battlespace awareness, and interoperable intelligence systems and architectures" would "improve precision intelligence capability." The Department decided to "focus on specific technical enhancements in response to Kosovo."126 The engineering approach to war was actually strengthened by its failures.

As the Department of Defense released its report on Kosovo, the Joint Staff was working on Joint Vision 2020 (JV2020). The extension of the vision another ten years gave technology more time to deliver on the capabilities that Kosovo drew into question. 127

The experience of Kosovo did, however, generate caveats in JV2020. JV2020 warned that "we should not expect war in the future to be either easy or bloodless" and stated that "friction is inherent in military operations" and derives from the following factors:

• effects of danger and exertion

• existence of uncertainty, and chance

31

• unpredictable actions of other actors;

• frailties of machines and information

• humans

Additionally, JV2020 asked readers to "remember that information superiority neither equates to perfect information, nor does it mean the elimination of the fog of war." These cautions appeared disconnected with other portions of the document, however, that highlighted the "information revolution" and the "profound changes" that it would create in the conduct of military operations. 128

Although JV2020 attempted to administer a corrective to the assumption that near-certainty would be the dominant characteristic of future war, caveats could not overcome the momentum behind the belief that technology would lift the fog of war. 129

As the Joint Staff prepared a revised Joint Vision document in July 2002, it based the effort on the following assumption: "Dramatic improvements in intelligence collection, analysis and dissemination capabilities will facilitate near-continuous surveillance of the battlespace. Analysis of this continuous information flow will produce the type of current and predictive intelligence that enables the US Armed Forces to achieve full spectrum dominance." The qualifiers and warnings of JV2020 disappeared. The words fog and friction were absent from the revision and the word uncertainty appeared only in connection with the future strategic environment. 130 Flawed assumptions about future war overcame the reality of Kosovo.

MAN'S NATURAL ELEMENT

Ground is man's natural element, and an infinitely complex one. War on land differs in three fundamental respects from war and sea, in the air or in space. War in the fluid media is ultimately concerned with the possession or control of ground—On land man can choose his degree of dependence on machines; in the fluid media, he cannot live or move without them. The fluid media are either uniform, or have an unchanged gradation of properties, except where they adjoin land —

—Richard E. Simpkin

While the Department of Defense called for more and better technologies in pursuit of dominant knowledge, the Army learned a different lesson from Kosovo. In 1999, a new Army Chief of Staff determined to reform Army organization based, in part, on the experience of Task Force Hawk, the only significant Army participation in Operation Allied Force. Task Force Hawk centered on twenty-four Apache Helicopters that were to conduct deep strikes against Serbian Army units in Kosovo. The task force grew from a planned deployment of 1,700 soldiers to approximately 6,000 soldiers including an infantry battalion task force of forty-two Bradley Fighting Vehicles and twelve M1A1 tanks, twenty-four Multiple Launch Rocket Systems, and a large headquarters of twenty-five expandable vans mounted on 5-ton trucks. It took five hundred fifteen C-17 sorties to transport the unit. To make matters worse, the force deployed into and operated from a small Albanian airfield surrounded by mud and standing water shared by twelve other NATO units and multi-national organizations. The Army brought in massive amounts of crushed rock and had to build helicopter-landing pads. Still, the airfield ramp became a clutter of munitions, repair parts, humanitarian supplies, vehicles and equipment. Although Task Force Hawk met its deployment schedule, it arrived later than many expected, including General Wesley Clark, the Supreme Allied Commander, Europe. The image of soldiers wading through the mud focused attention on Army organization and seemed a metaphor for what needed to change in the Army; it needed to be faster and lighter. When two Apache pilots died in a training accident, many believed that the unit was not prepared to operate at night in the demanding mountainous environment; any remaining interest in using Task Force Hawk waned and the unit was never employed.131 It was a profound embarrassment for the Army.

The Army was behind in organizational change and suffering from a degradation in readiness and morale. General Shinseki resolved to make immediate and substantial changes. It had been clear to many officers for years that the heavy force was powerful and possessed operational mobility, but was difficult to deploy, and dependent on a large logistical infrastructure. The Army's airborne and light infantry units possessed strategic mobility, but suffered from a lack of mobility, firepower, and protection once they arrived in a theater of operations. The Army discontinued its Force XXI program and shifted efforts to two initiatives: the Interim Brigade Combat Team (IBCT) and the Objective Force. The IBCT was to fill the short-term need for a strategically mobile force that possessed greater mobility and firepower than a light unit. The Objective Force had its roots in an earlier Army After Next initiative, a research and development effort to determine the optimal Army organization for 2020 and beyond. Between 1999 and 2003, General Shinseki defeated efforts to obstruct the formation of the IBCT, renamed the Stryker Brigade Combat Team (SBCT), and the Army began fielding the first three of six of these units in record time. In 2002, the Army moved up dramatically the target fielding date of the first Objective Force Unit of Action (UA) from 2015 to 2008, cancelled many programs, and shifted funds to research and development. 132

Both the Stryker Brigade and Objective Force hold promise to enhance Army capabilities, but the Army's uncritical acceptance of the assumption of near-certainty in future war is undermining both initiatives. Army experimentation in the mid to late 1990's had convinced many that "information dominance" provided the solution to the problem of future war. 133

Similar to the Joint, Navy, and Air Force transformation efforts, the belief that technology will lift the fog of war has corrupted the doctrinal basis for the Stryker Brigade's employment and the Objective Force's development. Unless the Army abandons its flawed vision of future combat, that vision could result in the employment of the Stryker Brigade in combat situations for which it is ill suited and create severe vulnerabilities in the Objective Force such that it is unable to fight successfully except under optimal conditions.

The Stryker Brigade's tactical doctrine is based on the assumption that the brigade's "integrated suite of intelligence reconnaissance and surveillance capabilities and digitized battle command systems" will permit the force to achieve "situational understanding and information superiority." The brigade will thus be able to "avoid surprise, develop rapid decisions, control the time and place for combat, conduct precision maneuver, shape the battlespace with precision fires and effects, and achieve decisive outcomes." Adopting the assumption of near-certainty in future war permitted the Stryker Brigade to achieve greater lightness while assuming virtually the same fighting capability of the mechanized force. In theory, information would compensate for limitations such as: light armor protection, no stabilized weapons to fire while moving, no fire control system tied to thermal sights to shoot weapons accurately at night, and a main armament of machine guns and grenade launchers instead of more powerful weapons like the 25 millimeter chain gun. 134

Despite the clear limitations of the technologies that are supposed to deliver it, the assumption of near certainty in future war has migrated to the present and has shaped current Army tactical doctrine. In the past, the Army anticipated having to fight for information because much of the situation remains uncertain until first contact due to enemy efforts to avoid detection and the human dimension of war. The Serbians employed countermeasures such as deception, camouflage, concealment, and intermingling with the civilian population. Important elements of information lie squarely in the human and psychological dimensions and are impossible to know until a ground maneuver formation closes with the enemy include: How will the enemy react? Will he use chemical munitions? How will he employ his reserve? What were the effects of bombing and artillery? Will he retreat or mount a resolute defense? How skilled is he? The first unit to fight always benefited from intelligence before contact with the enemy, but soldiers and commanders expected the unexpected. The Army relied on reconnaissance units that were prepared to fight to gain the part of the intelligence picture that remained concealed because of the limits of surveillance technology, enemy countermeasures, and the moral dimension of war. To fortify units for these encounter actions, the Army provided them with firepower, armor protection, and mobility. The Army also decentralized combined arms (e.g. engineers, infantry, armor, artillery, and aviation) capabilities to these units so they were capable of taking independent action. The all arms capability forced the enemy to deal with multiple threats simultaneously and allowed U.S. commanders to exploit opportunities and protect against dangers. Because battles of attrition tend to cause high casualties on both sides, emphasis was on maneuver and bold action to seize and retain the initiative. The Army sought temporal and psychological as well as physical advantages over the enemy. 135

According to the Army's capstone doctrinal manual, soldiers and units will now have near-perfect intelligence prior to contact with the enemy:

The Army must also gain information superiority. This means the operational advantage derived from the ability to collect, process, and disseminate an uninterrupted flow of information while exploiting or denying an enemy's capability to do the same—. Unmanned systems with artificial intelligence will augment human action and decision making through improved situational understanding—. The extensive information available to Army leaders will also allow unprecedented awareness of every aspect of future operations. Precise knowledge of the enemy and friendly situations will facilitate exact tailoring of units for mission requirements; tactical employment of precision fires; exploitative, decisive maneuver at extended ranges; and responsive, flexible support of those forces. Although knowledge will never be perfect, improved command and control systems will enable leaders to know far more than ever before about the nature of activities in their battlespace. They will have access to highly accurate information regarding enemy and friendly locations, the civil population, terrain, and weather—. The common operational picture provided through integration of real-time intelligence and accurate targeting reduces the need to fill space with forces and direct fire weapons. Agile forces can also improve the capacity of commanders to employ combat power with precision to achieve a desired outcome. The goal of future Army operations will be to simultaneously attack critical targets throughout the area of operations by rapid maneuver and precision fires to break the adversary's will and compel him to surrender. The cumulative effect of simultaneous shaping operations and nearly simultaneous decisive operations will be to reduce an adversary's ability to synchronize his effort and will establish the military conditions for friendly victory—decisive victory.136

The assumption of near perfect intelligence allows the army to declare the Stryker Brigade to be considered "optimized for combat in complex and urban terrain" even though these types of terrain are most resistant to sensors and provide the enemy with the best opportunities for concealment, deception, and surprise. The Army assumes, however, that the SBCT will be able to "understand the situation" such that it will encounter the enemy only at the times and places of its own choosing. 137

The Army is also designing the Objective Force based on the assumption of near certainty delivered by the "Global Information Grid" and a large number of unmanned air and ground sensors. The Objective Force's combat formation, the Unit of Action (UA), is intended to be a "system of systems" that is "empowered by dominant situational understanding resident in a vibrant knowledge network." In contrast to the Army's former emphasis on reconnaissance units capable of fighting, a "hallmark" of UA operations "will be the significant ability to develop situations out of contact." The UA will then "maneuver to positions of advantage with speed and agility, engage enemy beyond the range of their weapons systems, destroying them with enhanced fires, and assaulting at times and places of our choosing. " The Objective Force assumes that the technology will be available to deliver this high degree of clarity and that it will maintain that high fidelity of information throughout a campaign. It also assumes that joint fires, such as those applied against Serbian forces in Kosovo for seventy-eight days, will be successful "prior to forces being joined." Indeed, small UA units will be able to operate widely separated because these same fires will "shield" them from significant enemy threats. The UA organizational design is based on the assumption that it "will have situational understanding through all phases of the battle from alert to redeployment." A mathematical formula serves as the basis for organizational design: the sum of maneuver plus firepower plus protection multiplied by leadership, then raised to the power of information. Power is dependent on near-perfect information. 138

The Objective Force will be ineffective under conditions of uncertainty. The Unit of Action offers a doctrinal remedy for its organizational weaknesses. That doctrine, however, based as it is on the same assumption of near-certainty in future war, is also fundamentally flawed. The Unit of Action will fight "unlike any other tactical force" because it will fight only when it chooses and only when the enemy is "most vulnerable." Certainty in combat will allow the Objective Force to achieve a so-called "Quality of Firsts" such that the UA will "see first, understand first, act first, and finish decisively." The UA offers a clean break with even the most recent experiences in land warfare in Afghanistan and Operation Iraqi Freedom:

Historically, uncertainty about enemy and friendly conditions on the battlefield often dictated cautious movements to contact—.UA capabilities break this paradigm permitting future commanders to develop the situation before making contact, maneuver to positions of advantage largely out of contact, and, when ready initiate decisive action by destroying enemy systems beyond the range of their weapons to set conditions for decisive assault.

If a unit is capable of tactical overmatch, movements to contact need not be cautious, because the force is confident operating under conditions of certainty. The UA, however, must exercise caution to survive as it is designed only to operate when the situation is clear. Indeed, the Unit of Action doctrine acknowledges that it will only engage in what it knows in advance to be "profitable fights" in which it has "the best tactical advantage." The "empowerment" of "information dominance" is supposed to make land combat efficient, less dangerous, and certain in outcome. 139

It will also make it more cautious, deliberate, and highly selective. Because many believe that certainty will be the dominant condition of future war, "knowledge" is overtaking fighting as the primary basis for Army doctrine and organization. A section of the Army Transformation Roadmap entitled "Leveraging Information Technology and Innovative Concepts to Develop an Interoperable, Joint C4ISR Architecture and Capability that Includes a Tailorable Joint Operational Picture," announces that in combat, no maxim is truer than "knowledge is power." The anticipated knowledge will come mainly from "a seamlessly interoperable Joint C4ISR architecture, with the necessary space-based and terrestrial infrastructure."140 Because knowledge is power, it simplifies war and eliminates traditional tradeoffs between combat power and strategic mobility. Because units no longer have to hedge against uncertainty, "harnessing the power of information will enable the Objective Force units to increase their lethality, precision, and survivability even while dramatically reducing their mass and footprint."141

The primary difficulty with the Army's SBCT and Objective Force initiatives is that they are both advancing based on wishful thinking rather than analysis. There is no evidence that land forces will achieve anything like the level of knowledge assumed in the "Quality of Firsts." A recent RAND study that assumed perfect functioning of all emerging technologies in the year 2020 concluded that it would "be difficult if not impossible" to detect army forces that used "cover concealment, deception, intermingling, and dispersion." The study also found that the UA's air and ground sensors would only achieve dominant knowledge against an enemy in the open and that the precision fires on which the Objective Force depends would "provide attrition" but be insufficient to accomplish typical tactical missions. 142

It is as if the Army forgot that it operated on land and adopted wholesale the Air Force's and Navy's visions of future war. As Williamson Murray and Richard Sinnreich observed, "war on land is imbedded in and to a large extent driven by the ground itself, an extraordinarily disorderly environment in which the obstacles to knowledge, movement, and communications multiply friction, and in which, therefore, progress is slow, direction and momentum are difficult to sustain, the risk of surprise is omnipresent, and command and control are inherently fragile."143 Aside from fictional accounts of one-sided Unit of Action victories, interaction with the enemy and the unique challenges of the land environment are absent from the doctrine as the UA "acts first" then "finishes decisively by controlling the tempo of operations, denying the enemy freedom of action, and destroying the enemy's ability to fight."144

The assumption of near certainty in future war is depraving the Objective Force of its good intentions and undermining the effort. It is true that information, surveillance, and communications technology will help to produce invaluable awareness about the disposition and actions of ones own force, achieve a higher speed of action, integrate the efforts of Army units with the Joint Force, and generate valuable, albeit incomplete information about the enemy. The expectation that the enemy situation will be clear prior to contact and the associated unpreparedness to fight for the complete picture, however, will prevent the force from taking full advantage of vast improvements in command and control as well as joint interoperability. The enhanced strategic, operational, and tactical mobility of the force could prove irrelevant if the force lacks firepower and protection to defeat an enemy in complex terrain under uncertain conditions such as those encountered most recently in urban terrain in Iraq. The promising concept of distributed operations (under which Army formations arrive at various points in a theater of operations to conduct fast, simultaneous attacks) could generate multiple "Little Big Horns" if forces are unable to overmatch determined enemy attacks after the UA's arrival. Appropriate emphasis on teaching Objective Force leaders to be bold, aggressive and seize the initiative through surprise and speed will be for naught as leaders are compelled to wait for near-perfect intelligence as a pre-condition for operations. Decentralized combined arms capabilities provide tremendous potential to increase unit effectiveness, but weaknesses built into the force based on the assumption of near-perfect intelligence limit even those possibilities. Those limitations include inadequate protection to close aggressively with the enemy and a lack of integrated engineers to provide mobility support if mines and other obstacles go undetected. A reliance on long range fires at higher levels of command contradicts the doctrinal emphasis on decentralization, makes the force dependent on support from remote headquarters, and limits the force's freedom of action. Finally, the baseless assumption of certainty in future war risks the creation of an unrealistic picture of American "dominance" in efficient, relatively bloodless campaigns. When the actual experience of battle appears in stark contrast with that idealized vision of combat, it could generate fear and even paralysis. It is fortunate that soldiers today still train under conditions that aim to replicate the uncertainty of ground combat because the fighting in Afghanistan from 2001-2003 and in Iraq in March-April 2003 bore little resemblance to the battleground of the future on which the Objective Force is being designed to fight.

Until analysts began to assess the evidence concerning military operations during Operation Enduring Freedom, many observers viewed combat in Afghanistan as a demonstration of an American "way of war" that these observers had envisioned since the end of the 1991 Gulf War. The RMA technologies of sensors and precision munitions seemed decisive.145 Some ignored completely the role that a large Northern Alliance army played in the fight to defeat the Taliban. Others acknowledged the role of the Northern Alliance and suggested the possibility of applying an "Afghan Model" to future war; the United States would provide air and sea-based firepower to indigenous forces. Some suggested that the "Afghan model" applied to Iraq could win that war cheaply and quickly. The course of Iraqi Freedom once again revealed the tremendous capability associated with Special Operations Forces and precision strike assets. It also exposed the folly of relying on that capability to deliver cheap, rapid victory without a balanced joint force.

Dr. Stephen Biddle, who had ten years earlier warned about learning the wrong lessons from the Gulf War, corrected simplistic explanations for victory in Afghanistan. It is difficult to improve on his analysis:

The Afghan campaign was actually far less different or unusual than most now suppose: it was a surprisingly orthodox air-ground theater campaign in which heavy fire support decided a contest between two land forces. Of course, some elements were quite new: the fire support came almost exclusively from the air; the air strikes were directed mostly by commandos whose methods, equipment, and centrality to the outcome were unprecedented; and the ground armies were mostly not countrymen of the commandos and air forces who provided the firepower. In an important sense, though, the differences were less salient than the continuities: the key to success in Afghanistan as in traditional joint warfare was the close interaction of fire and maneuver, neither of which was sufficient alone and neither of which could succeed without significant ground forces trained and equipped at least as well as their opponents.146

Northern Alliance battles as well as those fought later with mainly American ground forces provided opportunities to evaluate the degree of certainty achieved in combat.

Biddle's study revealed that the outcome of these battles depended on factors beyond the influence of sensors and precision munitions. Geography was a critical factor in that the complexity of the terrain as well as the intermingling of Al Qaeda forces with civilians foiled attempts to kill or capture the enemy. Surveillance of the difficult terrain at Tora Bora, for example, could not compensate for the lack of ground forces to cover exfilteration routes. After a sixteen-day battle, many Al Qaeda forces, probably including Osama bin Laden, escaped across the Pakistan border. Deception might have contributed as well; Bin Laden's bodyguards used his cell phone transmissions to misdirect the manhunt aimed at capturing the Al Qaeda leader.147

Advantages in the human dimension of war proved more important than American military technology in generating tactical victories against the Taliban. Despite descriptions of U.S. Special Forces as "sensors," personal relationships between U.S. soldiers and faction leaders were more important than hitting targets with precision munitions. 148

It was Special Forces soldiers' interaction with leaders such as Rashid Dostrum and Hamad Karzai that proved most critical to success. The Special Forces and the firepower they accessed bolstered confidence in Northern Alliance leaders and galvanized into action forces that were otherwise predisposed toward inaction or retreat. When the tide turned it was due more to political and psychological effects than the physical impact of precision bombs. Overhead imagery was critical, especially during engagements, but the most valuable information came from human intelligence. Captain Jason Amerine who led the team assigned to Karzai's forces recalled that "the biggest tool in [Ahmed Karzai's] intelligence network was the [satellite] telephone—. He was able to get word right away of anything going on...."149

Even with intelligence from satellites and cellphones, tactical actions between the Special Forces-supported Northern Alliance militia and forces sympathetic to the Taliban remained profoundly uncertain; the outcome of battles often hinged on psychological factors impossible to predict. Special Forces teams sometimes recognized clear opportunities for victory only to see those opportunities slip away because Northern Alliance fighters perceived imminent defeat. Uncertainty spiked when the pro-Taliban occupied towns. CPT Amerine recalled one particular action: "I don't know how many guys were in the town. I don't. We'll just say somewhere between 30 and 50 guys were in town. They're opening up on my guys, and my guys start to withdraw. It was pretty withering fire. I had aircraft overhead the whole time, but I didn't want to bomb the town."

The friction inherent in combat also added difficulty and unpredictability, an example of which was the submission of faulty coordinates that resulted in the delivery of a 500 pound bomb on a friendly position, killing and wounding Americans and allied fighters.150

The "interaction" with the enemy increased the degree of uncertainty as the enemy adapted to U.S. capabilities. It was clear to those fighting in Afghanistan that Taliban forces were learning how to defeat American surveillance capabilities. Early Taliban positions were exposed and often silhouetted. By December 2001 the enemy began to employ extensive camouflage, concealment, and deception. Counterattacking forces used terrain to close within two hundred meters of Northern Alliance forces before they were detected. Enemy hid in culverts and burned out vehicles. They began to recognize the advantages of hiding among the civilian populace. On December 2-4 at Sayed Slim Kalay, enemy positions were not identified until Northern Alliance forces came under small arms fire.151

Even when enemy concentrations were identified, complex terrain and the cover of fortified positions frustrated attempts to predict the effects of bombing and made ground attack the only option to defeat the enemy. At Keshendeh-ye Pa'in, for example, two days of bombing was not enough to prevent the enemy from halting a ground advance. At the Qala-i-Gangi fortress, despite air attacks involving multiple AC-130 ammunition loads and seventy-two thousand-pound GPS-guided bombs, the defenders survived and resisted. From an American perspective, continued resistance was surprising. It took fighting the enemy in the close fight to determine his skill as well as determination to continue resisting. US forces learned that native Afghan Taliban had low morale, were oftentimes not resolute in defense, and tended to quit the field of battle when faced with significant air and ground combat power. Foreign al Qaeda fighters proved very determined and many threatened to kill Afghan Taliban who refused to fight. Discovering that qualitative difference as well as disparities in enemy training level and skill was only possible when engaged in close combat. 152

Perhaps the most direct test of technology's ability to lift the fog of war would come during Operation Anaconda in March 2002. US intelligence detected another concentration of Taliban forces in the Shah-i-Kot valley. US commanders deliberately planned an attack that would include two American infantry battalions reinforced with Aghan and other allied troops. It would be the largest combat operation of the war in Afghanistan.

Intelligence preparation for the operation spanned two weeks. The US focused every available surveillance and target acquisition capability including satellite imagery, unmanned aerial vehicles, and communications and signal intelligence assets on the ten by ten-kilometer box that defined the battleground. Every landing zone for the aerial insertions received the attention of four unmanned aerial vehicle overflights.

Enemy countermeasures to US sensors were effective and the fight during Operation Anaconda was characterized by a very high degree of uncertainty. On March 2, infantry air assaulted almost directly on top of undetected enemy positions. Soldiers came under immediate fire from small arms, mortars, rocket propelled grenades, and machineguns as their helicopters landed. Battalion and brigade command posts were pinned down and commanders fought alongside their men. Apache helicopters responding to provide direct fire support were hit and rendered inoperable. The planned second lift of soldiers had to be cancelled. Some units were pinned down by enemy fire during the first night of the battle and through the next day; they, including many of the wounded, could not be extracted until the following night. The unit had deployed with no artillery under the assumption that surveillance combined with precision fires from the air would be adequate. Even the most precise bombs proved ineffective against small, elusive groups of enemy infantry so soldiers relied heavily on small mortars. As the fight developed over the next ten days, it became apparent that over half of the enemy positions and at least three hundred fifty al Qaeda fighters had gone undetected. The enemy's reaction to the attack was also unexpected. American commanders had expected al Qaeda forces to withdraw upon contact with the superior allied force rather than defend as they did from fortified positions. As Sergeant Major Frank Grippe observed with a considerable degree of understatement, "The picture the intel painted was just a little bit different than the actual events happening on the ground by numbers of al Qaeda and the type of position they had set up and so forth."153

A combination of small unit skill, soldier initiative, and determined leadership permitted American forces to shake off the effects of tactical surprise, defeat al Qaeda attacks on the landing zones, then mount an offensive. Their ability to reduce the enemy positions depended heavily on Special-Forces directed precision air power, but especially the integration of air power with ground maneuver. The battle that ensued demonstrated clearly the tremendous capability of precision strikes, but also revealed some of its limitations. American aircraft heavily bombed al Qaeda positions on Objective Ginger for over one week, but the enemy was still able to fire on infantry as the Americans closed on their positions.154

The experience of Operation Anaconda revealed that geography, when combined with an enemy's determination to avoid detection creates a high degree of uncertainty in battle. Al Qaeda applied countermeasures to surveillance and precision munitions capabilities learned during previous engagements. As Stephen Biddle concluded:

How could such things happen in an era of persistent reconnaissance drones, airborne radars, satellite surveillance, thermal imaging, and hypersensitive electronic eavesdropping equipment? The answer is that the earth 's surface remains an extremely complex environment with an abundance of natural and manmade cover and concealment available for those militaries capable of exploiting it.

The experience of Operation Anaconda revealed the dangers of failing to take into account the "interaction" with the enemy and considering potential countermeasures to American technological capabilities. The course of the battle also demonstrated how friction encountered after initial contact with the enemy generated even greater uncertainty. The cancellation of subsequent lifts and other decisions such as the forced withdrawal of attack helicopters reveal that the future course of events depends not only on what one side plans to do, but upon enemy reactions and initiatives that are impossible to predict at the outset. Anaconda exposed the Army's "Doctrine of Firsts" as unrealistic. Despite the

40

experience of Anaconda, the belief in the certainty of future war persisted even as America's military prepared for an attack into Iraq under conditions of profound uncertainty.155

FIRST THE VERDICT, THEN THE TRIAL!

For after all allowances have been made for historical differences, wars still resemble each other more than they resemble any other human activity.

—Sir Michael Howard

War is the final auditor of military institutions. In theory, contemporary conflicts such as those in Afghanistan and Iraq provide opportunities for military innovation because of a high sense of urgency and opportunity for feedback based on actual experience.156 Analysis of the present combined with an understanding of history should permit a grounded projection into the near future and allow the strategist to meet what Sir Michael Howard identified as the challenge to: "steer between the danger of repeating the errors of the past because he is ignorant that they have been made, and the danger of remaining bound by theories deduced from past history although changes in conditions have rendered these theories obsolete." 157

The record of recent years is not encouraging, however, as a flawed vision of future war developed and grew despite contemporary experiences that ran directly counter to that vision. An element of classical hubris is man's belief that he has broken free from history. Many advocates of certainty in war disregard history because they believe that technology has generated unprecedented change; others misuse history to support their conception of change in warfare as linear and spurred almost exclusively by technology. 158

What is particularly surprising, however, is the neglect of recent wartime experience. Answers to questions that bore directly on the development of military plans and strategy for Operation Iraqi Freedom lay well outside the reach of sensors and computers. Those questions included: Will Iraq use biological or chemical weapons? Will military leaders obey Saddam if he orders them to employ those weapons? What will be the effects of those weapons? Will Iraq target civilians or strike Israel or Kuwait? Will Iraqi forces blow the bridges over the Euphrates River? How resolutely will the Iraqi Army defend? What are the combat potentials of different Iraqi units? Will the people of Baghdad welcome attacking U.S. forces? Will Saddam's Army defend forward or organize a defense nearer the center of Baghdad? How capable will our units be in urban operations? Will they set oil wells on fire as part of a larger scorched earth strategy? Will Saddam create a refugee crisis? Will Iraqi factions fight each other? How will each of the Kurdish factions react in the north? What will be Iran's reaction and what will be the actions of the Iranian-supported forces that had already entered eastern Iraq? Questions concerning a transition to military government and constabulary duty in post-conflict Iraq were fraught with even greater uncertainty. The best sensors or information technologies could not answer those questions and each bore directly on the conduct of operations. The United States and its allies devised a strategy for and fought under conditions of profound uncertainty, modifying the plan dramatically from the very beginning of hostilities.

Two factors obstruct the abandonment of the assumption of near-certainty in future war. First, some consider business, finance, and economic analogies more relevant to understanding future war than war itself. Second, there is a tendency to place unwarranted confidence in the fidelity of computer simulations that fail to replicate the conditions of war. Faulty analogies and flawed experiments are mutually reinforcing; the experiments promote the assumption of near-certainty in war and that assumption makes war appear comparable to business practices and the economy.

The military and business routinely share ideas and lessons in the areas of management and leadership. The military has clearly benefited from that relationship. Large portions of the military resemble business and require management efforts similar or identical to those in business. Specific military functions that benefit clearly from proven and emerging business management techniques include finance, budget, comptroller and accounting functions; transportation and supply management; and information management. More general lessons also apply such as WalMart's methods for assessing competition and remaining adaptive to the market. Lockheed-Martin's effort to forge a unifying culture and achieve efficiencies among its many sub-entities seems particularly relevant to joint integration. The military has applied and sometimes misapplied the latest management techniques such as Total Quality Management to improve operations.159 Problems arise when managerial practices and business principles influence military strategy, operations, or organization without sensitivity to the unique features and demands of war.

Uncertainty in war makes business and war incompatible and limits the utility of analogies between military conflict and the economy. Whereas military organizations must cope with inherent unpredictability, businesses rely on control and efficiency. Business fears the unpredictable and management emphasizes objective and quantifiable considerations rather than an embrace of the subjective and unpredictable.160

The uncertainties of war (such as the unanswered questions prior to Operation Iraqi Freedom) make precise calculation and control impossible. Interactions with the enemy and uncertainties associated with those interactions are fundamentally different from business interactions with either markets or competitors. Moreover, war cannot be prosecuted to business standards of efficiency because barely winning in war is an ugly proposition. In war one seeks to overwhelm the enemy such that he is unable to take effective action; the business principle of maximum payoff for minimum investment does not apply. Business relies on projections to gauge demand, control production, and manage supply chains. The human and psychological dimensions of war often make projecting demand for needs such as fire support or logistical supplies impossible to make with any degree of specificity. Consider, for example, an attack during which an enemy who was expected to offer stiff resistance collapses suddenly. If the means to exploit that transitory advantage, such as fuel, are not immediately at hand, forces may miss a fleeting opportunity. Unanticipated enemy actions, such as the interdiction of air or ground supply lines and weather, such as sandstorms that limit air and ground resupply operations, militate for decentralization of assets even if such an organization seems inefficient in peacetime. Business practices such as centralization of logistical assets and concepts such as just-in-time delivery, velocity management, and supply chain management are potentially disastrous if applied to the military without consideration of war's unique nature. In general, the complexity and uncertainty of war requires decentralization and a certain degree of redundancy, concepts that cut against business' emphasis on control and efficiency. The assumption that future war will lie mainly in the realm of certainty obscures differences between business and war fosters the belief that the influence of information technology on business and the economy is directly transferable to war.

In the late 1990s, a new concept called network-centric warfare formalized analogies between war and business. In a 1998 book that advanced the concept, David Alberts, John Gartska, and Frederick Stein indicated that network-centric warfare depended on a high performance information grid that "translates information into combat power by effectively linking knowledgeable entities in the battlespace."161 In an article that appeared in The Naval Institute's Proceedings during that same year, Vice Admiral Cebrowski and Mr. Gartska asserted that:" Network centric operations deliver to the US military the same powerful dynamics as they produced in American business. At the strategic level the critical element for both is a detailed understanding of the appropriate competitive space - all elements of the battlespace and battletime."162

While the authors of Network Centric Warfare stated that they saw the "lessons learned in the commercial sector not as gospel to be blindly followed, but as inputs to our concepts, development, and experimentation processes," they asserted that "the basic dynamics of the value-creation process are domain independent." They went on to apply their analogies without consideration for the unique dynamics of war.163 For example, the authors suggested a direct application of Metcalf's Law - the idea that as the number of nodes in a network increases linearly, the effectiveness of that network "increases exponentially as the square number of nodes in the network." Based on that "law," the network promised to deliver a "superior information position." The authors argued that the military and business shared interest in gaining access to an "information grid". As a "sensor grid" generates "competitive space awareness" for business, it would generate "battlespace awareness" for the military. As network centric businesses use "transaction grids" to translate high levels of awareness into specific actions such as shipping orders, increasing production, and ordering parts, the network centric military would use "engagement grids" to target and strike enemy assets.164 They assumed that an increase in access to relevant, accurate, and timely information would have the same effect on war as it did on business. The military could become more efficient, smaller and faster.

Network-centric advocates also believed that changes in the economy of the mid-to-late 1990s permitted similar changes in warfare - changes that could be engineered with information technology. Under the old economy, they argued, growth and profits were limited by competition with companies who produced comparable goods and services. Businesses, therefore, could not "lock in" market share and efforts to do so resulted in decreasing returns on investment. With information superiority, however, companies could generate extraordinary wealth and increasing returns on investment. Information permitted companies to "lock in" success and eliminate the constraints of market share equilibrium and competition. With information superiority in war and investment in the right technologies, it was argued that the U.S. military would achieve speed and precision to "lock out" enemy strategies and "lock in" success.165 To some, the information revolution in business provided nothing less than the answer to future war.

The concept of "lock out" assumed near-perfect intelligence. By connecting its information, sensor, and transaction grids, the military would achieve the same degree of visibility on the enemy that WalMart enjoyed on inventories and sales.166 Speed of action coupled with certain knowledge was the guarantor of victory. Admiral Cebrowski and Mr. Garstka depicted "old" warfare as attrition based; network-centric warfare would be cleaner, more humanitarian, and bring rapid victory. Under the old style of warfare, "reversals are possible, and frequently the outcome is in doubt," but network centric warfare appeared as "analogous to the new economic model, with potentially increasing returns on investment."167 The rapid growth of the information technology sector of the economy added arrogance to ignorance as an impediment to correcting the increasingly flawed vision of future war.

The economic bubble of the late 1990s increased enthusiasm for the concept of network-centric warfare. Futurists Alvin and Heidi Toffler argued that changes in warfare would parallel changes in the "information age" economy. Some of the Tofflers' ideas have proven generally correct such as the ability to use intelligence to strike targets with greater precision and less destructive power; the ability to employ smaller organizations over wider areas than in the past, and the integration of systems to achieve increased efficiency and speed of action.168 Advocates of network-centric warfare, however, emboldened by the booming economy, displayed irrational exuberance in connection with the degree of certainty that information technology could provide in war. The authors of Network Centric Warfare and others took inspiration from "profound changes in the nature of our world" including the possibility for dotcom executives to "become billionaires in periods measured in months.169 They built upon the Tofflers' ideas and suggested that the prosperity of the late 1990s signaled the advances that were possible in the conduct of war. It was against this backdrop in 1998, that the Secretary of Defense gave Joint Forces Command the mission to develop and test concepts for future war based on Joint Vision 2010. Joint Forces Command turned over a large portion of that work over to contractors.

A team comprised mainly of contractors used JV2010 as the basis for their efforts. They viewed the possibilities associated with information technology as the basis for new operational concepts. That vision of future war took shape under two complementary concepts: Rapid Decisive Operations (RDO) and Effects-Based Operations (EBO). Their names were inherently persuasive; criticism might be misconstrued as advocacy for "Ponderous Indecisive Operations" or "Randomly Generated Violence." Even beyond the names, the concepts had much to recommend them. The time it took to deploy forces to Southwest Asia and prepare for the 2003 invasion of Iraq supported RDO's call for forces capable of moving across strategic distances and transitioning immediately into combat. The need for concurrent, geographically dispersed actions at the outset of the war to secure the Kurdish population in Northern Iraq, control bridges across the Euphrates River, occupy oil fields in Northern and Southern Iraq, open ports in Southern Iraq, and prevent Iraq from firing missiles from the Western desert demonstrated the need for forces capable of conducting the simultaneous and distributed operations, called for in RDO. Concepts concerning speed of action and decision relative to the enemy (tempo and decision superiority) and improvements in interagency coordination to ensure mutually reinforcing efforts (an element of EBO) are also promising. 170

The persistent belief in near-certainty in future war, however, elevated anticipated capabilities of information technologies to the level of strategy, encouraged linear thinking, and undermined the positive features of the new concepts.

The concept of effects-based operations assumed near certainty in future war; it treated the enemy as a "system" that could be fully understood through a process called "operational net assessment (ONA)." Because ONA would produce "a comprehensive system-of-systems understanding of the enemy and the environment," operations could achieve a high degree of speed as well as precision in operational effects. The enemy would be unable to keep pace with the "high rates of change" imposed on him. Similar to WalMart's use of information technology, the military's knowledge would lock out opponents' courses of action. Because ONA permits commanders to understand even second and third order effects, military operations (essentially precision attacks against enemy "nodes") progress linearly and rapidly toward victory. The enemy is unable to respond effectively and falls victim to "cumulative and cascading effects." 45

It is assumed that because of near-perfect intelligence and knowledge of the enemy's reactions, actions necessary to achieve desired effects can be calculated with a great deal of precision and the application of force, therefore, can become very efficient and controlled. Under the concept of distributed operations, for example, it is assumed that commanders will have enough "knowledge" to "give distributed combat groups enough combat power to accomplish the required ends and survive the encounter." 172

Effects-based operations promise to influence enemy intentions and coerce the enemy before destructive power (or a large commitment of land forces) is necessary. Effects-based operations promise to bring "network-centric power to bear" with "coordinated sets of actions directed at shaping the behavior of friends, foes, and neutrals in peace, crisis, and war." EBO would seek to prevent wars or, if war became unavoidable, convince an adversary to desist from behavior contrary to United States interests. As Admiral Cebrowski and his assistant Dr. Thomas Barnett wrote in January 2003, "When 50% of something important to the enemy is destroyed at the outset, so is his strategy. 173

That stops wars - which is what network centric warfare is all about." It was this thinking that led some to believe that the "shock and awe" phase of Iraqi Freedom would lead to the regime's capitulation. During Operation Iraqi Freedom, however, coercive power seemed to come at least as much from ground forces advancing on the Iraqi capital as it did on the "shock and awe" strikes. Factors such as the desire to limit collateral damage and the hope of cajoling the Iraqis into surrendering complicated theoretical "calculations" of how much force to apply.

Confidence in predictability and rapid victory in war has generated interest in two other strategic concepts, "pressure" and "discriminate force." These concepts call for employing military force at low levels against critical nodes. While these ideas have met resistance, some within the Department of Defense and academia continue to argue for their adoption. In a November 2002 article, former U.S. Deputy Assistant Secretary of Defense Elizabeth Sherwood-Randall and former Israeli Deputy National Security Advisor Ariel Levite set forth perhaps the most comprehensive argument to appear for "discriminate force." The authors argued that a high degree of discrimination and control was now possible in war because of a "knowledge base that will enable aiming attacks at high-leverage targets, while avoiding irrelevant, politically sensitive, incorrectly identified, or illegitimate sites." The authors suggested that future military operations would emphasize "stand-off firepower over physical movement, software over hardware, and extensive deployment of light infantry as well as special forces over armored or mechanized forces."174 Some commentators suggested that the opening actions of Iraqi Freedom were consistent with "discriminate force" 175 The strategy for the war, however, included forces to impose the coalition's will on the enemy and the Iraqis, as in 1991, were incapable of challenging the initiative of U.S. and British joint forces. As the air war in Kosovo demonstrated in 1999, coercion could work if one's strategy includes the ability and the will to compel the enemy if coercion fails. As Operation Iraqi Freedom demonstrated in 2003, imposing one's will on the enemy requires a balanced joint force capable of operating under conditions of uncertainty and a strategy more sophisticated than a target list designed to achieve "shock and awe."

Simplistic strategic approaches to war that terms like discriminate force and pressure represent describe war as fast, efficient, controllable, and cost-effective. The approach was not really new. Those theories are not new. The belief in certainty in future war, in addition to influencing the intellectual foundation for defense transformation, had resurrected an old, failed strategy cloaked in a new lexicon.

Faith in American technological superiority, particularly in the information domain, has resurrected a belief, largely discredited during the Vietnam War, that military action can be calibrated and controlled with a great deal of precision to achieve strategic objectives. That belief combines faith in information technologies with old strategic bombing theories and the American tendency to view war as an engineering or business management problem that will succumb to systems analysis, reasoned judgment, and the application of superior technology. Elements of RDO, EBO and discriminate force replicate Secretary of Defense Robert McNamara's Vietnam strategy of graduated pressure as applied in Vietnam. Sherwood-Randall and Levite called for "capabilities and options for the highly discriminate, calibrated, and nuanced application of conventional military power" to effect the "cost/benefit calculations" of the enemy. With improvements in "intelligence and other situational awareness tools," war would become the application of "cutting edge air power." Because near-perfect intelligence would reduce the complexity and unpredictability of war, "organic armed formations" that possess "their own core components" would be "modified to meet the requirements of discriminate force."176 Because discriminate force closely parallels features in the emerging Department of Defense orthodoxy concerning future war, the authors provided a glimpse of how the flawed intellectual foundation of Defense Transformation could create vulnerabilities in force structure and organization. Some advocates are unaware of past failures associated with this approach and believe that they have invented a new strategic concept. Others acknowledge previous failures, but do not recognize the reductionism of their vision; they blame previous failures only on immature technology. 177

The emerging strategic concept for future war is nearly identical to the concept of "graduated pressure" that Secretary of Defense Robert McNamara and his principal subordinates developed during the Vietnam War. McNamara believed that fundamental changes in the nature of war made traditional military advice based on the need to impose one's will on the enemy irrelevant and even dangerous to national security. Similar to aspects of "effects based operations" McNamara developed a strategy that would use military force not to destroy, but to signal resolve and intentions to the enemy. Measured application of power using mainly bombing against carefully-selected targets but also small commando raids were designed to effect Vietnamese Communist "calculation of interests" and convince them to desist from their support for the insurgency in South Vietnam. Because the United States was so much more powerful - "full spectrum dominant" in today's language -Vietnamese communist leaders would desist from supporting the insurgency in South Vietnam. Emphasis was on control to send precisely the right message and produce the desired effects. In March of 1964, McNamara predicted that his strategy would "turn the tide" in Vietnam in four to six months. As in Kosovo, there seemed to be reason for confidence. Like Serbia in 1999, North Vietnam in 1964 was no "peer competitor."

Fundamental flaws in the Vietnam War strategy of graduated pressure are replicated in emerging doctrinal concepts. McNamara and his principal assistants were oblivious to the human and psychological dimensions of war. From the U.S. perspective bombing and limited raids might have appeared as coercion and communication short of war. From the perspective of the enemy, however, those were acts of war. War unleashes a dynamic that defies systems analysis quantification; McNamara and the architects of graduated pressure greatly underestimated the resolve of the North Vietnamese leadership and the ability of Vietnamese communist forces to suffer losses and continue fighting. The linear thinking of McNamara and his advisors kept them from recognizing that the future course of events depended not only on U.S. action, but also on enemy reactions and initiatives that were difficult to predict. Ho Chi Minh's response, the infiltration of North Vietnamese Army divisions into South Vietnam impelled the commitment of U.S. troops, precisely the action that graduated pressure was designed to avoid.

The situation in Vietnam was too complex a problem for bombing to solve. The source of Vietnamese communist strength was political as well as military; The enemy strategy to avoid American and South Vietnamese strength and attack weakness combined with the geography of South Vietnam and the mainly agrarian economy of North Vietnam to render America'spreferred method of fighting, the application of air power, unable to force a decision. 178

A September 1964 Pentagon war game, SIGMA II, exposed the flaws in the concept of graduated pressure. The games tested the thesis that: "By applying limited, graduated military actions, reinforced by political and economic pressures, against a nation providing external support for an insurgency, we could cause that nation to decide to reduce greatly, or eliminate altogether, its support for the insurgency. The objective of the attacks and pressures is not to destroy the nation's ability to provide support, but rather to affect its calculation of interests." The game was eerily prophetic. The hope that air power would be decisive was dashed as insurgents' low demand for supplies and the agrarian nature of North Vietnam's economy made the enemy resistant to bombing as a solution. Control of the situation passed to the enemy as the United States reacted to Vietnamese Communist initiatives and was forced to introduce large numbers of ground troops. Because of enemy resilience, measured and calculated application of force gave way to the destruction of all North Vietnamese targets and the mining of Haiphong Harbor. 179

The SIGMA II war game had no effect on American policy or strategy in Vietnam. Growing momentum behind the concept of graduated pressure prevented learning from the war game. Even planners who were personally convinced that graduated pressure could only lead to defeat suppressed their opinions because their bosses did not want to hear those opinions. Others went along because it was expedient to do so; they believed that, over time, they could erode barriers to more resolute military action. Similarly, the growing orthodoxy of near-certainty in future war overwhelmed practical experience that exposed it as fallacy. For example, Dr. David Alberts of the Department of Defense, a computer scientist and businessman-turned-strategist who has authored and co-authored much of the burgeoning literature on network-centric and information age warfare stated that "NCW proofs of concept are beginning to accumulate and convince even some of the diehard skeptics—. Experiences in Bosnia, Kosovo, and Afghanistan have proved real-world laboratories where important learning and proofs of concept have occurred." 180

Imprecision in language compounds the misreading of contemporary experience. It is unclear, for example, what Dr. Alberts' meant by "network-centric proofs of concept." In contrast to the SIGMA II test, joint experimentation failed to challenge the assumptions on which flawed concepts are based. Rather than expose flawed assumptions, joint experimentation has imparted those assumptions with false credibility derived from an appearance of impartiality associated with computer simulations. It is in this area of simulation that the military might learn a valuable lesson from business. The experience with joint experimentation is similar to the experiences of some companies during the information technology economic boom and the subsequent stock market crash of 2001.

Before the economic bubble of the late 1990s burst in 2001, there were indicators that businesses' expectations for continued growth were greatly inflated. The case of, CISCO, a computer network company, is particularly instructive. CISCO projected current growth linearly into the future similar to projections of America's military technological advantages into the future. CISCO persisted in those projections even as the market changed and every other company recognized the market slowdown. CISCO's faith in its network-centric method, however, blinded the company to market realities. Indeed, CISCO's "virtual close" software was designed to prevent earnings surprises. As one analyst concluded after CISCO's collapse: "I've come to realize how the use of computers - computer models to be precise - combined with hubris can lead to disaster—. While computers are wonderful tools for gathering and analyzing data, they cannot consistently and accurately predict the future of extremely complex systems—. This requires and, dare I say, always will require human judgment.'181 Like CISCO, the Department of Defense is ignoring the equivalent of the market - actual combat experience - in favor of computer simulations that reinforce flawed assumptions about the nature of future war.

Once Joint Vision 2010 identified information superiority as the foundation for defense transformation, the assumption of near-certainty in future war underpinned all concept development and experimentation efforts. 182

Because that assumption had the official sanction of the JCS Chairman and the Secretary of Defense, there was pressure to "validate" rather than scrutinize it. A close observer of joint experimentation remarked that the process reminded him of the Queen's declaration in Alice in Wonderland: "First the verdict, then the trial!"

Conflicts of interest present additional obstacles to effective experimentation. For example, J9 of Joint Forces Command has responsibility both for developing and testing future war concepts. 183

That conflict of interest appears similar to accounting firms such as Arthur Anderson having management consulting and auditing responsibilities. The continuous assertion of near-certainty in future war seems as obvious as false accounting at Worldcom and other companies, yet joint experimentation has failed to expose faults in visions of future war.

Nine months after soldiers fought against undetected enemy in hot landing zones during Operation Anaconda, Joint Forces Command reported to Congress that recent experiments had affirmed that future joint operations would be "knowledge centric" and U.S. forces would achieve "situational awareness superiority."184

In December 2002, Joint Forces Command reported that recent experiments demonstrated the "opportunity to replace the inefficient application of mass that was based on uncertainty with a more precise application of national power based on knowledge."185

Experiments determined that near-perfect intelligence became "knowledge through Operational Net Assessment (ONA), Common Relevant Operational Picture (CROP), and Joint Intelligence, Surveillance, and Reconnaissance (JISR)." Under the concept of Rapid Decisive Operations, experimentation demonstrated that knowledge about "the adversary, the operational environment, and ourselves" would permit American forces to win the next war:

with less risk of unintended consequences, and more efficient expenditure of national resources. Knowledge becomes a hedge against uncertainty, allowing deployment of more precisely tailored capabilities and enabling speed and degree of decisiveness of action. Knowledge-centric operations postulates that future operations will move beyond information superiority to decision superiority through a comprehensive, system-of-systems understanding of the enemy and the environment, as well as a shared integrated awareness of the friendly situation. Decision superiority is the ability of the commander, based upon information superiority and situational understanding to make effective decisions more rapidly than the adversary, thereby allowing a dramatic increase in the pace, coherence and effectiveness of operations. Advanced decision-support tools, knowledge-fusion, and horizontal and vertical integration of situational awareness will improve dissemination to decision -makers in an understandable and actionable format.186

The report indicated that experimentation "validated" the process of "Operational Net Assessment" and its ability to provide "knowledge in sufficient detail to apply integrated diplomatic, information, military, and economic (DIME) friendly actions decisively against an adversary's political, military, economic, social, information, infrastructure (PMESH) systems." ONA and the knowledge it generated created "decisive effects."187

While those charged with the development and testing of concepts clearly have the best intentions, many are contracted from large defense manufacturing companies such as Lockheed Martin, TRW, and General Dynamics. In addition to the incentive to develop sound concepts for future war, other influences such as the renewal of the consulting contract or the benefits to the parent company of developing concepts that demand that company's weaponry or communications equipment have potential to cloud judgment. The inherent limitations of computer simulations in replicating the complexity of war place a particularly high premium on independent, critical evaluation of concepts.

Joint experiments like Millenium Challenge 2002, described as "the largest most complex military experiment in history" fail to replicate the uncertainty of war because they are largely scripted. As the enemy conforms to the intelligence estimate, concepts like dominant battlespace knowledge and predictive intelligence are "validated." Retired Marine Corps Lieutenant General Paul Van Riper became so frustrated with constraints on enemy actions that he quit his role as opposing forces commander in Millennium Challenge. While all exercises contain a mix of scripting and free-play, the excessive restrictions placed on General Van Riper were designed primarily to protect the flawed assumption of information superiority. Another senior officer observed after the experiment, "it was in actuality an exercise that was almost entirely scripted to ensure a Blue win." It was important to preserve conditions of near-certainty because the military is already trading traditional sources of combat power, such as firepower and protection, for information dominance. The conflict of interest in Joint Forces Command was also apparent as the exercise director, who also had responsibility for supervising concept writers, changed Van Riper's scheme for employing the opposing force. Because of flaws in the experiment, Joint Forces Command failed to expose the limitations of "knowledge" in war and "validated" the concepts of Rapid Decisive Operations and Effects Based Operations – concepts that Van Riper criticized as representing little more than slogans. 188

Joint experiments also preserve the assumption of near-certainty in future war because they end before the adversary has the opportunity to adapt to U.S. strengths. Because near-perfect intelligence combined with precision weapons is supposed to deliver quick victory, experiments such as the Air Force's Global Engagement VI and the Army's Vigilant Warrior war games ended before strategic objectives were achieved. Because the war games assumed that a good beginning equated to a rapid decision and end of the war, they oversimplified the problem. Intelligence estimates are best at the outset of the campaign because they can be prepared deliberately before interaction with the enemy. Indeed, much of the uncertainty in war stems from that interaction under conditions that require rapid decisions based on imperfect information. As a retired senior officer who observed many joint and service experiments observed, the war games end when victory seems inevitable to the U.S. side, but not to the enemy. 189

Clausewitz observed that "war is a special activity, different and separate from any other pursued by man."190 He also observed that friction is what separates real war from war on paper; today we might add that friction also separates real war from war in computers. Because experiments that are supposed to test assumptions of future war are biased toward validating concepts and because primary causes of uncertainty in war are absent from those experiments, joint and service experimentation actually advance a flawed intellectual foundation for Defense Transformation. Many of the advocates of near-certainty in future war have assumed that their experience and education as systems analysts, economists, computer scientists, engineers and business managers gives them not only valuable insight into, but a holistic understanding of war. They overlook, however, war's human and psychological dimensions, the interactions with the enemy, the political nature of war, and other sources of uncertainty that make counterproductive their well-intentioned efforts to contribute to national defense.

The Army's Objective Force initiative is under review. There is much that the Army will want to retain such as decentralization of combined arms capabilities to lower levels and the ability to achieve improvements in mobility while reducing logistical requirements. What the Army has achieved in the area of command and control and sensor technologies will benefit the force of the future. The root cause of the Objective Force's difficulties, however, the assumption of near-certainty in future war, must be expunged along with its distortions in organization and doctrine. The Army might use the opportunity also to correct inflated claims about the SBCT's capability to fight in operations that will remain dominated by uncertainty.

Other efforts in the Department of Defense, hold promise for improving joint experimentation. Historian Williamson Murray has completed a study of past successes and failures in war gaming and experimentation. Although he noted that effective "red teaming" to test prevailing visions of future war rarely occurred, he identified the principal causes of those failures: organizational cultures that did not encourage debate and intellectual effort, arrogance, overconfidence in a simplistic solutions to future war, and a failure to understand the enemy.191 Although the same problems plague the development of concepts for future war and the conduct of joint experimentation, identifying them might serve as the first step in changing course. The Joint Staff has established a new process to subject concepts to greater scrutiny before they go to experimentation including panels of more junior officers not vested in concept development. Correcting the fundamental flaw in the vision of future war, however, does not require elaborate experimentation. The orthodoxies of knowledge centric warfare and near-certainty in future war are illogical and have been thoroughly discredited by recent experience.

IMPLICATIONS FOR DEFENSE TRANSFORMATION

"We must learn to live with a measure of uncertainty, paradox, and ambiguity. We must acknowledge that vital pieces of information may always be missing. That is the price we pay for entering into the lives of the cosmos, for becoming participators in nature instead of mere observers."

—F. David Peat

Operation Iraqi Freedom demonstrated the enduring uncertainty of war and thoroughly discredited portions of service and joint visions based on the assumption of near-certainty. It was clear before the war began that RMA technologies had neither lifted the fog of war nor provided the capability to achieve quick, cheap and decisive victory in Iraq. The key to victory in Iraqi Freedom was the joint capability that the coalition employed to impose its will on the enemy. In contrast to descriptions of war found in concepts such as Rapid Decisive Operations and Effects-Based Operations, the course of events in Iraqi Freedom depended very much on enemy and even allied reactions that proved difficult to predict. As reporters continuously asked officials if circumstances had forced military operations "off plan," they seemed not to understand that, in war, successful plans are not deterministic and are adaptable to a wide range of possibilities. Leaders adapted military plans and operations to changing circumstances, such as the denial of overland movement through Turkey. Because the force was capable of operating under conditions of profound uncertainty, the Coalition continued to make progress toward political goals and objectives.

An obvious observation emerged from early operations in Iraq: The best means of dealing with uncertainty was the flexible employment of joint and all-arms capabilities. Diverse means - including air, land, special operations, and naval forces as well as space-based assets - permitted innovations to retain the initiative. Coalition adaptability was clear, for example, in connection with operations in urban terrain and efforts to prevent injury to innocent civilians. When the enemy blended into the civilian population to force a protracted fight and escape Coalition air power, land forces closed with the enemy to identify and defeat them. When enemy forces, in turn, concentrated to defend against ground attacks, they became vulnerable to fires from artillery and aircraft. Uncertainty put a premium on flexibility rather than the detailed planning associated with concepts such as Effects-Based Operations. Uncertainty also demanded flexibility in operations conducted at sea and in the air. The plan for the air campaign, developed deliberately for months, did not survive the first moments of the war.

The enemy employed deception at sea; the Iraqis attempted to mine their own harbors with commercial boats. Coalition naval forces boarded and searched those boats and discovered many mines. Dynamic tasking of aircraft in which pilots received target instructions after take off greatly enhanced the ability of air forces to respond to real-time intelligence and support land forces. The uncertainty of the war and the adaptability it demanded revealed the strengths of the American military; it also revealed flaws in the deterministic aspects of concepts such as Effects-Based Operations and Rapid Decisive Operations.

In addition to freeing the Iraqi people from a brutal regime and removing the threat of weapons of mass destruction in the hands of Saddam, Operation Iraqi Freedom presents a tremendous opportunity to learn from that conflict and base visions of future war in reality rather than wishful thinking. If America fails to repair the intellectual foundation of defense transformation, future national security will be at risk. The fallacy of near-certainty in war will generate vulnerabilities in the force that future adversaries could exploit. These include flaws in strategic and operational concepts, an inability to capitalize on technological advances, confused priorities that result in wasted resources, diminished combat readiness, an impairment of joint interoperability, imbalances in force structure, and a military culture out of step with the realities of war.

The illusion of information dominance creates unrealistic expectations that long-range precision weapons systems can deliver quick, efficient, cheap, and decisive victory. Enthusiasm for impressive new technologies connected by the network into a "system of systems" led many to conclude prior to Operation Iraqi Freedom that those capabilities represented a "silver bullet" solution to the complex problem of war. Strategic and operational thinking suffers from that simplistic conception because of a tendency to mirror image the enemy and assume that the enemy will behave rationally.

The assumption that the use of force in war is susceptible to rational calculation and tight control is particularly dangerous. The illusion of control in war portrays the use of force innocuously and blurs distinctions between war and diplomacy. War, however, involving as it does killing and the prospect of death, unleashes a psychological dynamic that defies control. "Discriminate force" from the adversary's perspective is still an act of war, not a signal of resolve. If the adversary chooses to escalate, he is likely to gain the initiative over a country employing "deliberate force." When the enemy does not behave as planned, withdraw or the commitment to a level of effort not considered at the outset become the only options.

Unless the belief in near-certainty is rejected, future enemies will have greater opportunities to achieve surprise over U.S. forces. Faith that information technology combined with systematic methodology can "prevent surprise" encourages a tendency to discount factors that are not quantifiable such as cultural and historical influences on behavior. The vast literature on strategic and operational surprise reveals that a lack of information or the absence of systematic analysis rarely make principal contributions to so-called intelligence failures. The "noise" of conflicting information and the sheer volume of data often prevent warning of enemy action. Over time, false alarms generate a "cry wolf" syndrome that desensitizes commanders and staffs to actual warnings. Bureaucratic barriers and compartmentalized intelligence, often designed to preserve secrecy of sources, can prevent fusion of intelligence indicators. Other obstacles reside in the cognitive domain. Prejudices and a human tendency to pay attention mainly to information that reinforces current expectations often prevent the identification of specific threats and enemy actions that appear, in retrospect, to have been obvious. Even assuming that intelligence warnings are recognized, additional barriers exist between the perception of a specific danger and the translation of that perception into defensive or preemptive action. 192

This is not to suggest a defeatist attitude in connection with intelligence analysis, but declarations that the RMA has solved the complex problem of surprise in war could prevent real improvements in an area that has become especially critical given the terrorist threat and the proliferation of weapons of mass destruction. Initiatives such as the creation of a "collaborative information environment" and the process of "operational net assessment" should be pursued with vigor, but with also with realistic expectations.

A less deterministic approach will improve intelligence analysis at the operational and tactical levels as well. Operating with an appreciation for the uncertainty of war permits commanders to understand a range of possibilities and contingencies. Commanders will be better prepared to make decisions under the actual conditions of war; precise predictions are often precisely wrong. The recognition that war remains fundamentally uncertain will permit commanders to focus intelligence collection and combat reconnaissance efforts on what they cannot learn in advance and recognize the importance of initiative, adaptability, and bold action.

The orthodoxy of near-perfect intelligence inflates the importance of the headquarters and threatens to have a stultifying effect on high-level command. Terms like information dominance and decision dominance impart the idea that making near-perfect decisions based on near-perfect intelligence is the essence of command. To many, commanders are managers who mainly use tools such as the methodology in Operational Net Assessment. Command responsibility, however, is far more diverse. Commanders must be capable of conceptual thought and be able to communicate a vision of how the force will achieve its objectives. Their concepts of operation must harmonize the efforts of disparate entities and direct the force in a way that permits initiative and achieves synergy. As Martin van Creveld warned in Command in War, "communications and information processing technology merely constitutes one part of the general environment in which command operates. To allow that part to dictate the structure and functioning of command systems, as is sometimes done, is not merely to become the slave of technology, but also to lose sight of what command is all about." 193

The assumption of near-certainty also threatens to undermine forces' ability to fight. If commanders assume near-perfect intelligence, emphasis is likely to shift from mission-oriented orders and flexible execution of those orders toward the development of near-perfect plans based on deductive processes. Because those plans are regarded as near-perfect, commanders will be inclined to demand execution of specific tasks on time and within constraints of calculated resource allocations. The belief in near-perfect intelligence leads to an emphasis on firepower delivered from remote weapon systems under the control of higher headquarters. The illusion that war can be precisely managed and controlled leads to a preoccupation with efficiency, centralization, and control. Information displaces organic firepower and armor protection. This trend is already apparent. Displacement of fighting capability by perceived access to information was the foundation of the Army's division redesign in the late 1990s. Claims of what the SBCT can achieve in battle and the design of the Objective Force are also based on the same illusion. Computer simulations create a false impression that these organizations are capable. For example, analysts at RAND Corporation who are conducting computer simulation-based tests of the Objective Force are instructed not to let the unit get in close contact with the enemy.

Because information dominance and precision weapons permit efficiencies in force design, the weakness of future ground forces will demand that they avoid close battle. The force will be vulnerable under uncertain conditions. If the force loses communications, it will be isolated and even more vulnerable because it depends on remote fires. Michael Andrews, Army Deputy Assistant Secretary for Research and Technology observed that, "Everything relies on a reliable and secure network. Without it, our vulnerability is exposed." A widely circulated draft of an Objective Force white paper states clearly that the "Objective Force in 2015 requires knowledge dominance to succeed."194 Even if the force is able to prevent tactical surprises, operations are certain to be slow and deliberate because any degree of ambiguity will necessitate a reallocation of sensors and an analysis effort to avoid risks associated with encountering the enemy. Abandoning the assumption of knowledge dominance will help reverse the trend toward designing vulnerable units that are dependent on centralized resources and unable to overmatch the enemy in close combat.

The belief in near-certainty also undermines military culture, especially in connection with expectations of junior leaders. If leaders are not conditioned to cope with uncertainty, they are likely to experience paralysis and wait for orders when they confront chaotic circumstances. While much of the transformation literature stresses adaptability and initiative, the force's inability to overmatch the enemy in a close fight, a bias toward deductive reasoning, and the belief in dominant knowledge discourage risk taking. Leaders will be predisposed to wait for information rather than take resolute action. Indeed, they will have to act cautiously to ensure their force's survival. Ironically, a force that was designed to be fast and agile will operate ponderously.

Because belief in certainty or uncertainty as the dominant condition in war is relative, so are the consequences of that belief. Unique circumstances in combat will shift experiences, capabilities needed, and methods along a continuum between extremes of certainty and uncertainty. Assuming near-certainty, however, generates a series of derivative assumptions and predilections that are likely to lead to difficulties when that base assumption is proven false.

CERTAINTY	UNCERTAINTY
DEDUCTIVE REASONING AND PROCESSES	**INDUCTIVE REASONING AND INTUITION**
Detailed Planning, Targeting, Control	Mission Orders and Flexible Execution
Precision Firepower	Joint Integration; Fire and Maneuver
Centralization	Decentralization
Synchronization	Initiative
Deliberate execution	Speed of action

Forces prepared to fight under conditions of near-certainty in future war will be at a severe disadvantage relative to forces that embrace uncertainty and seek to turn it to their advantage.

The belief in near certainty has both derived from and reinforced American technological hubris, so much in evidence in the language of defense transformation. Phrases like Full Spectrum Dominance, Shock and Awe, Information Dominance, and Rapid Decisive Operations present a danger to our own efforts, embolden our adversaries, and offend our allies. As Colin Gray has observed, "When a capability appears almost too good to be true, especially when it pertains to an activity as complex, uncertain, and risky as war, the odds are that, indeed, it is too good to be true."195 The name of a concept should avoid presenting the object of difficult endeavors as a fait accompli. Potential hazards involve an underestimation of the challenges associated with military operations and false confidence that could lead to complacency or insensitivity to the limits of military technological advantages. Additionally, America's powerful military and economic strength relative to other nations has inspired considerable jealousy and suspicion; the immodesty associated with these terms serves only to cause further alienation.

Potential adversaries believe that the names of those concepts give expression to flaws in American thinking about future war; they are determined to capitalize on those flaws. For example, a recent study by two People's Liberation Army officers of the American vision of future war noted the belief in near-certainty and countered with the observation that while information technology "has made great strides, war still remains an unbroken mustang." The study went on to recommend to commanders that, "what is needed to grasp the ever-changing battlefield situation is greater use of intuition rather than mathematical deduction." In a passage that appears very close to Clausewitz's observation that uncertainty derives, in part, from an "interaction of opposites," the authors suggested that overconfidence in technology is America's principal vulnerability.

They believe that as long as the Edisons of today do not sink into sleep, the gate to victory will always be open to Americans. Self-confidence such as this has made them forget one simple fact - it is not so much that war follows the fixed racecourse of rivalry of technology and weaponry, as it is a game field with continually changing direction and many irregular factors—. It appears that Americans, however, do not pay attention to this. They drew the benefit of the Gulf War's technological victory and obviously have resolutely spared no cost to safeguard their leading position in high technology.196

Other militaries have also recognized the enduring uncertainty of war. If the U.S. military continues along the wrong path of defense transformation, others will learn from America's mistakes and plan to take advantage of vulnerabilities.

Potential adversaries view the importance that the American military has placed on network-centric concepts as a weakness and are developing technological countermeasures to attack components of emerging capabilities. News concerning the development of electromagnetic bombs or the sale of GPS jammers to Iraq highlight the danger of assuming linear progression toward greater clarity and precision on the battlefield. Historically, countermeasures have limited the effects of all "dominant" weapons on the battlefield. A cursory examination of twentieth century conventional weapons development reveals technological interactions that limited the effects of new technology. On land, the machine gun seemed decisive until the introduction of mobile protected firepower; the tank seemed decisive until the introduction of tank-killing systems. In the air, the development of radar limited the effectiveness of the bomber. The submarine may have dominated the seas were it not for the invention of sonar and battleships controlled the ocean's surface until the advent of naval aviation. Although Nazi Germany's strategic communications seemed invulnerable, the Allies had access to transmissions after capturing an Enigma machine and breaking the codes. Advocates of decisive weapons or technological capabilities have a history of ignoring countermeasures. Today, potential adversaries are closely monitoring American military operations and defense transformation initiatives to develop countermeasures to US capabilities. As Secretary of Defense Donald Rumsfeld observed, "In a networked environment, information assurance is critical." He warned that "No nation relies more on space for its national security than the United States. Yet elements of the U.S. space architecture—ground stations, launch assets and satellites in orbit—are threatened by capabilities that are increasingly available." 56

The U.S. must avoid the tendency to think linearly about technological countermeasures, especially when many capabilities and countermeasures can be purchased off-the-shelf.

Technological hubris and the associated neglect of countermeasures has led some to conclude that national defense should rely on a combination of small, light ground forces and preponderant air and naval power. This is one of the paradoxes of the RMA orthodoxy. American technological advantages have pushed adversaries out of the air and sea domains, yet RMA advocates suggest further investment in forces that are already dominant and reductions in the only forces that are capable of contending with potential adversaries' responses - a shifting of the venue of conflict to complex and urban terrain. Such an imbalance of forces would create vulnerabilities and thereby undermine America's ability to deter conflict or win wars if deterrence fails. As operations in Afghanistan demonstrated, the best results are achieved with synergistic joint capabilities. As the 1999 air war in Kosovo demonstrated, the absence of one of the components leads to extreme difficulties and results inconsistent with objectives. As Operation Iraqi Freedom demonstrated, the joint force must be able to fight under conditions of uncertainty on land, close with and defeat enemies employing countermeasures to joint fires, control terrain, and impose order. Iraqi Freedom demonstrated that, fighting together, joint forces are able to overcome challenges and uncertainties associated with complex geography (especially urban areas), political and humanitarian constraints on the use of firepower, and enemy actions such as deception, dispersion, concealment, and intermingling with the civilian population. As land, sea, and air forces were amassing to invade Iraq, however, Admiral Cebrowski and his assistant in the Office of Force Transformation wrote that future wars would be fought with air and sea-based precision munitions and small, "elite" special operations forces. They stated that a new "American Way of War moves the military toward an embrace of a more sharply focused global cop role: we increasingly specialize in neutralizing bad people who do bad things."198 Admiral Cebrowski seemed to overlook the fact that "bad people" are sometimes positioned at the head of bad armed forces that are determined to fight and might be savvy enough to evade long-range detection and precision munitions. The need to change the geopolitical landscape in Iraq demanded the presence of land forces to establish security and dismantle the Baath Party apparatus. It was important to defeat Iraqi Army units and it was equally important to separate physically the population from the Fedayeen militia. The belief in certainty, rooted as it is in technological hubris, masks the human dimension of war and creates the illusion that sensors and long-range fires can solve complex military and political problems. Only balanced joint forces will represent an effective deterrent or be able to win future wars.

While defense transformation has been distracted by the unrealistic objective of achieving near-certainty, organizational changes that could deliver immediate improvements in the ability to fight have not received focused attention. Indeed, the flawed assumption of near-certainty has led to changes in the wrong direction. Organizational reform would permit the joint force to take full advantage of the capabilities associated with communications, sensor, and information technologies. While some positive organizational initiatives are underway (such as the establishment of Joint Task Force Headquarters), changes made under the assumption of near-certainty, are generally unsound. To fight effectively under conditions of uncertainty and complexity, organizations must be flexible and agile. Flatter, or less hierarchical organizations are, in general, more capable of operating in uncertain environments than hierarchical organizations. Diverse capabilities at lower levels of command, to include all-service and all arms, will increase the effectiveness, albeit not the efficiency of the force.199 The assumption of near certainty, however, has resulted in a centralization of capabilities and the preservation of hierarchical organizations.

The flawed vision of future war impedes service cooperation; its abandonment will foster more effective integration of service capabilities. If the intellectual foundation of joint transformation acknowledges the complexity and uncertainty of war and the associated need for balanced forces, all services will have a greater incentive to work together. Understanding the limits of technology will bolster efforts to solve complex operational problems as a joint team through doctrine, organizational reform, training, tactics, and education.

In addition to creating an imbalance of forces and impeding joint integration, the irrational faith in certainty threatens to waste resources and create an imbalance between readiness and acquisition. It is easy to understand how precision strike technologies contribute to military operations. It is harder to understand the qualitative factors and skill level necessary to make that strike happen. It is perhaps even more difficult to understand the elements of combat power in land formations. Like air and sea forces, Army and Marine Corps units generate power from weapons, equipment and individual skill, but the main source lies in the collective psychology of the organization. In battle, strength comes from resistance to fear and disintegration that fear can impel. Imponderables such as confidence in one another and in one's leaders are most important in that connection. That confidence derives, in part, from bonds of mutual trust and respect that develop during tough, realistic training. Because it is easier to understand the sources of an F-22's capabilities, for example, than understand the source of an infantry platoon's combat power, those who make resource decisions must understand how investments in manning, forming, and training ground units are vital to maintaining a balanced joint capability. That training should occur in a joint environment whenever possible. If the bonds of trust and mutual understanding that exist within ground, air, and sea units could be transferred to joint organizations, the results would be powerful.

The consequences of the assumption of near certainty are wide ranging and potentially damaging to American national security. The belief in near-certainty has misdirected and undermined defense transformation efforts. Unless it is abandoned, the consequences will be negative and potentially severe.

CONCLUSION

In armed conflict no success is possible - or even conceivable - which is not grounded in an ability to tolerate uncertainty, cope with it, and make use of it." —Martin Van Creveld

The abandonment of the assumption of near-certainty in war will accelerate defense transformation. Unrealistic assumptions about the nature of future war polarize the debate and obstruct change. The promise of omniscience in the future discredits and dilutes the transformation effort by deferring changes until an ambiguous future capability becomes available; it encourages recidivism and resistance to changes that are long overdue. The potential effects of the orthodoxy of near-certainty in future war reveal that bad ideas have bad consequences. Indeed, the migration to the present of what were considered theoretical features of future war is already damaging national defense capabilities. Repairing the intellectual foundation of defense transformation will repair the damage done and permit real progress in building the force of the future. The following are recommendations for improving the joint force's ability to fight and win under conditions of complexity and uncertainty:

• Denounce the orthodoxy of near-certainty in future war and make an explicit statement that future war will remain in the realm of uncertainty.

• Develop joint and service operational concepts or idealized visions of future war that are consistent with the uncertainty and complexity of war. Make these concepts "fighting-centric" rather than "knowledge-centric." Build these concepts on an understanding of battle at the tactical level as well as operational and strategic considerations. Identify continuities as well as changes in warfare. Discard the concepts of Rapid Decisive Operations and Effects-Based Operations after salvaging their positive features.

• Reform joint and service organizations. Retain interoperability as a top priority for reform. Establish a balance between air, sea, and land capabilities. Push all arms and joint capabilities to lower levels of command. Decentralize assets and create the highest degree of autonomy possible while flattening the overall organization. Retain necessary redundancies, but eliminate overhead that does not contribute to effectiveness. Use effectiveness rather than efficiency as the principal criterion for evaluating organizations.

Emphasize mobility and adaptability to achieve speed of action without compromising overmatch in the aerospace, sea, and land domains.

• Eliminate service parochialism, but preserve positive aspects of service culture that derive from unique characteristics of operations in their domains. Forge a common understanding of service interdependence. Emphasize the mutual effort necessary to achieve objectives in complex environments. Encourage officers to expand their scope of identity and gain an appreciation for the capabilities and contributions of other services as well as for the complexity of war. Reinforce reforms in joint education with practical joint training at lower levels of command.

• Abandon the idea that lightness, ease of deployment, and reduced logistical infrastructure are virtues in and of themselves. Invest in air and sealift to improve strategic deployment capabilities. Develop technologies to reduce the demands on strategic lift and logistical support, but do not assume that information eliminates tradeoffs between combat power, deployability, and sustainability. The Army, for example, must fundamentally redesign the Objective Force. It should retain the SBCT, but acknowledge its limitations as well as its capabilities.

• Maintain the emphasis on improving joint training and education. Adopt tiered readiness that aligns each of the services for both training and deployment.

• Eliminate the ambiguous language of defense transformation. Be skeptical of concepts and presentations that rely on superlatives, theoretical models, flashy graphics, and futuristic videos.

• Declare a moratorium on joint experimentation and concept development. Study Operation Iraqi Freedom in context of military operations since 1991. Reform the organization for joint concept development and experimentation. Increase free-play in experimentation and remove conflicts of interest. Recognize that fundamentally flawed ideas can be discarded without elaborate experimentation. Eliminate the practice of contracting out the intellectual responsibilities of military professionals and civilian defense leaders. Whenever possible, include live deployments and tactical operations in joint experimentation and recognize that iterations in constructive or virtual simulations can neither replicate the fog and friction of war nor substitute for thought and analysis.

• Continue to pursue initiatives to lessen the degree of uncertainty and friction in war and consolidate gains already made. However, recognize limitations as well as possibilities. Pay particular attention to countermeasures and anticipate them by hardening the network and creating redundant capabilities. Pursue network-centric warfare as a vital capability, not a strategy.

• Declare that the revolution in sensor, communication, information, and precision engagement technologies has occurred. Study these advances in the context of recent conflicts and focus on integration of what is available (or what will become available shortly) and abandon the idea of "skipping a generation" of technology. Make appropriate changes now.

These measures would help the Department of Defense, Joint Staff, and each of the services reverse the damage to defense transformation incurred from unrealistic assumptions about the nature of war, advance American national security, and secure progress already made in defense reform.

What is certain about the future is that even the best efforts to predict the conditions of future war will prove erroneous. What is important, however, is to not be so far off the mark that visions of the future run counter to the very nature of war and render American forces unable to adapt to unforeseen challenges. An embrace of the uncertainty of war, balanced Joint Forces, effective joint integration, and adaptive leaders will permit the flexibility that is key to future victories.

ENDNOTES

1 The block quotation is from William A. Owens, "Introduction," in Stuart E. Johnson and Martin C. Libicki, eds., Dominant Battlespace Knowledge, (Washington, D.C.: National Defense University Press, 1996), p. 4. Other definitions are from Joint Vision 2020, The DOD Dictionary of Military Terms, and Joint Publication 1-02. See the Joint Electronic Library on the worldwide web at http://www.dtic.mil/doctrine (3 November 2002).

2 The discussion of "predictive intelligence" as a component of "robust intelligence" is from The Joint Staff, "Joint Operations Concept: Full Spectrum Dominance Through Joint Integration," Predecisional Draft Version 4.8, 10 February 2003, , pp. 33-35. A subsequent draft removed the definition, but retained the term robust intelligence.

3 Those studies included the 1989-1990 Base Force, 1993 Bottom-Up Review, and 1997 Quadrennial Defense Review. See Eric V. Larson, David T. Orletsky, and Kristin Leuschner, Defense Planning in a Decade of Change: Lessons from the Base Force, Bottom-Up Review and Quadrennial Defense Review (Washington, D.C.: RAND, 2001). See also, Andrew Krepinevich, "Why No Transformation?" National Interest, 4 February 1999. <http//www.csbaonline.org> (3 October 2002).

4 George W. Bush, Speech delivered to Citadel Cadets, 11 December 2001. http://www.whitehouse.gov/news/releases/2001/12/20011211-6.htm (15 January 2003).

5 Donald Rumsfeld, Memorandum from Secretary of Defense to Secretaries of the Military Departments, Chairman of the Joint Chiefs of Staff, Undersecretaries of Defense, et. al., "Legislative Priorities of Fiscal Year 2004," 17 September 2002.

6 Department of Defense, "Quadrennial Defense Review Report," 30 September 2001, pp. 29-31. http://www.defenselink.mil/pubs/qdr2001.pd (15 December 2002). Hereafter cited as 2001 QDR Report.

7 There has been no shortage of activity within the services. The Air Force is working toward the establishment of ten air expeditionary forces capable of organizing into strike packages based on the mission. The Navy has organized its efforts around the areas of sea basing, sea strike, and sea shield and is establishing a communications infrastructure called "NetForce." The Army is integrating digital communications and command and control systems into existing organizations, considering radical changes in personnel management that would permit unit rather than individual replacement, fielding a new organization designed to increase strategic mobility, and continuing work on Objective Force organizations, doctrine, and technology. For summaries and analyses of service and

joint transformation, see Hans Binnendijk, ed., Transforming America's Military (Washington, D.C.: NDU Press, 2002).

8 Under Secretary of Defense for Acquisition, "Evolutionary Acquisition and Spiral Development," 12 April 2002, as quoted in John Hanley, "Rapid Spiral Transformation," Transformation Trends, 3 February 2003, p. 3. http://www.oft.osd.mil/library/transformation trends/trends.cfm#past (15 March 2003). "Efforts Underway to Promote Jointness," DOD Update, 4 February 2003, pp. 6-7. http://www.dfi-intl.com/shared/updates/dod/2003-02-04DoDUpdate.pd (15 February 2003)

9 For example, the Office of Force Transformation reviewed service "Transformation Roadmaps" and recommended changes to make them consistent with DOD plans.

10 Speech, President George W. Bush, Norfolk Naval Air Station, February 13, 2001. http://frwebgate6.access.gpo.go See also 2001 QDR Report, p. 13.

11 Memorandum from Secretary Donald Rumsfeld to General Myers, Subject: Concept of Operations, 12 August 2002.

12 The Joint Staff, "Joint Operations Concepts," Final Draft, 20 February 2003, p. 3. Hereafter cited as "Joint Operations Concepts Final Draft." See also Kim Berger, "US DoD Presses for Joint Operations Concept," Jane's Defense Weekly, 25 September 2002. < http://jdw.janes.com/> (7 December 2002). "Pace Asserts JROC's Importance in Developing CONOPS," Defense Daily, 24 January 2003. www.defensedaily.com (9 December 2002). "JROC Takes More Active Role in Acquisition Process," Aerospace Daily, 24 January 2003. http://aviationnow.com/aviationnow/aerospacedaily (15 January 2002). Separately, Secretary Of Defense Rumsfeld affirmed his intention to use the concept to "test proposals from the various services" as quoted in "Services, Joint Staff Forming Joint Operational Concepts," Inside the Navy, 24 November 2002, p.4. Admiral Cebrowski, the head of the Office of Force Transformation has developed "information age metrics" to assist the Department in making resource decisions. Arthur K. Cebrowski, "New Rules for a New Era," Transformation Trends, 21 October 2002. http://www.oft.osd.mil/library/transformation trends/past (18 March 2003).

13 On importance of the concept see Paul K. Davis, "Integrating Transformation Programs," in Binnendijk, ed, Transforming America's Military, pp. 193-219. Stephen Peter Rosen, Winning the Next War: Innovation and the Modern Military,(Ithaca, NY: Cornell University Press, 1991), p. 20. The FYO4 budget, for example, cancelled 24 Army programs and 50 Navy programs and shifted those funds to "transformation initiatives." See "President's FY04 Budget Released," DOD Update, 4 February 2003, pp. 1-5. http://www.dfi-intl.com/shared/updates/dod/2003-02-04DoDUpdate.pd (20 February 2003). See also "Rumsfeld's Budget Favors Weaponry of Tomorrow," Washington Times, 4 February 2003, p. 8. Colonel David Fastabend suggested that an operational concept has four fundamental characteristics. It should provide an idealized vision of war, it should reflect the strategic environment, it should connect theory, strategic context and doctrine, it should present a clear choice concerning the technique for success in war, and it should be regarded as a "component of conflict" between potential adversaries rather than an inflexible construct. David Fastabend, "That Elusive Operational Concept," Army, June 2001. <http://www.ausa.org/www/armymag.nsf> (10 January 2003).

14 "Efforts Underway to Promote Jointness," DOD Update, 4 February 2003, pp. 6-7.

15 2001 QDR Report, p. 29.

16 For discussions of strategic and operational environments, see Joint Vision 2020, the 2001 QDR Report, and the Joint Operations Concepts Final Draft.

17 William A. Owens, Lifting the Fog of War (Baltimore: Johns Hopkins, 2001), p. 96. Peter Reddy, "Joint Interoperability: Fog or Lens for Joint Vision 2010?," Research Report Number 97-0137, (Maxwell Air Force Base, Alabama: Air Command and Staff College, March 1997).

18 "Joint Operations Concepts Final Draft," pp. 14-15, 20.

19 The paper lists "increasing political, economic, ethnic and religious divisions, globalization, the diffusion of power to hostile non-state actors, population growth, urbanization , a scarcity of natural resources, and the proliferation of dangerous technologies and weaponry" as some of the factors that make war "dynamic, uncertain, and complex." Joint Operations Concepts, p. 7.

20 "Joint Operations Concepts Final Draft," pp. 7-9.

21 "Joint Operations Concepts Final Draft," pp. 9, 20-21.

22 Interviews with officers and civilians in J7 and J8, the Joint Staff, conducted in December 2002. For the concepts of robust intelligence and predictive intelligence, see "Joint Operations Concept: Full Spectrum Dominance Through Joint Integration," Predecisional Draft Version 4.8, 10 February 2003, , pp. 33-35.

23 The literature that questions the idea of dominant knowledge in future war continues to grow. For a sample, see: Stephen Biddle, "Victory Misunderstood: What the Gulf War Tells Us About the Future of Conflict," International Security, Vol. 21, No. 2 (Fall 1996) http://www.comw.org/rma/fulltext/victory.html (10 September 2002). Michael O'Hanlon, Technology and Future War, esp. pp. 106-142. Richard J. Harknett, "The Risks of a Networked Military," Orbis, Winter 2000. John A. Gentry, "Doomed to Fail: America's Blind Faith in Military Technology, Parameters, Winter 2002-2003, pp. 88-103. Mark Helprin, "Revolution or Dissolution?" Forbes, 23 February 1998, vol. 161, no 4. Franklin Spinney, "What Revolution in Military Affairs?" Defense Week, 23 April 2001 vol. 222, issue 17, p. 2. For an excellent critique of RMA claims in connection with the certainty of war, see Christopher Kolenda, "Transforming How We Fight: A Conceptual Approach," Naval War College Review, (Spring 2003, Vol. LVI, No. 2) http://www.nwc.navy.mil/press/Review/2003/Spring/art6-sp3.htm (28 March 2003). For a bibliography of articles concerning "second thoughts on the RMA," see The RMA Debate website at http://www.comw.org/rma/fulltext/second.htm.

24 Consider the following excerpt from a definition of the "knowledge centric" characteristic of Rapid Decisive Operations, an overarching concept billed as "the solution" to future joint operations. "Advanced decision support tools, knowledge fusion, accurate compression, and horizontal and vertical integration of situational awareness will improve dissemination to decision-makers in an understandable and actionable format. Future operations will move beyond information superiority to decision superiority—better decisions faster—

based on knowledge developed through a comprehensive, system-of-systems understanding of the enemy and the environment, and a shared integrated awareness of the friendly situation. This will reduce operational risk, and dramatically increase the pace, coherence, and effectiveness of operations. A knowledge-centric joint force will enable a better balance of effectiveness and efficiency; it will ensure increased rapidity of our operations." US Joint Forces Command, J9 Joint Futures Lab, "Toward a Joint Warfighting Concept: Rapid Decisive Operations," RDO Whitepaper 2.0, 18 July 2002, pp. 6-7.

25 An example is the Army's determination to retain the division structure despite compelling arguments that alternative organizations were more appropriate for the post-Cold War era. See Douglas A. Macgregor, Breaking the Phalanx: A New Design for Landpower in the 21st Century (Westport, CT: Praeger, 1997).

26 "An Interview with the Director," Fateful Lightning, A Newsletter of The Information Technology Association of America," October 2002, p. 2. http://www.afei.org/transformation/pdf/Cebrowski ITAA interview.pdf(15 December 2002).

27 "U.S. Programs Future May Turn on C4ISR, Defense News, 25 November 2002, p. 18. See also Arthur Cebrowski, "New Rules for a New Era," Transformation Trends, 21 October 2002. http://www.afei.org/transformation/pdf/TransTrends 02 10 21.pdf(15 December 2002).

28 See, for example, Lawrence Kaplan, "The Coming Anarchy," The Atlantic (February 2004). http://www.theatlantic.com/politics/foreign/anarchy.htm (10 October 2002). Samuel P. Huntington, "The Clash of Civilizations," Foreign Affairs, (Summer 1993, vol. 72, no. 3) http://www.foreignaffairs.org/1993/3.html (15 September 2002). Benjamin Barber, Jihad vs. McWorld, (New York: Times Books, 1995).

29 Andrew F. Krepinevich, "Cavalry to Computer: The Pattern of Military Revolutions," The National Interest, 37, (1994), 30. The idea of a contemporary revolution in military affairs actually had its origin with Russian military thinkers in the 1960s who predicted that America's combination of precision munitions with computer technologies and sensors had introduced a "military-technical revolution." See Notra Trulock III, Kerry Hines, Ann Herr, Soviet Military Thought in Transition^ Implications for the Long-Term MilitaryfCompetition (Arlington: Pacific-Sierra Research Corp., May 1988). This idea gained wide acceptance in America, however, only after the 1991 Gulf War. , pp. 2, 28, 31. For a superb study of military revolutions, see Macgregor Knox and Williamson Murray, eds., The Dynamics of Military Revolution 1300-2050, (New York: Cambridge University Press, 2001).

30 Harlan K. Ullman, James P. Wade, L.A. "Bud" Edney, et. al., Shock & Awe: Achieving Rapid Dominance (Washington, D.C.: NDU Press, Dec. 1996), esp. chapters 1 and 2. Quotation is from chapter 2. www.ndu.edu/inss (10 January 2003).

31 John Warden, "Employing Air Power in the Twenty-first Century," in Richard H. Shultz, Jr. and Robert L. Pfaltzgraff, Jr., eds., The Future of Air Power in the Aftermath of the Gulf War (Maxwell Air Force Base, Alabama: Air University Press, 1992), pp. 78-81.

32 See, for example, George and Meredith Friedman, The Future of War: Power, Technology, and American World Dominance in the Twenty-First Century (New York: St. Martin's Griffin, 1996), pp. 278-281. Alvin and Heidi Toffler, War and Anti-War: Survival at

the Dawn of the 21st Century (New York: Little, Brown, and Company, 1993), pp. 64-80. For a balanced summary of the issue, see Elliot Cohen and Keaney, Revolution in Warfare?: Air Power in the Persian Gulf (Annapolis, Maryland: US Naval Institute Press, 1995), pp. 188-212.

33 See Biddle, "Victory Misunderstood." For critiques, see: Daryl G. Press, "Lessons from Ground Combat in the Gulf: The Impact of Training and Technology," International Security, Vol. 21, No. 2 (Fall 1997), pp. 137-146. Thomas Keaney, "The Linkage of Coalition Air and Ground Power in the Future of Conflict," International Security, Vol. 21, No. 2 (Fall 1997), pp. 147-150. Thomas G. Mahnken and Barry D. Watts, "What the Gulf War Can (and Cannot) Tell Us about the Future of Conflict," International Security, Vol. 21, No. 2 (Fall 1997), pp. 151-162. For Biddle's summary of the discussion and counterarguments, see Stephen Biddle, "The Gulf Debate Redux: Why Skill and Technology Are the Right Answer," International Security, Vol. 21, No. 2 (Fall 1997), pp. 163-174. See also, Stephen Biddle, "Commentary on Victory Misunderstood," paper published by the Institute for Defense Analysis, September 1997. <http://www.ida.org/DIVISIONS/sfrd/crp/d-2014 Full Paper.pd> (10 January 2003).

34 Barry D. Watts, Clausewitzian Friction and Future War, McNair Paper 52, October 1996, Institute For National Strategic Studies, pp. 37-53.

35 Richard M. Swain, Lucky War: Third Army in Desert Storm (Fort Leavenworth Kansas: US Army Command and General Staff College Press, 1994), pp. 250-255, 333-335.

36 Watts, Clausewitzian Friction and Future War, pp. 37-53. David R. Mets, "The Long Search for Surgical Strike: Precision Munitions and the Revolution in Military Affairs," Cadre Paper No. 12, October 2001, Air University, Maxwell Air Force Base, Alabama, p. 37.

37 Michael Gordon and Bernard Trainor, The Generals' War: The Inside Story of the Conflict in the Gulf (New York: Little Brown, 1994), pp. 400-432.

38 Conduct of the Persian Gulf War Final Report to Congress, (Washington: Government Printing Office, April 1992), p.140. Barry D. Watts and Thomas A. Keaney, The Gulf War Air Power Study: Effects and Effectiveness (Washington: Government Printing Office, 1993), .pp. 360-363. Hereafter cited as GWAPS. Daryl G. Press, "The Myth of Air Power in the Persian Gulf War and the Future of Warfare," International Security, Vol. 26, No. 2 (Fall 2001), pp. 2938.

39 Daryl G. Press, "The Myth of Air Power in the Persian Gulf War and the Future of Warfare,", pp. 44. Mets, "The Long Search for Surgical Strike: Precision Munitions and the Revolution in Military Affairs," pp. 48-50.

40 Martin van Creveld et al, Air Power and Maneuver Warfare, p. 219. For another perspective on the ineptitude of the Iraqis, see "The Perfect Enemy: Assessing the Gulf War," Security Studies, Vol. 5, No. 1 (Autumn 1995), p.101. See also Swain, Lucky War, p. 343.

41 GWAPS, vol. II, pp. 360-363.

42 GWAPS, vol. II pp. 360-361.

43 Daryl Press, "The Myth of Air Power in the Persian Gulf War and the Future of Warfare," International Security, Vol. 26, No. 2 (Fall 2001), pp. 5-44.

44 General Norman Schwartzkopf briefed reporters concerning the success of the "Great SCUD Hunt." Instead of SCUDs, however, the video showed a strike on fuel trucks. Iraqi deception and "shoot and scoot" tactics were very successful and, despite pilot reports of mobile launchers being destroyed, it seems certain that none of the mobile launchers and only fourteen of the twenty-eight fixed launchers were hit. "Counter-Force in Desert Storm," available on the worldwide web at http://www.cdiss.org/scudnt6.htm. See also, Gordon and Trainor, The Generals' War, pp. 227-248. On Khafji, see Earl Tilford, "Halt Phase Strategy: A New Wine in Old Skins—With PowerPoint," Strategic Studies Institute Monograph, Carlisle Barracks, PA, 23 July 1998, pp. 7-9. http://www.fas.org/man/dod-101/usaf/docs/halt.pdf (August 2002). For an example of a persistent views despite the evidence, see Daniel Goure and Stephen Cambone, "The Coming Age of Air and Space Power," in Daniel Goure and Christopher Szara, eds., Air and Space Power in the New Millenium (Washington, D.C.: Center for Strategic and Internatio nal Studies, 1997), pp. 8-11.

45 GWAPS, vol. II, p. 361.

46 Williamson Murray, "Clausewitz Out, Computers In: Military Culture and Technological Hubris," The National Interest, 1 June 1997. http://www.clausewitz.com/CWZHOME/ClauseSComputers.htm (August 20, 2002).

47 To review what Clausewitz identifies as the various causes of uncertainty in war, see Carl von Clausewitz, On War, ed. and trans. Michael Howard and Peter Paret (Princeton, NJ: Princeton University Press, 1976), pp. 80-90, 101, 113-114, 117-118, 119-121, 136-140, 148150, 161, 184-191,198-203, 577-578, 585, 605-610.

48 The idea of "war as an extension of politics" included far more than the connection between military strategy and national policy. Clausewitz was particularly sensitive to the emotions and social forces unleashed by the French Revolution. For an analysis of Clausewitz's views of Politik and war, see Antulio J. Echevarria II, "War Politics, and the RMA -The Legacy of Clausewitz," Joint Force Quarterly, Winter 1995-96, pp. 76-80.

49 Clausewitz, On War, pp. 86, 101.

50 John Keegan, The Face of Battle: A Study of Agincourt, Waterloo, and The Somme (New York: Penguin Books, 1976), p. 303.

51 Clausewitz,, On War, pp. 113-114.

52 Clausewitz,, On War, pp. 572-573.

53 Clausewitz, On War, pp.139, 149.

54 Alan D. Beyerchen, "Clausewitz, Nonlinearity and the Unpredictability of War, International Security, vol. 17, no. 3 (Winter 1992), pp. 59-90. See also Stephen J. Cimbala, Clausewitz and Chaos: Friction in War and Military Policy (Westport, CT: Praeger, 2000). Katherine L. Herbig, "Chance, and Uncertainty in On War," in Clausewitz and Modern Strategy, ed., Michael I. Handel (London: Frank Cass, 1986), pp. 95-116.

55 Clausewitz, On War, p. 101.

56 Clausewitz, On War, p. 101.

57 Admiral William Owens as quoted in Williamson Murray, "Clausewitz Out Computers In," p. 62.

58 The tendency to claim that technological solutions can create certain solutions to complex problems is not limited to defense transformation. A new counter-terrorism system plans to use information technology to identify and defeat terrorist plans prior to attacks. The Total Information Awareness (TIA) system would use data retrieval, biometric identification and other technologies to analyzed information in databases to lift the fog of homeland security. Shane Harris, "Critics Say 'Total Information Awareness' Impractical," GovExec.com, 12 December 2002.< http://www.govexec.com/dailyfed/1102/112002ti.htm> (1 December 2002). On Americans' tendency to view war as an engineering problem, see Richard Sinnreich and Williamson Murray , "Joint Warfighting in the 21st Century," unpublished paper prepared for the Office of Net Assessment, Department of Defense, 2002.

59 Clifford J. Rogers, 'Clausewitz, Genius, and the Rules," Journal of Military History, October 2002. < http://www.clausewitz.com/CWZHOME/RogersRules.htm> (10 January 2003).

60 Clauswitz, On War, p. 136.

61 See Clausewitz, On War, pp, 75-89.

62 Admiral William Owens as quoted in Williamson Murray, "Clausewitz Out Computers In," p. 62.

63 Alan Beyerchen, "Clausewitz, Nonlinearity, and the Unpredictability of War," Internat6i4onal Security, vol 17: no. 3 (Winter, 1992), pp. 59-90.

64 General Anthony Zinni, interview, "Ambush in Mogadishu," http://www.pbs.org/wgbh/pages/frontline/shows/ambush/interviews. (5 February 2003). On the same point, see Kenneth Allard, Somalia Operations: Lessons Learned (Washington DC, National Defense University Press, 1995), p. 74.

65 David Halberstam, War in a Time of Peace: Bush, Clinton, and the Generals (New York: Scribner, 2001), p. 258.

66 The Pakistanis, for example, were reluctant to enter into a combat situation after the 5 June incident without receiving permission from their government. Because TF Ranger operations were classified, the multi-national reaction force was not privy to the plan and, therefore, was not well prepared to respond.

67 Kenneth Allard, Somalia Operations, pp. 55-66.

68 Allard, pp. 55-61

69 Captain Haad (sector commander in General Aidid's militia), interview, http://www.pbs.org/wgbh/pages/frontline/shows/ambush/interviews (5 February 2003). See

also, Charles J. Dunlop, Jr., "21st Century Land Warfare: Four Dangerous Myths." Parameters, 27 (Autumn 1997), pp. 27-37.

70 For a description of the action as well as the perspective of the command group, see Mark Bowden, Blackhawk Down: A Story of Modern War (New York: Atlantic Monthly Press, 1999). Many of the confusing circumstances were not limited to the desperate fight of 3-4 October. The Somalis used civilian shields, for example, as a routine tactic. "Throngs of women and children crowded around UN peacekeepers, allowing armed Somalis to get close enough to wipe out the UN troops with automatic weapons. While a risky tactic, the Somalis knew it had a good chance of success. If the opponents are bloody-minded enough, they will always exploit the humanitarian attitudes of their adversaries." James F. Dunnigan, Digital Soldiers: The Evolution of High-Tech Weaponry and Tomorrows Brave New Battlefield (New York: St. Martin's Press, 1996), p. 219.

71 Anatol Lieven, "Hubris and Nemesis: Kosovo and the Pattern of Western Military Ascendancy and Defeat," in Cohen and Bacevich, eds., War Over Kosovo: Politics and Strategy in a Global Age (New York: Columbia University Press, 2001), p. 113.

72 Owens, Lifting the Fog of War, p. 96.

73 An example of the belief in American dominance is found in Harlan K. Ullman, James P. Wade, L.A. "Bud" Edney, et. al., Shock & Awe: Achieving Rapid Dominance (Washington, D.C.: NDU Press, Dec. 1996). The book is available on-line at <http://www.dodccrp.org/shockIndex.html>. The authors state that "The military posture and capability of the United States of America are, today, dominant. Simply put, there is no external adversary in the world that can successfully challenge the extraordinary power of the American military in either regional conflict or in "conventional" war as we know it once the United States makes the commitment to take whatever action may be needed." See the following on the 1990s as the ideal time for experimentation and the lack of a "peer competitor." James R. Blaker, "The American RMA Force: An Alternative to the QDR," Strategic Review, vol. 25, no. 3 (Summer 1997), pp. 21-30; See also Richard K. Betts, Military Readiness: Concepts, Choices, Consequences (Washington, D.C.: Brookings, 1995), pp. 35-84. John Arquilla, "The 'Velvet' Revolution in Military Affairs," World Policy Journal (Winter 1997/98), p. 42.

74 John Arquilla and David Ronfeldt, "A New Epoch—and Spectrum—Of conflict," in John Arquilla and David Ronfeldt, eds., In Athena's Camp: Preparing for Conflict in the Information Age, (Washington, D.C.: RAND, 1997), pp. 1-2.

75 Still other matters demanded the attention of the Department of Defense and the Joint Staff including the 1994 nuclear crisis in Korea and efforts to dismantle the nuclear arsenals in former Soviet Republics.

76 Various reviews including the 1989-1990 Base Force, 1993 Bottom-Up Review, and 1997 Quadrennial Defense Review resulted in little fundamental change. See Eric V. Larson, David T. Orletsky, and Kristin Leuschner, Defense Planning in a Decade of Change: Lessons from the Base Force, Bottom-Up Review, and Quadrennial Defense Review(Washginton, D.C.: RAND, 2001).

77 On the issue of the fractious nature of and paralysis in defense reform during the 1990's, see Owens, Lifting the Fog of War, pp. 32-41, 207-230. See also, Richard H. Kohn, "The Erosion of Civil Control of the Military in the United States Today," Naval War College Review (Summer 202, Volume LV, Number 3), pp. 12-14. Lawrence Korb, interview by PBS Frontline, at www.pbs.org/wgbh/pages/frontline/shows/future.

78 The Joint Staff, Joint Vision 2010, p. 1. < http://www.dtic.mil/jv2010/jvpub.htm> (2 September 2002). Hereafter cited as JV2010.

79 JV2010, p. 13.

80 JV2010, pp. 13, 32. William S. Cohen, Report of the Quadrennial Defense Review; May 1997, pp. vi, see also p. 39. <http://www.defenselink.mil/pubs/qdr/> (15 January 2003).

81 For an uncritical summary of the Army's division redesign, see Billy J. Jordan and Mark J. Reardon, "Restructuring the Division: An Operational and Organizational Approach, Military Review, May-June 1998. http://www.fas.org/man/dod-101/army/unit/docs/mr-98may-june-jor.htm (12 January 2003).

82 Eugenia C. Kiesling, Arming Against Hitler: France and the Limits of Military Planning (Lawrence Kansas: University Press of Kansas, 1996), pp.136-143, 175-181. Quotation is from page 180.

83 Robert Doughty, The Breaking Point: Sedan and the Fall of France, 1940 (Hamden, Conn.: Archon Books, 1990), esp. 27-32.

84 Conrad Crane, Bombs, Cities and Civilians: American Airpower Strategy in World War II (Lawrence, Kansas: University Press of Kansas, 1993), p. 158. Tami Biddle, Rhetoric and Reality in Air Warfare:The Evolution of British and American Ideas About Strategic Bombing, 1914-1945 (Princeton, NJ: Princeton University Press, 2002), p. 300. See also Michael Sherry, The Rise of American Airpower: The Creation of Armageddon (New Haven: Yale University Press, 1987), esp. pp. 22-46. For pronouncements of air power's decisiveness prior to World War II, see William Mitchell, Winged Defense (New York: GP Putnam's Sons, 1925) and Alexander P. DeSeversky, Victory Though Airpower (New York: Simon and Schuster, 1942). Air power enthusiasts' claims of decisiveness after a conflict despite evidence to the contrary has been a pattern. See, for example, the position of the Air Force historian that air power was decisive in both Korea and Vietnam in "Why American Needs to Maintain Its Air Superiority," Washington Times, 6 July 1998, p. 13. At the end of the 1991 Gulf War, the Air Force Chief of Staff announced that Desert Storm was "the first time in history" that an enemy Army was "defeated by Air Power." "Transcript of McPeak Briefing on Air Force Air Power in the Iraqi War," Inside the Air Force, 22 March 1991, p. 18.

85 Most observers date the dawn of the new age of precision weapons to the USAF's destruction of the Thanwa Bridge in Vietnam in 1972. See Mark Clodfelter, The Limits of American Airpower: The American Bombing of North Vietnam (New York: Free Press, 1986).

86 Ronald Fogleman, "Strategic Vision and Core Competencies: Global Reach - Global Power," Vital Speeches, 1 December 1996, vol. 63, no. 4, pp. 98-100.

87 Tilford, "Halt Phase Strategy: Old Wine In New Skins—. With PowerPoint," pp. 16-19, 21-25. A RAND study took a "quantitative approach" to estimate the "ability of U.S. forces to damage and halt an invading mechanized ground force" of over twelve heavy armored divisions. The study concluded that "in theaters that do not feature heavily foliated or urbanized terrain" long range weapons systems "will be able to rapidly halt armored invasions short of their objectives" if "sufficient investments are made in the emerging information and firepower systems." See David A. Ochmanek, Edward R Harshberger, David E. Thaler, and Glesnn A. Kent, To Find and Not to Yield: How Advances in Information and Firepower Can Transform Theater Warfare (Santa Monica, CA: RAND, 1998). The assumptions and limitations of the study did not prevent air power advocates from recommending that the Army convert heavy forces to the National Guard so the nation could afford more aircraft to carry out the strategy. Rebecca Grant, Airpower and the Total Force: A Gift of Time, Arlington, VA, IRIS Independent Research, 1998.

88 Daryl Press, "The Myth of Air Power in the Persian Gulf War and the Future of Warfare," pp. 33-34.

89 Department of the Air Force, "The USAF Transformation Flight Plan, FY03-07," HQUSAF/XPXT, Transformation Division, 2002, quotations are from pages viii, 3, and 40.

90 Owens, Lifting the Fog of War, pp. 136-138. See pages 100-112 for the argument that dominant battlespace knowledge will lead to near-perfect mission assignment. Owens' use of history to support his assertions was striking for lack of depth and reasoned argument. Owens contrasted costly land battles such as the Battle of Gettysburg with the initial air strikes in Desert Storm to suggest that technology would make the "inefficient, costly, and bloody" features of war "obsolete." He compares casualties during the landings at Normandy in WWII to the casualties suffered during Desert Storm and asserts technology as the principal cause in the vast difference, failing even to mention geography or the qualitative differences between the German and Iraqi forces. Owens' book has many strengths, however, and the author makes a compelling case and sound suggestions for improvements in joint interoperability.

91 Admiral Vern Clark, "Sea Power 21: Projecting Decisive Joint Capabilities," Proceedings, October 2002, www.usni.org/PROCEEDINGS/ARTICLES02/PROCNO10.HTM (15 November 2002). In the early to mid 1990s, the Navy, in the midst of the dramatic reductions of force that attended the end of the Cold War, shifted emphasis from deep-ocean operations and nuclear deterrence to power projection in regional conflicts. In two documents, "—From the Sea," published in 1992 and "Forward — From the Sea" published in 1994, the Navy focused on expeditionary warfare. In the meantime, naval officers were among those who embraced the revolution in military affairs and the belief that emerging technologies would reduce greatly the degree of uncertainty in future war.

92 All quotations are from Vice Admiral Richard W. Mayo and Vice Admiral John Nathman, "ForceNet: Turning Information into Power," Proceedings, February 2003. Article is available on the worldwide web at www.usni.org/PROCEEDINGS/Articles03/PROmayo02.htm

93 Admiral Vern Clark, "Sea Power 21: Projecting Decisive Joint Capabilities," Proceedings, October 2002, Available on the internet at www.usni.org/PROCEEDINGS/ARTICLES02/PROCNO10.HTM.

94 Vice Admiral Richard W. Mayo and Vice Admiral John Nathman, "ForceNet: Turning Information into Power," Proceedings, February 2003. <http//www.usni.org/PROCEEDINGS/Articles03/PROmayo02.htm> (15 March 2003).

95 One contracted concept developer identified "posited advances in genetic algorithms/intelligent agents and general acceptance of a new paradigm for maneuver warfare in the twenty-first century" as the assumptions on which he based his efforts. He observed that any consideration of combat on land was too specific for his level of interest. E-mail to author, October 2002.

96 Daniel Goure and Stephen Cambone, "The Coming Age of Air and Space Power," in Daniel Goure and Christopher Szara, eds., Air and Space Power in the New Millenium," (Washington, D.C.: Center for Strategic and International Studies, 1997) pp. 8-11. The authors used anti-Scud missile launcher operations in Desert Storm to make the point that the United States had the ability to acquire information from half-way around the world, then "communicate the knowledge so gained in a useful form anywhere in the world. Moreover it demonstrated that we can act on that information." They failed to mention that, based on enemy countermeasures such as frequent movement, concealment, and deception, not one mobile Scud missile launcher was destroyed during these operations.

97 C. Kenneth Allard, "Information Warfare: The Burden of History and the Risk of Hubris," in Stuart J.D. Schwartzstein, ed., The Information Revolution and National Security: Dimensions and Directions (Washington, D.C.: Center For Strategic and International Studies, 1996).

98 Naval operations are also characterized by a strong tradition of decentralization of authority to the captains of ships whom must be prepared to make quick decisions on which the fate of his ship, crew and mission rest.

99Terrorists used an explosive laden civilian craft to ram the ship and blow a hole in her side, almost sinking her. An investigation concluded that is was very unlikely that the attack could have been identified and prevented. Roberto Suro, "Pentagon Avoids Individual Punishment in Cole Attack," Washington Post, January 20, 2001; Page A01.

100 Headquarters United States Marine Corps, "Expeditionary Maneuver Warfare: Marine Corps Capstone Concept," undated, <http//www.doctrine.usmc.mil/emw.htm> (5 January 2003). These views are consistent with an earlier document, "Operational Maneuver From the Sea," available on the worldwide web at http://www.dtic.mil/jv2010/usmc/omfts.pdf (5 January 2003).

101 Halberstam, War in a Time of Peace, p. 56.

102 Halberstam, War in a Time of Peace, pp. 309-357. Benjamin S. Lambeth, The Transformation of American Airpower (Ithaca, NY: Cornell University Press, 2000), pp. 173-180.

103 Department of Defense, Report to Congress, "Kosovo/Operation Allied Force After Action Report," 30 January 2000, pp. 2, A7.

104 Madeline Albright as quoted in Earl Tilford, "Operation Allied Force and the Role of Air Power," Parameters, Winter 1999-2000, pp. 24-38.

105 Greece and France were the primary nations who opposed more resolute military action against Milosevic's forces and in Serbia.

106 Halberstam, War in a Time of Peace, pp. 444-453. See also Michael Ignatieff, "The Virtual Commander: How NATO Invented a New Kind of War," New Yorker, 2 August 1999, pp. 33-35.

107 Andrew J. Bacevich, "Neglected Trinity: Kosovo and the Crisis in Civil-Military Relations," in Cohen and Bacevich, eds., War Over Kosovo, pp. 155-157. See also Halberstam, War in a Time of Peace, pp. 420-435. See also Michael Ignatieff, Virtual War: Kosovo and Beyond, (London: Random House, 2000), pp. 176-179.

108 Benjamin Lambeth, NATO's Air War for Kosovo: A Strategic and Operational Assessment (RAND: Santa Monica, CA, 2001), pp. 199-204.

109 Philip A. Haun, "Air Power versus a Fielded Army: A Construct for Air Power in the 21st Century," Research Project, Air University, Maxwell Air Force Base, Alabama. April 2001, pp. 17-18. https://research.maxwell.af.mil/papers/student/ay2001/acsc/01-054.pd (15 January 2003).

110 Lambeth, NATO's Air War for Kosovo, pp. 32-33.

111 Lambeth, NATO's Air War for Kosovo, pp. 21-22, 26, 64, 117-118.

112 For a summary of the impediments to target identification and other factors that limited military operations, see Phillip M. Haun, "Air Power versus a Fielded Army," pp. 13-23.

113 Michael Ignatieff, Virtual War, p. 97.

114 Earl Tilford, "Operation Allied Force and the Role of Air Power," Parameters, Winter 1999-2000, pp. 24-38. Lambeth, NATO's Air War for Kosovo: A Strategic and Operational Assessment, pp. 24-25, 28-29, 60.

115 Earl Tilford, "Operation Allied Force and the Role of Air Power," Parameters, Winter 1999-2000, pp. 24-38. Benjamin Lambeth, NATO's Air War for Kosovo, pp. 128-133. See also, Richard J. Newman, "The Bombs that Failed in Kosovo," U.S. News and World Report, 20 Septembe r 1999, p. 29.

116 William Cohen as quoted in Thomas, "Kosovo and the Current Myth—", Parameters.

117 Lambeth, NATO's Air War for Kosovo, pp. 144-147.

118 Thomas, "Kosovo and the Current Myth of Information Superiority," Parameters,

119 Lambeth, NATO's Air War for Kosovo, pp. 136-139.

120 Lambeth, NATO's Air War for Kosovo, pp. 138-139.

121 Lambeth, NATO's Air War for Kosovo, pp. 136-147.

122 Lambeth, NATO's Air War for Kosovo, pp. 242-248.

123 Lambeth, NATO's Air War for Kosovo, pp. 56-59, 68-86. See also Ivo H. Daalder and Michael E. O'Hanlon, Winning Ugly: NATO's War to Save Kosovo (Washington, D.C.: Brookings Institution, 2000), pp. 3-5, 199, 203-205.

124 O'Hanlon, Technology and Future War, pp. 132-133, 194. The most significant new sensor capability in Kosovo was the UAV. As a comprehensive study on emerging technologies concluded, "UAVs have a limited ability to deal with ambiguity—.UAVs should be able to deal with ambiguity, but this ability exceeds the existing technological capabilities of sensors and computers." David B. Glade II, "Unmanned Aerial Vehicles," in William C. Martel, ed., The Technological Arsenal: Emerging Defense Capabilities, p. 192. John Matsumura et. al., Exploring Advanced Technologies for the Future Combat Systems Program, (Santa Monica, CA: RAND, 2002), esp. pp. 11-19, 59.

125 Benjamin Lambeth, NATO's Air War for Kosovo, p. 179.

126 Department of Defense, Report to Congress, "Kosovo/Operation Allied Force After-Action Report," 31 January 2000, pp. xxii, 52, 55,59,132.

127 An author of JV2020 indicated that the purpose of the document was to expand the vision another ten years based on "the advancement of information technologies" and how those technologies "changed the modern battlefield." Dan Cateriniccia, "Pentagon Revamping 2020 Vision," Federal Computer Week, 24 May 2002.

128 The Joint Staff, Joint Vision 2020, Washington, D.C., June 2000, pp. 1, 8-13, 28-29. http://www.dtic.mil/jointvision/jvpub2.htm (8 August 2002). Hereafter cited as JV2020.

129 In addition to the Department of Defense Report to Congress cited above, see "DARPA Tackles Kosovo Problems, " Aviation Week and Space Technology," 2 August 199, p. 55.

130 Department of Defense, The Joint Staff, "Joint Vision Revision Final Draft," July 2002, p. 10. Near certainty is an assumed precondition for success in war and the basis for Defense Transformation. The following is from pages 26-27. "—C4ISR is the catalyst for transformational change and provides the foundation to help achieve a 'decision superior' joint force. This capability will provide a fused, secure, tailored presentation of the battlespace that enables enhanced awareness and understanding, integrates real and near-real time information with historical data, and supports the joint commander's ability to plan future actions, make and communicate decisions, and assess consequences. This increased ability to generate and share information provides commanders with enhanced C2 capabilities that integrate and fuse both data and information to facilitate decision superiority—. The joint C4ISR infrastructure will create an information synergy that assists decision superiority at all levels. Networked communications and automated processing, exploitation and dissemination of collected intelligence, surveillance, and reconnaissance (ISR) data and information have dramatically increased the quality and timeliness of intelligence available to commanders. The next step will provide more predictive intelligence assessments as part of a common relevant operational picture produced through secure virtual collaboration among geographically dispersed analysts and integrated with operations data. Additionally, technological advances in long-dwell

collection assets - such as unmanned aerial vehicles, distributed undersea and unattended ground sensors and space-based collection platforms - combined with ever-improving process capabilities have initiated a revolutionary paradigm shift. Persistent surveillance over large portions of the battlespace will become increasingly possible and improve our ability to anticipate adversary actions, and enhance rapid decision-making. The products of long-dwell assets, coupled with improved human intelligence, highly trained reconnaissance personnel, and enhanced organic sensor and ISR platforms, will enable future joint forces to better maneuver and apply precision fires, while countering an adversary's use of camouflage, concealment and deception."

131 For a detailed analysis of Task Force Hawk, see Bruce R. Nardulli, Walter L. Perry, Bruce Pirnie, et. al., Disjointed War: Military Operations in Kosovo, 1999, (Washington, D.C.: RAND, 2002), pp. 57-97. For a detailed list of lessons the Army identified in Kosovo, see United States General Accounting Office, "Kosovo Air Operations: Army Resolving Lessons Learned Regarding the Apache Helicopter," March 2001.

132 For a summary of Army Transformation Efforts in the 1990s, see Bruce R. Nardulli and Thomas L. McNaugher, "The Army: Toward the Objective Force," in Hans Binnendijk, ed., Transforming America's Military, pp. 101-128. On funding shifts, see "Objective Force Funds Boosted At The Expense Of Legacy Efforts,"7nsKfe The Army, February 3, 2003 , p. 14.

73 In 1996, for example, training and doctrine command commander General William Hartzog wrote, "The information age is upon us—The very nature of warfare is changing—The view of the future we see envisions a new battlefield; one where we gather, process, and use information differently than ever before. This information will then empower us as we field and fight the most lethal land force in the world." U.S. Army Training and Doctrine Command, Land Combat in the 21st Century, 1996, page 1

134 On the original tactics for the Interim Brigade Combat Team and assumptions concerning "situational understanding," see Center for Army Lessons Learned Newsletter No. 118, "Army Transformation Taking Shape—Interim Brigade Combat Team Tactics, Techniques, and Procedures," July 2001, U.S. Army Center for Army Lessons Learned, Fort Leavenworth, Kansas. For a summary of the origins and initial progress of the Objective Force and Interim Brigade Combat Team initiatives, see Bruce R. Nardulli and Thomas L. McNaugher, "The Army: Toward the Objective Force," in Hans Binnendijk, ed., Transforming America's Military (Washington, D.C.: National Defense University Press, 2002), pp. 101-128.

135 See, for example, Department of the Army, FM3-90, Tactics, (Washington, D.C.: Government Printing Office, 2001), pp. 1-5—1-9, 1-11—1-15, 6-10—6-14, 9-2, 13-13—13-19.

136 FM1 The Army, Headquarters, Department of the Army, Washington, DC, 14 June 2001. < http://www.army.mil/features/FMl+FM2/FMIFM2.htm> (15 January 2003).

137 This view pervades most Army documents written since 2001. Honorable Thomas E. White and General Eric K. Shinseki, A Statement on the Posture of the United States Army 2003, 11 February 2003, p. 32. Department of the Army, Army Transformation Roadmap, 2002 http//www.army.mil/vision/Transformation Roadmap.pdf (1 March 2003).

138 Department of the Army, Unit of Action Maneuver Battle Lab, "Change 1 to TRADOC Pamphlet 525-3-90 O&O: The United States Army Objective Force Operational and Organizational Plan Unit of Action," US Army Armor Center, Fort Knox, KY, 22 November 2002, pp. 1-4—1-11, 3-1. Emphasis in quotation is in the original.

139 Department of the Army, Unit of Action Maneuver Battle Lab, "Change 1 to TRADOC Pamphlet 525-3-90 O&O: The United States Army Objective Force Operational and Organizational Plan Unit of Action," US Army Armor Center, Fort Knox, KY, 22 November 2002, pp. 4-1—4-5. See also, Department of the Army, Army Transformation Roadmap, 2002, p. 7.

140 Department of the Army, Army Transformation Roadmap, 2002, p. F1.

141 Department of the Army, Army Transformation Roadmap, 2002, p. 7, p. G-3.

142 John Matsumura et. al., Exploring Advanced Technologies for the Future Combat Systems Program, (Santa Monica, CA: RAND, 2002), esp. p. 59.

143 Williamson Murray and Richard Sinnreich, "Joint Warfighting in the Twenty-first Century," unpublished paper, p. 23. See also Richard Simpkin, Race to the Swift: Thoughts on Twenty-First Century Warfare (London: Brassey's, 1985), pp 57-77.

144 Department of the Army, Unit of Action Maneuver Battle Lab, Change 1 to TRADOC Pamphlet 525-3-90 O&O: The United States Army Objective Force Operational and Organizational Plan Unit of Action, US Army Armor Center, Fort Knox, KY, 22 November 2002, pp. 4-4—4-5.

145 For a list of these article and statements, see Stephen Biddle, "Afghanistan and the Future of Warfare: Implications for Army and Defense Policy," Strategic Studies Institute, Carlisle Barracks, PA, November 2002, pp. 1-3.

146 Biddle, "Afghanistan and the Future of Warfare," p. 6.

147 Biddle, "Afghanistan and the Future of Warfare," p.11. On bin Laden's deception, see Peter Fin, "Bin Laden Used Ruse to Flee," Washington Post, 21 January 2003, Page A01

148 Admiral Arthur Cebrowski as quoted in "An Interview with the Director," Fateful Lightning, October 2002. Available on the worldwide web at http://e-reservist.net/SPRAG/TransformationInterview.

149 Jason Amerine as quoted in an interview on PBS Frontline. www.pbs.org/wgbh/pages/frontline/shows/campaign/interviews/amerin (1 March 2003).

150 Ibid.

151 On the enemy's ability to adapt, see Biddle, "Afghanistan and the Future of Warfare" and Robert Andrews, "Al Qaeda's Troops Have Adapted. Have Ours?" Washington Post, 22 September 2002, p. B2.

152 Biddle, Afghanistan and the Future of Warfare, pp. 15-19.

153 Dodge Billingsley, "Ice, Snow And Bullets," March 8, 2002, www.cbsnews.com (15 March 2003).

154Except as otherwise noted, the above account of Operation Anaconda is summarized from Biddle, "Afghanistan and the Future of Warfare," pp. 28-38. See also pages 43-45.

155 Joint Experiments scheduled for May 2003 and beyond were to test concepts that were "knowledge centric" and assumed "anticipatory understanding." US Joint Forces Command J9, "Pinnacle Series Game Overview: 'A Wargame and a Discovery Experiment,'" undated briefing. US Joint Forces Command J9, "Campaign Plan 2003-2009 Information Briefing," 14 March 2003. Knowledge centric operations are assumed to replace mass and "produce desired effects with the right amount of force." They also permit commanders to "avoid unfavorable engagements" and "create cascading efficiencies while employing limited resources."

156 Rosen, Winning the Next War, pp. 109-110.

157 Michael Howard, "The Use and Abuse of Military History, in Michael Howard, ed., The Causes of War and Other Essays, (Cambridge, Mass.: Harvard University Press, 1983), p. 195.

158 Williamson Murray, "Thinking About Innovation," Naval War College Review Spring 2001, Vol. LIV, No. 2, pp. 126-127. Colin Gray, Modern Strategy (New York: Oxford University Press, 1999), p. 201. For an example of a linear, simplistic interpretation of the influence of technology on war, see David Alberts, John Gartska, and Frederick Stein, Network Centric Warfare: Developing and Leveraging Information Superiority (Washington, D.C.: Command and Control Research Program, 1999), p. 27.

159 Earl Tilford, "The Revolution in Military Affairs: Prospects and Cautions," 23 June 1995, Strategic Studies Institute, Carlisle Barracks, Pennsylvania, pp. 10-13. http://www.carlisle.army.mil/ssi/pubs/1995/rmapros/rmapros.pd (3 February 2003).

160 This point if from Tilford, "The Revolution in Military Affairs," pp. 11-12

161 David Gompert and Irving Lachow, "Transforming U.S. Forces: Lessons from the Wider Revolution,", RAND Issue Paper, 2000, p. 2. <www.rand.org/publications> (15 November 2002). On the general assumption that IT would have an effect on war similar to its effect on business and the economy, see Alberts, Gartska, and Stein, Network Centric Warfare, pp. 25-85. For a summary and critique of this viewpoint see Earl Tilford, "The Revolution in Military Affairs."

162 Arthur K. Cebrowski and John J. Gartska, "Network Centric Warfare: Its Origin and Future," Proceedings, January 1998, p. 32.

163 Alberts, et. al. Network Centric Warfare, p. 26.

164 Ibid. p. 36, pp. 245-265.

165 Cebrowski and Garstka, "Network Centric Warfare: Its Origin and Future." See also, Alberts, Garstka, and Stein, Network Centric Warfare, pp. 15-85.

166 Cebrowski and Garstka, "Network Centric Warfare: Its Origin and Future."

167 Ibid.

168 Alvin and Heidi Toffler, War and Anti War, pp. 38, 57-80.

169 ,Alberts, Garstka, and Stein, Network Centric Warfare, pp. 22-23.

170 The most succinct description that blends all of these concepts in a way that appears sound and cogent relative to much of the literature can be found in the draft Joint Operations Concept. "Major Combat Operations are conducted in a campaign consisting of sequential, parallel, and simultaneous actions distributed throughout the physical, information, and cognitive domains of the global battlespace Operations will attempt to sustain an increased tempo, placing continuous pressure on the adversary, and will harmonize military action with the application of other instruments of national power. The campaign is designed to dismantle an adversary's system of offense and defense. It will preempt their freedom of action, destroy critical capabilities, and as rapidly as possible, isolate enemy forces and deny them sanctuary, the ability to maneuver and reconstitute, thereby allowing their defeat or destruction through the integrated application of air, ground, maritime, space, and information capabilities." The Joint Staff, Joint Operations Concept, "Full Spectrum Dominance Through Joint Integration," Joint Staff Working Draft Version 4.8, 10 February 2003, p. 28.

171 This is summarized from multiple sources that discuss Rapid Decisive Operations and Effects-Based Operations. Joint Capstone Concept, version 4.8, pp. 14-19. J9 Concepts Department, US Joint Forces Command, "A Concept Framework for Joint Experimentation: Effects-based Operations," 20 July 2001. See J9 Joint Futures Lab, U.S. Joint Forces Command, "Toward a Joint Warfighting Concept: Rapid Decisive Operations," RDO Whitepaper Version 2.0, 18 July 2002, esp. pp. 6-17. Quotations are from p. 7. In his recent book on Effects-based Operations, Edward Smith stated that effects would be "cumulative over time." Edward Smith, Effects Based Operations: Applying Network-Centric Warfare in Peace, Crisis, and War. (Washington D.C.: CCRP), November 2002, p. xv.

172 US Joint Forces Command, Notes from Distributed Operations Workshop 3-4, December 2002. Concept developers identified "knowledge" as the critical enabler of distributed operations and also identified the risks associated with conducting distributed operations without information superiority.

173 Arthur K. Cebrowski and Thomas P.M. Barnett, "The American Way of War," Proceedings, January 2003, pp. 42-43. Others have even higher hopes for Effects Based Operations. Air Force Major General David Deptula suggested the following: "I want to see a set of integrated physical and cognitive effects models that could help this nation achieve its national security objectives without the adversary even knowing that he's been influenced." Major General David Deptula, USAF, A Dialogue on Analyzing Effects Based Operations (EBO), an interview by Dr. Jacqueline Henningsen, Director, Air Force Studies & Analyses Agency, www.mors.org/publications/phalanx/mar02/Lead2.htm (3 January 2003).

174 Ariel E. Levite and Elizabeth Sherwood-Randall, "The Case for Discriminate Force," Survival, vol. 44, no. 4, Winter 2002-2003, pp. 81-98.

175 Thomas Picks, "Calibrated War Makes Comeback" The Washington Post, 21 March 2003 page A1.

176 Levite and Sherwood-Randall, "The Case for Discriminate Force," pp. 81-98.

177 See, for example, Cebrowski, "New Rules for a New Era."

178 H.R. McMaster, Dereliction of Duty: Lyndon Johnson, Robert McNamara, The Joint Chiefs of Staff and the Lies that Led to Vietnam (New York: HarperCollins, 1997), pp. 72-85, 182-189, 217-221. On the fundamental problems with using air power for coercion, see Robert A. Pape, Bombing to Win: Air Power and Coercion in War (Ithaca, NY: Cornell University Press, 1996), esp. pp. 314-331.

179 179 McMaster, Dereliction of Duty, 155-158

180 David S. Alberts, Information Age Transformation: Getting to a 21st Century Military, 2d. ed., (Washington, DC: CCRP, 2002), pp. 13-14.

181 Whitney Tilson, "Cisco's Hubris," The Motley Fool, 14 August 2001, available on the internet at www.fool.com

182 The JV2010 concepts of Dominant Maneuver, Precision Engagement, Focused Logistics, and Full-Dimensional Protection are all based on "improved command, control, and intelligence, which can be assured by information superiority." Dominant Maneuver assumed a "full picture of the battlefield." Precision Engagement was based on "near real-time information about the target" and a "common awareness of the battlespace." Full Dimension Protection required "a joint architecture built upon information superiority." Focused logisitics also depended on highly accurate information to track logistical status and predict demands. Joint Vision 2010, esp. p. 19.

183 Government Accounting Office, "Military Transformation: Actions Needed to Better Manage DOD's Joint Experimentation Program," August 2002, pp. 5-6.

184 See, for example, United States Joint Forces Command, "2002 Joint Experimentation Annual Report to Congress, 1 December 2002. Hereafter cited as "2002 Joint Experimentation Annual Report."

185 "2002 Joint Experimentation Annual Report," p. 8, 11.

186 "2002 Joint Experimentation Annual Report," p. 5.

187 "2002 Joint Experimentation Annual Report," p. 17.

188 The account of Millenium Challenge 2002 is summarized from the following sources. Quotation is from Richard Hart Sinnreich, "Cooking the Books Won't Help the Military Transform," Lawton Constitution, 18 August 2002, p. 4. See also"Get the Facts:Was it a Test or a PR Exercise?" Fayetteville Observer, 20 August 2002. Sean Naylor, "War Games Rigged? General Says Millenium Challenge 02 was Almost Entirely Scripted," Army Times, 16 August 2002. Mackubin Thomas Owens, "War Games are Still Just Games," Wall Street Journal, 29 August 2002.

189 Huba Wass de Czega, "02 Wargaming Insights," unpublished paper, December 2002, esp. pp. 1-3.

190 Carl, von Clausewitz, On War, p. 187.

191 Williamson Murray, "Red Teaming: Its Contribution to Past Military Effectiveness," unpublished paper, Department of Defense, Joint Advanced Warfighting Project, 2002.

192 The following books examine causes of surprise and failures to act on warnings. Michael I. Handel, ed., Strategic and Operational Deception in the Second World War (London: Frank Cass, 1987). Donald C. Daniel and Katherine L. Herbig, eds., Strategic Military Deception (New York: Pergamon, 1982). Roberta Wohlstetter, Pearl Harbor: Warning and Decision (Stanford: Stanford University Press, 1962).

193 Martin van Creveld, Command in War (Cambridge, Massachusetts: Harvard University Press, 1985), p. 275.

194 Michael Andrews as quoted in Dylan Machan, "A Few Good Toys," Forbes, Dec. 9, 2002. Department of the Army, "The Objective Force," Objective Force Task Force White Paper, 8 December 2002, p. 18. Comment on RAND analysts is based on conversations with people involved in the tests.

195 Colin S. Gray, "Defining and Achieving Decisive Victory," Strategic Studies Institute, Carlisle Bks, PA, April 2002, p. 25.

196 Qiao Liang and Wang Xiangsui, Unrestricted Warfare, trans. FBIS (Beijing: Peoples Liberation Army Literature and Arts Publishing House, February 1999), pp. 215, 221.

197 For Secretary Rumsfeld's comments, see Molly Peterson, "Defense Chief Outlines Challenges of Information Warfare," Government Executive Magazine, 16 August 2002. Available on the worldwide web at www.govexec.com. For countermeasures under development that threaten American communications and "network-centric" capabilities, see: O'Hanlon, Technology and Modern War, pp. 58-61, 195-196. The Chinese are pursuing electo-magnetic pulse weapons and other countermeasures. Mark A. Stokes, "Chinese Ballistic Missile Forces in the Age of Global Missile Defense: Challenges and Responses," in Andrew Scobell and Larry Wortzel, eds., China's Growing Military Power: Perspectives on Security, Ballistic Missiles, and Conventional Capabilities, (Carlisle Barracks, PA: Strategic Studies Institute, 2002), pp. 135-136. See also, Susan Pushka, "Rough But Ready Force Projection: An Assessment of Recent PLA Training," in the same volume, pp. 240-241. See also essays in Steven Lambakis, James Kiras, and Kristin Kolet, eds., Understanding "Asymmetric" Threats to the United States, (Washington D.C.: National Institute for Public Policy, 2002). Marie Squeo, "US Military's GPS Reliance Makes a Cheap, Easy Target," Wall Street Journal, 24 September 2002.

198 Arthur Cebrowski and Thomas P.M. Barnett, "The American Way of War," Transformation Trends, 13 January 2003. http://www.oft.osd.mil/ (20 March 2003).

199 In addition to the numerous examples already provided, diversification of capabilities and the formation of smaller, autonomous units is consistent with general methods for coping with uncertainty and complexity. See F. David Peat, From Certainty to Uncertainty: The Story of Science and Ideas in the Twentieth Century (Washington, D.C.: Joseph Henry Press, 2002), esp. pp. 143-144.

BIBLIOGRAPHY

Alberts, David S. Information Age Transformation: Getting to a 21st Century Military, 2d. ed. Washington, DC: CCRP, 2002.

Alberts, David, John Gartska, and Frederick Stein, Network Centric Warfare: Developing and Leveraging Information Superiority. Washington, D.C.: Command and Control Research Program, 1999.

Allard, C. Kenneth. "Information Warfare: The Burden of History and the Risk of Hubris," in Stuart, J.D. ed., The Information Revolution and National Security: Dimensions and Directions . Washington, D.C.: Center For Strategic and International Studies, 1996.

Allard, Kenneth. Somalia Operations: Lessons Learned. Washington DC, National Defense University Press, 1995.

Amerine, Jason. Interview on PBS Frontline. www.pbs.org/wgbh/pages/frontline/shows/campaign/interviews/amerin (1 March 2003).

"An Interview with the Director," Fateful Lightning, A Newsletter of The Information Technology Association of America," October 2002, p. 2.

http://www.afei.org/transformation/pdf/Cebrowski ITAA interview.pdf(15 December 2002).

Andrews, Robert. "Al Qaeda's Troops Have Adapted. Have Ours?" Washington Post, 22 September 2002, p. B2.

Arquilla, John "The 'Velvet' Revolution in Military Affairs," World Policy Journal

Arquilla, John and David Ronfeldt, eds., In Athena's Camp: Preparing for Conflict in the Information Age. Washington, D.C.: RAND, 1997

Barber, Benjamin. Jihad vs. McWorld. . New York: Times Books, 1995.

Berger, Kim. "US Department of Defense Presses for Joint Operations Concept," Jane's Defense Weekly, 25 September 2002. journal on-line; Available from <http://jdw.janes.com/>. Internet. Accessed 7 December 2002.

Betts, Richard K. Military Readiness: Concepts, Choices, Consequences. Washington, D.C.: Brookings, 1995.

Beyerchen, Alan D. "Clausewitz, Nonlinearity and the Unpredictability of War." International Security 17, no. 3 (Winter 1992): 59-90.

Biddle, Stephen, "Afghanistan and the Future of Warfare: Implications for Army and Defense Policy," Strategic Studies Institute, Carlisle Barracks, PA, November 2002.

Biddle, Stephen, "Victory Misunderstood: What the Gulf War Tells Us About the Future of Conflict," International Security, Fall 1996. Journal on-line. available from <http://www.comw.org/rma/fulltext/victory.html>. Internet. Accessed 10 September 2002.

Biddle, Stephen. "Commentary on Victory Misunderstood," Institute for Defense Analysis September 1997. Available on-line <http://www.ida.org/DIVISIONS/sfrd/crp/d-2014 Full Paper.pdf> Internet. Accessed 10 January 2003.

Biddle, Stephen. "The Gulf Debate Redux: Why Skill and Technology Are the Right Answer," International Security, 21, No. 2 (Fall 1997): 163-174.

Biddle, Tami. Rhetoric and Reality in Air Warfare:The Evolution of British and American Ideas About Strategic Bombing, 1914-1945. Princeton, NJ: Princeton University Press, 2002

Billingsley, Dodge. "Ice, Snow And Bullets," March 8, 2002, www.cbsnews.com (15 March 2003).

Binnendijk, Hans, Transforming America's Military. Washington, D.C.: NDU Press, 2002.

Blaker, James R. "The American RMA Force: An Alternative to the QDR," Strategic Review25, no. 3 (Summer 1997): 21-30

Bowden, Mark. Blackhawk Down: A Story of Modern War. New York: Atlantic Monthly Press, 1999.

Bush, George W. Speech delivered to Citadel Cadets, 11December 2001. Available on-line <http://www.whitehouse.gov/news/releases/2001/12/20011211-6.htm> Internet; accessed 15 January 2003.

Cateriniccia, Dan. "Pentagon Revamping 2020 Vision," Federal Computer Week, 24 May 2002.

Cebrowski, Arthur "New Rules for a New Era," Transformation Trends, 21 October 2002. Journal on-line. Available from http://www.afei.org/transformation/pdf/TransTrends 02 10 21.pdf> Internet. Accessed15 December 2002.

Cebrowski, Arthur and Thomas P.M. Barnett, "The American Way of War," Transformation Trends, 13 January 2003. http://www.oft.osd.mil/ (20 March 2003).

Cebrowski, Arthur K. "New Rules for a New Era," Transformation Trends, 21 October 2002. Journal on-line. Available from <http://www.oft.osd.mil/library/transformation trends/past>. Internet. Accessed 18 March 2003

Cebrowski, Arthur K. and John J. Gartska, "Network Centric Warfare: Its Origin and Future," Proceedings, January 1998, p. 32.

Cebrowski, Arthur K. and Thomas P.M. Barnett, "The American Way of War," Proceedings, January 2003, pp. 42-43.

Cebrowski, Arthur. "U.S. Programs Future May Turn on C4ISR", Defense News, 25 November 2002, p. 18.

Cimbala, Stephen J. Clausewitz and Chaos: Friction in War and Military Policy. Westport, CT: Praeger, 2000

Clark, Admiral Vern. "Sea Power 21: Projecting Decisive Joint Capabilities," Proceedings. (October 2002,) Available on-line <www.usni.org/PROCEEDINGS/ARTICLES02/PROCNO10.HTMHnternet. Accessed 15 November 2002.

Clausewitz, Carl von. On War. Ed. and trans. Michael Howard and Peter Paret. Princeton, NJ: Princeton University Press, 1976.

Clodfelter, Mark. The Limits of American Airpower: The American Bombing of North Vietnam. New York: Free Press, 1986.

Cohen, Elliot and Thomas Keaney. Revolution in Warfare? Air Power in the Persian Gulf. Annapolis, Maryland: US Naval Institute Press, 1995.

Cohen, William S. Report of the Quadrennial Defense Review, May 1997, Available on-line <http://www.defenselink.mil/pubs/qdr/> Internet. Accessed 15 January 2003.

"Counter-Force in Desert Storm," undated. Available on the worldwide web at http://www.cdiss.org/scudnt6.htm.

Crane, Conrad. Bombs, Cities and Civilians: American Airpower Strategy in World War II. Lawrence, Kansas: University Press of Kansas, 1993.

Creveld, Martin van. Air Power and Maneuver Warfare. Maxwell Air Force Base, Alabama: Air University Press,1994.

Daniel, Donald C. and Katherine L. Herbig, eds., Strategic Military Deception. New York: Pergamon, 1982.

"DARPA Tackles Kosovo Problems, " Aviation Week and Space Technology," 2 August 1999.

Department Of Defense Update, Efforts Underway to Promote Jointness available on-line <http://www.dfi-intl.com/shared/updates/dod/2003-02-04DoDUpdate.pd>; Internet; accessed 15 February 2003.

Department of Defense, "Quadrennial Defense Review Report," 30 September 2001, available on-line <http://www.defenselink.mil/pubs/qdr2001.pd>; Internet accessed 15 December 2002.

Department of Defense, Conduct of the Persian Gulf War Final Report to Congress, Washington: Government Printing Office, April 1992,

Department of Defense, Report to Congress, "Kosovo/Operation Allied Force After-Action Report," 31 January 2000, pp. xxii, 52, 55,59,132.

Department of the Army, "The Objective Force," Objective Force Task Force White Paper, 8 December 2002.

Department of the Army, Army Transformation Roadmap, 2002. http//www.army.mil/vision/Transformation Roadmap.pdf (1 March 2003).

Department of the Army. FM1, The Army, Headquarters, Washington, DC, 14 June 2001. < http://www.army.mil/features/FMI+FM2/FMIFM2.htm> (15 January 2003).

Department of the Army. FM3-90, Tactics. Washington, D.C.: Government Printing Office, 2001.

Deptula, David USAF, "A Dialogue on Analyzing Effects Based Operations (EBO)," an interview by Dr. Jacqueline Henningsen, Director, Air Force Studies & Analyses Agency, www.mors.org/publications/phalanx/mar02/Lead2.htm (3 January 2003).

DeSeversky, Alexander P., Victory Though Airpower. New York: Simon and Schuster, 1942.

Dunlop, Charles J. Jr. "21st Century Land Warfare: Four Dangerous Myths." Parameters, 27 (Autumn 1997): 27-37

Dunnigan, James F. Digital Soldiers: The Evolution of High-Tech Weaponry and Tomorrow's Brave New Battlefield. New York: St. Martin's Press, 1996

Echevarria II, Antulio J. "War Politics, and the RMA - The Legacy of Clausewitz," Joint Force Quarterly. (Winter 1995-96): 76-80.

Fastabend, David.A. "That Elusive Operational Concept," Army Magazine Online. June 2001. Journal on-line. Available from http://www.ausa.org/www/armymag.ns; Internet; accessed 10 January 2003.

Fin, Peter "Bin Laden Used Ruse to Flee," Washington Post, 21 January 2003, Page A01

Fogleman, Ronald. "Strategic Vision and Core Competencies: Global Reach - Global Power," Vital Speeches. 63, no. 4 (1December 1996): 98-100.

Friedman, George and Meredith Friedman, The Future of War: Power, Technology, and American World Dominance in the Twenty-First Century. New York: St. Martin's Griffin, 1996

General Anthony Zinni, interview, "Ambush in Mogadishu," Available on-line http://www.pbs.org/wgbh/pages/frontline/shows/ambush/interviews> Internet. Accessed 5 February 2003.

Gentry, John A. "Doomed to Fail: America's Blind Faith in Military Technology," Parameters. (Winter 2002-2003): 88-103.

"Get the Facts:Was it a Test or a PR Exercise?" Fayetteville Observer, 20 August 2002.

Gompert, David and Irving Lachow, "Transforming U.S. Forces: Lessons from the Wider Revolution,", RAND Issue Paper, 2000, p. 2. <www.rand.org/publications> (15 November 2002).

Gordon, Michael and Bernard Trainor,. The Generals' War: The Inside Story of the Conflict in the Gulf. New York: Little Brown, 1994.

Goure, Daniel and Stephen Cambone, ed., Air and Space Power in the New Millenium. Washington, D.C.: Center for Strategic and International Studies, 1997.

Goure, Daniel and Christopher Szara ed. Air and Space Power in the New Millenium, Washington, D.C.: Center for Strategic and International Studies, 1997.

Grant, Rebecca. Airpower and the Total Force: A Gift of Time. Arlington, VA: IRIS Independent Research, 1998.

Gray, Colin S. "Defining and Achieving Decisive Victory," Carlisle Barracks, PA: Strategic Studies Institute, April 2002, p. 25.

Gray, Colin. Modern Strategy. New York: Oxford University Press, 1999.

Halberstam, David. War in a Time of Peace: Bush, Clinton, and the Generals. New York: Scribner, 2001.

Handel, Michael I. ed. Strategic and Operational Deception in the Second World War. London: Frank Cass, 1987.

Hanley, John, "Evolutionary Acquisition and Spiral Development," in,TransformationTrends,available on-line <http://www.oft.osd.mil/library/transformation trends/trends.cfm#past>: Internet; acessed 15 March 2003.

Harknett, Richard J. "The Risks of a Networked Military," Orbis, (Winter 2000).

Harris, Shane. "Critics Say 'Total Information Awareness' Impractical," GovExec.com 12 December 2002. Available on-line <http://www.govexec.com/dailyfed/1102/112002ti.htm> Internet. accessed 1 December 2002.

Haun, Philip A. "Air Power versus a Fielded Army: A Construct for Air Power in the 21st Century," Research Project, Air University, Maxwell Air Force Base, Alabama. April 2001, pp. 17-18. https://research.maxwell.af.mil/papers/student/ay2001/acsc/01-054.pd (15 January 2003).

Helprin, Mark. "Revolution or Dissolution?" Forbes, 23 February

Herbig, Katherine L. "Chance, and Uncertainty in On War," in Clausewitz and Modern Strategy, ed. Michael I. Handel. London: Frank Cass, 1986.

Howard, Michael. The Causes of War and Other Essays, Cambridge, Mass.: Harvard University Press, 1983.

Huntington, Samuel P. "The Clash of Civilizations," Foreign Affairs,

Ignatieff, Michael. "The Virtual Commander: How NATO Invented a New Kind of War," New Yorker, 2 August 1999, pp. 33-35.

Ignatieff, Michael. Virtual War: Kosovo and Beyond, (London: Random House, 2000), pp. 176179.

Johnson, Stuart E. and Martin C. Libicki, eds. Dominant Battlespace Knowledge. Washington, D.C. National Defense University Press, 1996.

The Joint Staff, "Joint Vision 2010," Available on-line <http://www.dtic.mil/jv2010/jvpub.htm> Internet. Accessed 2 September 2002

The Joint Staffs "Joint Operations Concept: Full Spectrum Dominance Through Joint Integration," Predecisional Draft Version 4.8, 10 February 2003.

The Joint Staff, "Joint Operations Concept: Full Spectrum Dominance Through Joint Integration, Final Draft"

The Joint Staff, "Joint Vision 2020," available from < http://www.dtic.mil/doctrine> Internet. Accessed 3 November 2002.

Jordan, Billy J. and Mark J. Reardon, "Restructuring the Division: An Operational and Organizational Approach, Military Review. (May-June 1998). Available on-line

<http://www.fas.org/man/dod-101/army/unit/docs/mr-98may-june-jor.htm> Internet. Accessed 12 January 2003.

"JROC Takes More Active Role in Acquisition Process," Aerospace Daily, 24 January 2003. http://aviationnow.com/aviationnow/aerospacedaily (15 January 2002).

Kaplan, Lawrence "The Coming Anarchy," The Atlantic. February 2004. Journal on-line. Available from <http://www.theatlantic.com/politics/foreign/anarchy.htm> Internet. Acessed10 October 2002.

Keaney, Thomas. "The Linkage of Coalition Air and Ground Power in the Future of Conflict," International Security. 21, No. 2 (Fall 1997).

Keegan, John. The Face of Battle: A Study of Agincourt, Waterloo, and The Somme New York: Penguin Books, 1976

Knox, Macgregor and Williamson Murray, ed. The Dynamics of Military Revolution 1300-2050. New York: Cambridge University Press, 2001.

Kohn, Richard H. "The Erosion of Civil Control of the Military in the United States Today," Naval War College Review. LV (Summer 2002) :2-14.

Kolenda, Christopher. "Transforming How We Fight: A Conceptual Approach," Naval War College Review, 2 (Spring 2003).

Korb, Lawrence, interview by PBS Frontline. Available on-line <www.pbs.org/wgbh/pages/frontline/shows/future>

Krepinevich, Andrew F. "Cavalry to Computer: The Pattern of Military Revolutions," The National Interest, 37 (1994): 30.

Krepinevich, Andrew. "Why No Transformation?" National Interest, 4 February 1999. journal online; Available from <http//Error! Hyperlink reference not valid.; accessed 3 October 2002.

Lambakis, Steven, James Kiras, and Kristin Kolet, eds., Understanding "Asymmetric" Threats to the United States. Washington D.C.: National Institute for Public Policy, 2002.

Lambeth, Benjamin S. The Transformation of American Airpower. Ithaca, NY: Cornell University Press, 2000.

Lambeth, Benjamin. NATO's Air War for Kosovo: A Strategic and Operational Assessment. RAND: Santa Monica, CA, 2001.

Larson, Eric V, David T Orletsky, and Kristin Leuschner. Defense Planning in a Decade of Change: Lessons from the Base Force, Bottom-Up Review, and Quadrennial Defense Review Washington, D.C.: RAND, 2001

Larson, Eric V. David T. Orletsky, and Kristin Leuschner, Defense Planning in a Decade of Change: Lessons from the Base Force, Bottom-Up Review, and Quadrennial Defense Review. Washington, D.C.: RAND, 2001.

Levite, Ariel E. and Elizabeth Sherwood-Randall, "The Case for Discriminate Force," Survival, vol. 44, no. 4, Winter 2002-2003.

Macgregor, Douglas A. Breaking the Phalanx: A New Design for Landpower in the 21st Century. Westport, CT: Praeger, 1997.

Machan, Dylan "A Few Good Toys," Forbes, Dec. 9, 2002.

Mahnken, Thomas G. and Barry D. Watts, "What the Gulf War Can (and Cannot) Tell Us about the Future of Conflict," International Security. 21, No. 2 (Fall 1997):151-162.

Martel, William C., ed., The Technological Arsenal: Emerging Defense Capabilities. Washington: Smithsonian, 2001.

Matsumura, John et. al., Exploring Advanced Technologies for the Future Combat Systems Program. Santa Monica, CA: RAND, 2002.

Mayo, Richard W Vice Admiral. and Vice Admiral John Nathman, "ForceNet: Turning Information into Power," Proceedings.(February 2003). Available on-line <www.usni.org/PROCEEDINGS/Articles03/PROmayo02.htm>

McMaster, H.R. Dereliction of Duty: Lyndon Johnson, Robert McNamara, The Joint Chiefs of Staff and the Lies that Led to Vietnam. New York: HarperCollins, 1997.

Mets, David R. "The Long Search for Surgical Strike: Precision Munitions and the Revolution in Military Affairs," Cadre Paper No. 12, October 2001, Air University, Maxwell Air Force Base, Alabama.

Mitchell, William. Winged Defense. New York: GP Putnam's Sons, 1925.

Mueller, John. "The Perfect Enemy: Assessing the Gulf War," Security Studies. 5, No. 1 (Autumn 1995): 101.

Murray, Williamson. "Clausewitz Out, Computers In: Military Culture and Technological Hubris," The National Interest, 1 June 1997. Available from <http://www.clausewitz.com/CWZHOME/Clause&Computers.htm> Internet. Accessed August 20, 2002.

Murray, Williamson. "Red Teaming: Its Contribution to Past Military Effectiveness," unpublished paper, Department of Defense, Joint Advanced Warfighting Project, 2002.

Murray, Williamson. "Thinking About Innovation," Naval War College Review Spring 2001, Vol. LIV, No. 2, pp. 126-127.

Nardulli, Bruce R., Walter L. Perry, Bruce Pirnie, et. al., Disjointed War: Military Operations in Kosovo, 1999. Washington, D.C.: RAND, 2002.

Naylor, Sean. "War Games Rigged? General Says Millenium Challenge 02 was Almost Entirely Scripted," Army Times, 16 August 2002.

Newman, Richard J. "The Bombs that Failed in Kosovo," U.S. News and World Report, 20 September 1999. "Objective Force Funds Boosted At The Expense Of Legacy Efforts," Inside The Army, February 3, 2003 , p. 14.

O'Hanlon, Michael. Technology and Future War. Washington, D.C.: Brookings Institution Press, 2000.

Ochmanek, David A. Edward R Harshberger, David E. Thaler, and Glesnn A. Kent, To Find and Not to Yield: How Advances in Information and Firepower Can Transform Theater Warfare. Santa Monica, CA: RAND, 1998.

O'Hanlon, Michael E. Winning Ugly: NATO's War to Save Kosovo. Washington, D.C.: Brookings Institution, 2000.

Owens, Mackubin Thomas. "War Games are Still Just Games," Wall Street Journal, 29 August 2002.

Owens, William A. Lifting the Fog of War. Baltimore: Johns Hopkins, 2001 "Pace Asserts JROC's Importance in Developing CONOPS," Defense Daily, 24 January 2003. www.defensedaily.com (9 December 2002).

Pape, Robert A. Bombing to Win: Air Power and Coercion in War. Ithaca, NY: Cornell University Press, 1996.

Peat, F. David From Certainty to Uncertainty: The Story of Science and Ideas in the Twentieth Century. Washington, D.C.: Joseph Henry, 2002.

Peterson, Molly. "Defense Chief Outlines Challenges of Information Warfare," Government Executive Magazine, 16 August 2002.

"President's FY04 Budget Released," Department Of Defense Update, Available on-line <http://www.dfi-intl.com/shared/updates/dod/2003-02-04DoDUpdate.pd> Internet. Accessed 20 February 2003

Press, Daryl "The Myth of Air Power in the Persian Gulf War and the Future of Warfare," International Security26, No. 2 (Fall 2001):5-44.

Press, Daryl G. "Lessons from Ground Combat in the Gulf: The Impact of Training and Technology," International Security,21, No. 2 (Fall 1997):137-146.

Press, Daryl G. "The Myth of Air Power in the Persian Gulf War and the Future of Warfare," International Security. 26, No. 2 (Fall 2001): 29-38.

Qiao Liang and Wang Xiangsui, Unrestricted Warfare, trans. FBIS, Beijing: Peoples Liberation Army Literature and Arts Publishing House, February 1999.

Reddy, Peter "Joint Interoperability: Fog or Lens for Joint Vision 2010?," Research Report Number 97-0137. Maxwell Air Force Base, Alabama: Air Command and Staff College, March 1997

Ricks, Thomas. "Calibrated War Makes Comeback" The Washington Post, 21 March 2003 page A1.

Rogers, Clifford J. "Clausewitz, Genius, and the Rules," Journal of Military History October 2002. Available on-line <http://www.clausewitz.com/CWZHOME/RogersRules.htm> Internet. Accessed 10 January 2003

Rosen, Stephen Peter Winning the Next War: Innovation and the Modern Military. Ithaca, NY: Cornell University Press, 1991.

Rumsfeld, Donald, Secretary of Defense. "Legislative Priorities of Fiscal Year 2004," Memorandum from Secretary of Defense to Secretaries of the Military Departments, Chairman of the Joint Chiefs of Staff, Undersecretaries of Defense, 17 September 2002.

"Rumsfeld's Budget Favors Weaponry of Tomorrow," Washington Times. 4 February 2003, p. 8.

Scobell, Andrew and Larry Wortzel, eds., China's Growing Military Power: Perspectives on Security, Ballistic Missiles, and Conventional Capabilities.Carlisle Barracks, PA: Strategic Studies Institute, 2002.

Shultz, Richard H. and Robert L. Pfaltzgraff, eds., The Future of Air Power in the Aftermath of the Gulf War. Maxwell Air Force Base, Alabama: Air University Press, 1992.

Sherry, Michael. The Rise of American Airpower: The Creation of Armageddon. New Haven: Yale University Press, 1987.

Simpkin, Richard. Race to the Swift: Thoughts on Twenty-First Century Warfare. London: Brassey's, 1985.

Sinnreich, Richard and Williamson Murray. "Joint Warfighting in the 21st Century." unpublished paper prepared for the Office of Net Assessment, Department of Defense, 2002.

Sinnreich, Richard Hart. "Cooking the Books Won't Help the Military Transform," Lawton Constitution, 18 August 2002, p. 4.

Smith, Edward. Effects Based Operations: Applying Network-Centric Warfare in Peace, Crisis, and War. Washington D.C.: CCRP, November 2002.

Spinney, Franklin. "What Revolution in Military Affairs?" Defense Week, 23 April 2001 vol. 222, issue 17, p. 2.

Squeo, Marie. "US Military's GPS Reliance Makes a Cheap, Easy Target," Wall Street Journal, 24 September 2002.

Summer 1993, vol. 72, no. 3. Journal on-line. http://www.foreignaffairs.org/1993/3.html (15 September 2002).

Suro, Roberto. "Pentagon Avoids Individual Punishment in Cole Attack," Washington Post. January 20, 2001; Page A01.

Swain, Richard M. Lucky War: Third Army in Desert Storm. Fort Leavenworth, Kansas: US Army Command and General Staff College Press, 1994.

Tilford, Earl "Halt Phase Strategy: A New Wine in Old Skins...With PowerPoint," Strategic Studies Institute Monograph, Carlisle Barracks, PA., 23 July 1998. Available from <http://www.fas.org/man/dod-101/usaf/docs/halt.pdf>. Internet. Accessed August 2002.

Tilford, Earl. "The Revolution in Military Affairs: Prospects and Cautions," 23 June 1995, Strategic Studies Institute, Carlisle Barracks, Pennsylvania, pp. 10-13. http://www.carlisle.army.mil/ssi/pubs/1995/rmapros/rmapros.pd (3 February 2003).

Tilford, Earl. "Operation Allied Force and the Role of Air Power," Parameters, Winter 1999-2000, pp. 24-38.

Tilson, Whitney. "Cisco's Hubris," The Motley Fool, 14 August 2001, available on the internet at www.fool.com.

Toffler, Alvin and Heidi Toffler,. War and Anti-War: Survival at the Dawn of the 21st Century..New York: Little, Brown, and Company, 1993.

"Transcript of McPeak Briefing on Air Force Air Power in the Iraqi War," Inside the Air Force, 22 March 1991

Trulock, Notra III, Kerry Hines and Ann Herr. Soviet Military Thought in Transition: Implications for the Long-Term Military Competition Arlington: Pacific-Sierra Research Corp.1988.

Ullman, Harlan K., James P Wade, et al. Shock & Awe: Achieving Rapid Dominance. Washington, D.C.: NDU Press, Dec. 1996.

United States Joint Forces Command, "2002 Joint Experimentation Annual Report to Congress, 1 December 2002.

United States Marine Corps, "Expeditionary Maneuver Warfare: Marine Corps Capstone Concept," undated, <http//www.doctrine.usmc.mil/emw.htm> (5 January 2003). These views are consistent with an earlier document, "Operational Maneuver From the Sea," available on the worldwide web at http://www.dtic.mil/jv2010/usmc/omfts.pdf (5 January 2003).

US Joint Forces Command, J9 Joint Futures Lab, "Toward a Joint Warfighting Concept: Rapid Decisive Operations," RDO Whitepaper 2.0, 18 July 2002.

Van Creveld, Martin. Command in War. Cambridge, Massachusetts: Harvard University Press, 1985.

Wass de Czega, Huba. "02 Wargaming Insights." unpublished paper, December 2002.

Watts, Barry D. "Clausewitzian Friction and Future War," McNair Paper 52, Washington, D.C.: Institute For National Strategic Studies, October 1996.

Watts, Barry D. and Thomas A. Keaney. The Gulf War Air Power Study: Effects and Effectiveness. Washington: Government Printing Office, 1993.

White, Thomas E. and General Eric K. Shinseki, A Statement on the Posture of the United States Army 2003, 11 February 2003.

"Why American Needs to Maintain Its Air Superiority," Washington Times. 6 July 1998, p. 13.

Wohlstetter, Roberta. Pearl Harbor: Warning and Decision. Stanford: Stanford University Press, 1962.

Moral, Ethical, and Psychological Preparation of Soldiers and Units for Combat

Address delivered on 14 May 2010 at the Naval War College Spring Ethics Conference by Brigadier General H. R. McMaster, U.S. Army

I want to begin by thanking you for volunteering to serve our nation and humankind in time of war. We are engaged, as previous generations were engaged, against enemies who pose a great threat to all civilized peoples. As those generations defeated Nazi fascism, Japanese imperialism, and communist totalitarianism, we will defeat these enemies, who cynically use a perverted interpretation of religion to incite hatred and violence.

The murder of more than three thousand of our fellow Americans on September 11, 2001, is etched indelibly in all of our memories. Since those attacks, our nation has been at war with those who believe that there are no innocent Americans. It is those of you who have volunteered for military service in time of war who will continue to stand between terrorists who murder innocents— including children—as they do almost every day in places like Afghanistan, Iraq, Pakistan, Somalia, and Yemen—and those whom those terrorists would victimize.

As the recent attempt to commit mass murder on a flight bound for Detroit reminds us, battlegrounds overseas are inexorably connected to our own security. Our enemies seek to enlist masses of ignorant, disaffected young people with a sophisticated campaign of propaganda and disinformation. They work within and across borders.

And our fight against this networked movement is unprecedented, for several reasons. It is a new kind of threat because of the enemy's ability to communicate and mobilize resources globally. Moreover, the enemy employs mass murder of innocent civilians as its principal tactic. We recognize that if these terrorists and murderers were to gain access to weapons of mass destruction, attacks such as those on September 11th and those against innocents elsewhere would pale in comparison.

As President Obama observed in Oslo on 10 December 2009, "To say that force may sometimes be necessary is not a call to cynicism—it is a recognition of history; the imperfections of man and the limits of reason." He observed that "a non-violent movement could not have stopped Hitler's armies. Negotiations cannot convince al Qaeda's leaders to lay down their arms." America, he observed, has used its military power in places like the Balkans and today in Haiti "because we seek a better future for our children and grandchildren, and we believe that their lives will be better if other peoples' children and grandchildren can live in freedom and prosperity."(1) I firmly believe that the servicemen and -women here today are both warriors and humanitarians.

The Army's recently published Capstone Concept is a document that describes the Army's vision of future armed conflict. It identifies a continuing need for "cohesive teams and resilient soldiers who are capable of overcoming the enduring psychological and moral challenges of combat."(2)

I would like to focus my remarks on military leaders' connected responsibilities of ensuring moral and ethical conduct in war while also preparing our soldiers psychologically for the extraordinary demands of combat. It is likely that you will be called on to advise your commanders in that connection, and I thought that I might share some thoughts on the moral and ethical preparation of soldiers and units for the challenges they are likely to face in combat.

Prior to the wars in Afghanistan and Iraq, much of the debate over the nature of future armed conflict focused on the importance of emerging technologies. Many believed that these technologies would completely transform war. They called this a "revolution in military affairs." New communications, information, surveillance, and precision-strike technologies would permit technologically advanced military forces to wage war rapidly, decisively, and efficiently. We were seduced by technology.

Yet this ahistorical definition of armed conflict divorced war from its political nature. It tried to simplify the problem of future war to a targeting effort. All we had to do was target the enemies' conventional forces—which, conveniently, looked just like ours. This approach did little to prepare us for the challenges we subsequently faced in Iraq and Afghanistan. As Lieutenant General Sir John Kiszely of the British army observed,

for many military professionals, warfare—the practice of war, and warfighting— combat, were synonymous, thereby misleading themselves that there was no more to the practice of war than combat. True, some armed forces found themselves involved in other operations. . . . But these missions were largely considered by many military establishments to be aberrations—Operations Other Than War, as they came to be known in British and American doctrine—distractions from the "real thing": large scale, hi-tech, inter-state conflict.(3)

The lack of intellectual preparation limited military effectiveness and made it harder for our leaders and forces to adapt to the reality of the wars in Afghanistan and Iraq. But our military is a learning institution, and we adapted to the demands of the conflicts after the removal of the Taliban and Hussein regimes. The U.S. military undertook a range of adaptations, from improving our military education and training to refining our tactics, to investigating abuses and other failures. These adaptations derived, in part, from a better appreciation for the political complexity of the wars we were in—and the complexity of war in general. Many of these lessons were formalized in the December 2006 publication of a counterinsurgency manual. This manual was meant to provide the doctrinal foundation for education, training, and operations.(4) Our forces have adapted, and leaders have ensured ethical conduct. Every day, our soldiers take risks and make sacrifices to protect innocents.

The orthodoxy of the revolution in military affairs had conflated warfare and warfighting. It had dehumanized our understanding of war, ignored critical continuities in warfare, and exaggerated the effect of technology on the nature of armed conflict. As John Keegan observed in The Face of Battle, his classic 1976 study of combat across five centuries, the human dimension of war exhibits a high degree of continuity:

What battles have in common is human: the behaviour of men struggling to reconcile their instinct for self-preservation, their sense of honour and the achievement of some aim over which other men are ready to kill them. The study of battle is therefore always a study of fear and usually of courage, always of leadership, usually of obedience; always of compulsion, sometimes of insubordination; always of anxiety, sometimes of elation or catharsis; always of uncertainty and doubt, misinformation and misapprehension, usually also of faith and sometimes of vision; always of violence, sometimes also of cruelty, self-

sacrifice, compassion; above all, it is always a study of solidarity and usually also of disintegration—for it is toward the disintegration of human groups that battle is directed.(5)

Keegan was obviously sensitive to the social and psychological dimensions of combat, but he argued against turning the study of war over to sociologists or psychologists. Keegan contended that understanding war and warriors required an interdisciplinary approach and a "long historical perspective."

If you take away one thing from our discussion tonight, I ask you to embrace your duty to study, as a complement to your expertise in the law of war and operational law, the history, literature, psychology, and philosophy of war and warfare, as well as memoirs and accounts of combat experiences. It is our duty as leaders to develop our own understandings of our profession and the character of armed conflict. But I would also like to talk with you about how you might help your commanders ensure your troopers' ethical conduct in war and steel your units against the disintegration that Keegan observes can occur under the extraordinary physical and psychological strains of combat.

Because our enemy is unscrupulous, some argue for a relaxation of ethical and moral standards and the use of force with less discrimination, because the ends—the defeat of the enemy—justify the means employed.(6) To think this way would be a grave mistake. The war in which we are engaged demands that we retain the moral high ground despite the depravity of our enemies.

Ensuring ethical conduct goes beyond the law of war and must include a consideration of our values—our ethos. Prior to the experiences of Iraq and Afghanistan, ethical training in preparation for combat was centered on the law of war. The law of war codifies the principal tenets of just-war theory, especially jus in hello principles of discrimination and proportionality. Training covered the Geneva Conventions and the relevant articles of the U.S. military's Uniform Code of Military Justice. As Christopher Coker observes in The Warrior Ethos, however, individual and institutional values are more important than legal constraints on immoral behavior; legal contracts are often observed only as long as others honor them or as long as they are enforced.(7) Experience in Afghanistan and Iraq inspired the U.S. military to emphasize values training as the principal means of ensuring moral and ethical conduct in combat.

Utilitarianism and the thinking of philosopher John Stuart Mill would have us focus on achieving good consequences in this conflict. As the Army and Marine Corps counterinsurgency (COIN) manual points out, the insurgent often hopes to provoke the excessive or indiscriminate use of force.(8) We are fighting this war on two battlegrounds—intelligence and perception. We must — locally in Afghanistan and Iraq, and broadly in the war on terror — be able to separate terrorists and insurgents from the population. This means treating people with respect and building relationships with people that lead to trust. And this trust leads to intelligence about the enemy. We have to counter what is a very sophisticated enemy propaganda and disinformation campaign and clarify our true intentions — not just with words but with our deeds. This is particularly difficult because the enemy seeks to place the onus of indiscriminate warfare on us by provoking overreactions, denying us positive contact with the population, and blaming his own murderous attacks on us. You know the line: if Americans were not in Iraq or Afghanistan, we would not have detonated this car bomb at this funeral, in the marketplace, at the mosque, etc.

Immanuel Kant would say that it is your duty to ensure ethical and moral conduct in this war. Kant would have us treat people as ends, not means — the essence of the ethics of respect. Indeed, today's wars are contests for the trust and allegiance of the people. Moral and ethical conduct despite the brutality of this enemy will permit us to defeat enemies whose primary sources of strength are coercion and the stoking of hatreds based on ignorance.

This might sound a bit theoretical to you, so I would like to talk to you about your specific components of ensuring moral and ethical conduct despite the uncertain, complex, and dangerous environments in which our forces are operating.

Breakdowns in discipline that result in immoral or unethical conduct in war can often be traced to four factors. (If you are looking for a case study that illuminates these factors, I recommend that you read Jim Frederick's recently published Black Hearts).(9)

• Ignorance—concerning the mission or the environment or a failure to understand or internalize the warrior ethos or professional military ethic. This results in the breaking of the covenant, the sacred trust that binds soldiers to our society and to each other.

• Uncertainty. Ignorance causes uncertainty, and uncertainty can lead to mistakes, mistakes that can harm civilians unnecessarily. Warfare will always remain firmly in the realm of uncertainty, but leaders must strive to reduce uncertainty for their troopers and units.

• Fear. Uncertainty combines with the persistent danger inherent in combat to instill fear in individuals and units. Leaders must strive not only to reduce uncertainty for their troopers but also to build confident units. Confidence serves as a bulwark against fear and fear's corrosive effect on morale, discipline, and combat effectiveness.

• Combat trauma. Rage is often a result of combat trauma. Fear experienced over time or in a traumatic experience can lead to combat trauma, and combat trauma often manifests itself in rage and actions that compromise the mission.

The counterinsurgency manual recognizes that ensuring moral conduct during counterinsurgency operations is particularly difficult, because "the environment that fosters insurgency is characterized by violence, immorality, distrust, and deceit." The COIN manual directs leaders to "work proactively to establish and maintain the proper ethical climate of their organizations" and to "ensure that the trying counterinsurgency environment does not undermine the values of their Soldiers and Marines." Soldiers and marines "must remain faithful to basic American, Army, and Marine Corps standards of proper behavior and respect for the sanctity of life."(10) To inoculate soldiers and units against the four aforementioned causes of moral and ethical breakdowns, leaders should make a concerted effort in four areas:

• Applied ethics or values-based instruction

• Training that replicates as closely as possible situations that soldiers are likely to encounter

• Education about cultures and historical experiences of the peoples among whom the wars are being fought

• Leadership that strives to set the example, keep soldiers informed, and manage combat stress.

Applied Ethics and Values-Based Instruction

Our Army's values aim, in part, to inform soldiers about the covenant between them, our institution, and society.(11) The service's seven values of loyalty, duty, respect, selfless service, honor, integrity, and personal courage are consistent with Aristotelian virtue as well as the ancient philosophy of Cicero and the modern philosophy of Immanuel Kant. It is easy, for example, to identify the similarity between the Army's definition of respect as beginning "with a fundamental understanding that all people possess worth as human beings" and Cicero's exhortation in On Duties that "we must exercise a respectfulness towards men, both towards the best of them and also towards the rest."(12) The U.S. Army's values have obvious implications for moral conduct in counterinsurgency, especially in connection with the treatment of civilians and captured enemy.

Applied ethics indoctrination for new soldiers is perhaps even more important today than in the past, because of the need to differentiate between societal and military professional views on the use of violence. In much of the media to which young soldiers are exposed — such as action films, video games, and "gangsta rap" music—violence appears justifiable as a means of advancing personal interests or demonstrating individual prowess.(13) In contrast, the law of war, like the military's code of honor, justifies violence only against combatants.

A way to offset or counter this societal pressure is found in the collective nature of Army ethics training. This is immensely important. Soldiers must understand that our Army and their fellow soldiers expect them to exhibit a higher sense of honor than that to which they are exposed in popular culture. As Christopher Coker observed, "In a world of honor the individual discovers his true identity in his roles and [that] to turn away from the roles is to turn away from oneself."(14) Particularly important is the soldier's recognition that he or she is expected to take risks and make sacrifices to accomplish the mission, protect fellow soldiers, or safeguard innocents. Use of force that reduces risk to the soldier but places either the mission or innocents at risk must be seen as inconsistent with the military's code of honor and professional ethic.(15)

Values education can ring hollow unless it is pursued in a way that provides context and demonstrates relevance. While we emphasize ethical behavior as an end, we must also stress the utilitarian basis for sustaining the highest moral standards. Showing soldiers the enemy's propaganda helps emphasize the importance of ethical behavior in countering disinformation. Respectful treatment, addressing grievances, and building trust with the population ought to be viewed as essential means toward achieving success in counterinsurgency operations.

Historical examples and case studies of how excesses or abuse in the pursuit of tactical expediency have corrupted the moral character of units and undermined strategic objectives are particularly poignant. You might consider using films like The Battle of

Algiers (1966) to inspire discussions on topics such as torture, insurgent strategy, terrorist tactics, and propaganda.

Training

Applied ethics education, however, cannot steel soldiers and units against the disintegration that can occur under the stress of combat. Training our new troopers and integrating them into cohesive, confident teams must be your first priority as leaders. Tough realistic training builds confidence and cohesion that serve as "psychological protection" and bulwarks against fear and psychological stress in battle. As Keegan observed, much of the stress that soldiers experience in combat stems from "uncertainty and doubt." Training endeavors to replicate the conditions of combat as closely as possible and to reduce thereby soldiers' uncertainty about the situations they are likely to encounter.

Units experiencing the confusion and intensity of battle for the first time in actual combat are susceptible to fear. Fear can cause inaction or, in a counterinsurgency environment, might lead to an overreaction that harms innocents and undermines the counterinsurgent's mission. In her book Stoic Warriors, Nancy Sherman quotes Seneca to emphasize the importance of training as a form of "bulletproofing" soldiers against the debilitating effects of fear and combat stress: "A large part of the evil consists in its novelty," but "if evil has been pondered beforehand the blow is gentle when it comes."(16) We must base training scenarios directly on recent experiences of units in Afghanistan or Iraq and conduct training consistent with Aristotle's observation that virtues are formed by repetition. Repetitive training under challenging and realistic conditions prepares units to respond immediately and together to encounters with the enemy, using battle drills — rehearsed responses to a predictable set of circumstances. Demonstrating their ability to fight and operate together as a team will build the confidence and cohesion necessary to suppress fear and help soldiers and units cope with combat stress while preserving their professionalism and moral character.

Soldiers trained exclusively for conventional combat operations may be predisposed toward responding with all available firepower upon contact with the enemy. Such a reaction in a counterinsurgency environment, however, might result in the unnecessary loss of innocent life and run counter to the overall aim of operations. In training, we should still evaluate units on their ability to overwhelm the enemy but also evaluate them on how well they protect innocents and apply fire power with discipline and discrimination.

Our training should include civilian role-players to replicate as closely as possible the ethnic, religious, and tribal landscapes of the areas in which units will operate. As in Iraq and Afghanistan, the enemy in these exercises blends into the population. When role players are not available, cultural experts should train soldiers to play the role of civilians while their fellow soldiers are trained and evaluated. Using soldiers as civilian role-players has a secondary benefit: it is very useful for soldiers to view their own force from the perspective of the civilian population. Exercises that include civilian role-players help soldiers understand better the importance of restraint and respectful, professional conduct. Role players and soldiers come together at the end of the exercise for an "afteraction review" to identify lessons and consider how the unit might apply those lessons to future training and operations.

Cultural and Historical Training

Because unfamiliarity with cultures can compound the stress associated with physical danger, ensuring that soldiers are familiar with the history and culture of the region in which they are operating is critical for sustaining combat effectiveness and promoting respectful treatment of the population. Use professional reading programs; discuss books and articles with your soldiers. Use lectures and film. Excellent documentaries are available on the history of Islam, as well as on the history of Iraq and Afghanistan.

Cultural training has practical applications. An understanding of ethnic, cultural, and tribal dynamics allows soldiers to evaluate sources of information and anticipate potential consequences of their actions. Leaders who have a basic understanding of history and culture can also recognize and counter the enemy's misrepresentation of history for propaganda purposes.

Perhaps most important, education and training that include history and culture promote moral conduct by generating empathy for the population. The COIN manual describes "genuine compassion and empathy for the populace" as an "effective weapon against insurgents."(17) If soldiers understand the population's experience, feelings of confusion and frustration might be supplanted by concern and compassion. As Roman emperor and Stoic philosopher Marcus Aurelius observed, "Respect becomes concrete through empathy." Cicero reminds us that a soldier's respect must extend to the enemy and civilians: "We ought to revere, to guard and to preserve the common affection and fellowship of the whole of humankind."

Leaders must also learn history to evaluate themselves and place contemporary operations in the context of previous experience. Examining previous counterinsurgency experiences allows leaders to ask questions about contemporary missions, avoid some of the mistakes of the past, recognize opportunities, and identify effective techniques.

A critical examination of history also allows soldiers to understand the fundamentals of counterinsurgency theory and thereby equips them to make better decisions in what are highly decentralized operations. Soldiers need to recognize that the population must be the focus of the counterinsurgent's effort and that the population's perceptions—of their government, the counterinsurgent forces, and the insurgents—are of paramount importance. This highlights the need for soldiers to treat the population respectfully and to clarify their intentions through their deeds and conduct.

While it is important that all soldiers possess basic cultural knowledge, it is also important that leaders and units have access to cultural expertise. Soldiers often share what they learn with other members of their team. So sending even just a few soldiers from each platoon or company to language or cultural training can have a broad positive effect on the organization. In a counterinsurgency environment, cultural expertise, such as "human terrain teams," can help units distinguish between reconcilable and irreconcilable groups through an analysis of each group's fears and aspirations.(18)

Ultimately, the counter insurgent hopes to reduce violence and achieve enduring security by mediating between factions that are willing to resolve differences through politics rather than violence.(19) Cultural expertise contributes to the ethical conduct of war by helping soldiers and units understand their environment. This richer understanding can help them determine how to apply force discriminately and to identify opportunities to resolve conflict, short of force.

Combat Stress

Education or indoctrination in professional military ethics and tough, realistic training are important. However, they are insufficient to preserve moral character under the intense emotional and psychological pressures of combat. Soldiers and units must also be prepared to cope with the stress of continuous operations in a counterinsurgency environment; combat stress often leads to unprofessional or immoral behavior.(20)

Counterinsurgency operations can be even more stressful than more conventional wars. Control of stress is a command responsibility. Leaders must be familiar with grief counseling and "grief work." Grieving our losses must be valued, not stigmatized. Understand how to "communalize" grief so units can get through difficult times together.

Watch soldier behavior carefully to identify warning signs. These include social disconnection, distractibility, suspiciousness toward friends, irrationality, and inconsistency. If units experience losses, get them combat-stress counseling. Watch for soldiers who become "revenge driven," as they can break down the discipline of the unit and do significant damage to the mission and their fellow troopers. Commitment to fellow troopers and mission must be the motivating factor in battle — not rage.

Additionally, soldiers' knowledge that they have behaved in a professional, disciplined, moral manner when confronting the enemy is one of the most important factors in preventing post-traumatic stress and various dysfunctions that come with it. Developing and maintaining unit cohesion is critical in preventing disorders associated with combat stress and combat trauma. As Jonathan Shay notes, "What a returning soldier needs most when leaving war is not a mental health professional but a living community to whom his experience matters."

Military education is thin on the psychological dynamics of combat, perhaps because its importance becomes obvious only in wartime. You might read and discuss such books as J. Glenn Gray's The Warriors: Reflections on Men in Battle (Bison Books, 1998), Jonathan Shay's Achilles in Vietnam: Combat Trauma and the Undoing of Character (Simon and Schuster, 1995), and David Grossman and Loren Christensen's On Combat: The Psychology and Physiology of Deadly Conflict in War and in Peace (Warrior Science, 3rd ed., 2008).

Leadership

Common to all of these efforts to preserve the moral character of soldiers and units is leadership. Lack of effective leadership has often caused combat trauma. Sun Tzu had it right 2,500 years ago, in his classic The Art of War—"Leadership is a matter of intelligence, trustworthiness, humaneness, courage, and sternness." Humaneness in the face of the ambiguous and difficult situations we are facing today and will face tomorrow will permit soldiers to remain psychologically ready, and it must be an area that our leaders focus on. Sternness involves ensuring that leaders are in positions of leadership. Emphasize leader development but do not hesitate to remove those who do not enjoy the trust or confidence of their troopers.

Effective communication is vital. Explain to troopers the importance of their mission (the stakes) and make sure that they understand the higher commander's intent and concept for defeating the enemy and accomplishing the mission. A key part of the psychological well-being of soldiers is a sense of agency, or control; preserving discipline and moral conduct in combat depends in large measure on it.(21) It is vital that troopers understand how the risks they take and sacrifices they make contribute to the achievement of objectives worthy of those risks and sacrifices. Ultimately, positive feedback in the form of success in combat reinforces ethical and moral conduct.

Senior commanders must establish the right climate and send a simple, clear message continuously to their troopers: "Every time you treat a civilian disrespectfully, you are working for the enemy." It is, however, junior officers and noncommissioned officers who will enforce standards of moral conduct. Preparing leaders at the squad, platoon, and company levels for that responsibility is vitally important.

In Black Hearts, a headquarters company commander commenting on the cause of the horrible rape and murder of civilians south of Baghdad said the following: "Clearly a lot of what happened can be attributed to a leadership failure. And I'm not talking about just at the platoon level. I'm talking about platoon, company, battalion. Even I feel in some way indirectly responsible for what happened out there. I mean, we were all part of the team. We just let it go. And we let it go, and go, and go. We failed those guys by letting them be out there like that without a plan."

It is the warrior ethos that permits soldiers to see themselves "as part of an ongoing historical community," a community that sustains itself through "sacred trust" and a covenant that binds them to one another and to the society they serve. The warrior ethos forms the basis for this covenant. It is composed of such values as honor, duty, courage, loyalty, and self-sacrifice. The warrior ethos is important because it makes military units effective and because it makes war "less inhumane."

As our commander in chief observed in Oslo, "Make no mistake: Evil does exist in the world." Your advice and leadership will help our forces remain true to our values as we fight brutal and murderous enemies who pose a grave threat to all civilized people. I am proud to serve alongside you. My thanks to you and your families for your invaluable service to our nation in time of war.

BRIGADIER GENERAL H. R. MCMASTER, USA

Brigadier General McMaster, well-known for his 1998 book Dereliction of Duty, has, since its appearance, commanded 1st Squadron, 4th Cavalry Regiment, and the 3rd Armored Cavalry Regiment (in combat in Iraq), serving also on the U.S. Central Command Staff, at the International Institute for Strategic Studies, and in U.S. Army Training and Doctrine Command. He is now serving on the staff of Commander, U.S. Forces Afghanistan.

FOOTNOTES

(1) "Remarks by the President at the Acceptance of the Nobel Peace Prize," The White House: President Barack Obama, www.whitehouse.gov.

(2) U.S. Army Dept., The Army Capstone Concept, TRADOC Pamphlet 525-3-0 (Fort Leavenworth, Kans.: Training and Doctrine Command, 21 December 2009), available at www.tradoc.army.mil.

(3) John Kiszely, Post-modern Challenges for Modern Warriors, Shrivenham Paper 5 (Shrivenham, U.K.: Defence Academy of the United Kingdom, December 2007), p. 6, available at www.da.mod.uk.

(4) U.S. Army Dept./U.S. Navy Dept., Counterinsurgency, Field Manual (FM) 3-24/Marine Corps Warfighting Publication (MCWP) 3-33.5 (Washington, D.C.: U.S. Army Combined Arms Center/Headquarters, U.S. Marine Corps, December 2006) [hereafter COIN manual], available at www.fas.org/.

(5) John Keegan, The Face of Battle (New York: Viking, 1976), p. 83.

(6) For example, some French army officers made this argument during the War of Algerian Independence. See Lou DiMarco, "Losing the Moral Compass: Torture and Guerre Revolutionnaire in the Algerian War," Parameters (Summer 2006), pp. 70-72, available at www.carlisle.army.mil/.

(7) Christopher Coker, The Warrior Ethos: Military Culture and the War on Terror (London: Routledge, 2007), pp. 135-38.

(8) COIN manual, p. 7-5.

(9) Jim Frederick, Black Hearts: One Platoon's Descent into Madness in Iraq's Triangle of Death (New York: Harmony Books, 2010).

(10) COIN manual, p. 7-1.

(11) For the Army values, see "Soldier Life: Being a Soldier," Goarmy.com. For comprehensive analyses of the Army profession and military ethics, see Don Snider and Lloyd Mathews, eds., The Future of the Army Profession, 2nd ed., rev. and exp. (New York: McGraw-Hill, 2005). The counterinsurgency manual states that "the Nation's and the profession's values are not negotiable," also that "violations of them are not just mistakes; they are failures in meeting the fundamental standards of the profession of arms." COIN manual, p. 7-1.

(12) Marcus Tullius Cicero, On Duties, ed. and trans. M. T. Griffin and E. M. Atkins (Cambridge, U.K.: Cambridge Univ. Press, 1991), p. 39.

(13) Coker, The Warrior Ethos, p. 92.

(14) Ibid., p. 137.

(15) Don M. Snider, John A. Nagl, and Tony Pfaff, Army Professionalism, the Military Ethic, and Officership in the 21st Century (Carlisle, Pa.: U.S. Army War College, Strategic Studies Institute, December 1999), available at www.strategicstudiesinstitute.army.mil/.

(16) Nancy Sherman, Stoic Warriors: The Ancient Philosophy behind the Military Mind (New York: Oxford Univ. Press, 2005), p. 117.

(17) COIN manual, p. 7-2.

(18) Teams of regional experts, linguists, and area-studies specialists, such as anthropologists (military and civilian), embedded at the brigade level to advise the command. See Human Terrain System, hts.army.mil/.

(19) Education in negotiation and mediation techniques represents a gap in leaders' education that can be filled with self-study until the military begins to incorporate this instruction into its formal education programs. For relevant work conducted in this area by the Harvard Negotiation Project, see Program of Negotiation at Harvard Law School, www.pon.harvard.edu/. For a book useful in connection with preparing for negotiation and mediation in a counterinsurgency environment, see Roger Fisher and Daniel Shapiro, Beyond Reason: Using Emotions as You Negotiate (New York: Viking, 2005).

(20) Evidence for this conclusion comes from the business world. A 1997 survey on the "Sources and Consequences of Workplace Pressure," for instance, found that workers responded to workplace pressure by resorting to unethical behavior—for instance, "cutting corners on quality control, engaging in insider trading, falsifying reports, accepting kickbacks, and having an affair with a business associate." Edward S. Petry, Amanda E. Mujica, and Dianne M. Vickery, "Sources and Consequences of Workplace Pressure: Increasing the Risk of Unethical and Illegal Business Practices," Business and Society Review 99, no. 1 (2003), p. 26.

(21) Sherman, Stoic Warriors, p. 126.

* * * * * * * * * * * *

Continuity and Change: The Army Operating Concept and Clear Thinking About Future War

* * * * * * * * * * * *

Lt. Gen. H.R. McMaster, Ph.D., U.S. Army

March-April 2015 MILITARY REVIEW

* * * * * * * * * * * *

Anticipating the demands of future armed conflict requires an understanding of continuities in the nature of war as well as an appreciation for changes in the character for armed conflict. —The U.S. Army Operating Concept

Expert knowledge is a pillar of our military profession, and the ability to think clearly about war is fundamental to developing expert knowledge across a career of service. Junior leaders must understand war to explain to their soldiers how their unit's actions contribute to the accomplishment of campaign objectives. Senior officers draw on their understanding of war to provide the best military advice to civilian leaders. Every Army leader uses his or her vision of future conflict as a basis for how he or she trains soldiers and units. Every commander understands, visualizes, describes, directs, leads, and assesses operations based, in part, on his or her understanding of continuities in the nature of war and of changes in the character of warfare.

1st Lt. Robert Wolfe, security force platoon leader for Provincial Reconstruction Team (PRT) Farah, provides rooftop security during a key leader engagement 25 February 2013 in Farah City, Afghanistan. Civilian and military representatives from the PRT visited a newly constructed family guidance center run by Voice of Women in Farah City, an Afghan-operated nongovernmental organization, to discuss gender issues, conduct a site survey, and monitor programming.

A failure to understand war through a consideration of continuity and change risks what nineteenth century Prussian philosopher Carl von Clausewitz warned against: regarding war as "something autonomous" rather than "an instrument of policy," misunderstanding "the kind of war on which we are embarking," and trying to turn war into "something that is alien to its nature."1 In recent years, many of the diiculties encountered in strategic decision making, operational planning, training, and force development stemmed from neglect of continuities in the nature of war. The best way to guard against the tendency to try to turn war into something alien to its nature is to understand four key continuities in the nature of war and how the U.S. experience in Afghanistan and Iraq validated their importance.

First, War is Political

Army forces are prepared to do more than fight and defeat enemies; they must possess the capability to translate military objectives into enduring political outcomes.

—The U.S. Army Operating Concept (2)

In the aftermath of the 1991 Gulf War, defense thinking was dominated by theories that considered military operations as ends in and of themselves rather than essential components of campaigns that integrate the broad range of efforts necessary to achieve campaign objectives. Advocates of what became the orthodoxy of the "revolution in military affairs" (RMA) predicted that advances in surveillance, communications, and information technologies, combined with precision strike weapons, would overwhelm any opponent and deliver fast, cheap, and efficient victories. War was reduced to a targeting exercise.3 These conceits complicated efforts in Afghanistan and Iraq as unrealistic and underdeveloped war plans confronted unanticipated and underappreciated political realities. In particular, coalition forces failed to consider adequately how to consolidate military gains in the wake of the collapse of the Taliban regime in Afghanistan and the Hussein regime in Iraq. In Afghanistan, after proxy forces helped topple the Taliban regime, those forces and their leaders undermined state-building efforts. Mujahideen-era militias pursued narrow agendas and competed for power and resources within nascent institutions. In Iraq, policies that exacerbated the fears of the minority Sunni Arab and Turkmen populations strengthened the insurgency as Shia Islamist militias and Iranian proxies subverted the government and security forces. In both Afghanistan and Iraq, political competition for power, resources, and survival drove violence and weakened institutions critical to the survival of the state.

With these lessons in mind, the recently published U.S. Army Operating Concept (AOC) observes that "compelling sustainable outcomes in war requires land forces to defeat enemy organizations, establish security, and consolidate gains."4 Army forces are prepared to reinforce and integrate the efforts of partners as a fundamental part of campaign design.5 Military professionals should be particularly skeptical of ideas and concepts that divorce war from its political nature and promise fast, cheap, and eicient victories through the application of advanced military technologies.

Second, War is Human

Conventional and special operations forces work together to understand, influence, or compel human behaviors and perceptions. Army commanders understand cognitive, informational, social, cultural, political, and physical influences affecting human behavior and the mission.

—The U.S. Army Operating Concept (6)

People fight today for the same fundamental reasons that the Greek historian Thucydides identified nearly 2,500 years ago: fear, honor, and interest.7 The orthodoxy of the RMA, however, dehumanized as well as depoliticized war. In Iraq and Afghanistan, understanding and addressing the fears, interests, and sense of honor among communities was essential to reducing support for insurgent and terrorist organizations. In Afghanistan, coalition forces struggled to understand local drivers of conflict and instability. Coalition forces sometimes unintentionally empowered predatory and criminal actors, fostered exclusionary political and economic orders, and alienated thereby key elements of the population. The Taliban, regenerating in safe houses in Pakistan, portrayed themselves as patrons and protectors of aggrieved parties in Afghanistan. In Iraq, an inadequate understanding of tribal, ethnic, and religious drivers of conflict at the local level sometimes led to military operations (such as raids against suspected enemy networks) that exacerbated fears or offended the sense of honor of populations in ways that strengthened the insurgency. Later, in both wars, as U.S. Army and Marine Corps forces "surged" into areas that had become enemy safe havens, they developed an understanding of local drivers of violence, often acting as mediators between the population and indigenous army and police forces. Ultimately, more inclusive and legitimate governance and security forces helped U.S. and Iraqi forces move Iraqi communities toward temporary political accommodations that removed support for illegal armed groups that were perpetuating violence and instability.

(Photo by Pfc. David Devich, 55th Signal Company Combat Camera)

An Afghan National Army Commando and a U.S. Special Forces soldier assigned to Combined Joint Special Operations Task Force–Afghanistan direct ANA soldiers during a firefight with insurgents in Gelan District, Ghazni Province, Afghanistan, 8 February 2014.

The cultural, social, economic, religious, and historical considerations that comprise the human aspects of war must inform wartime planning as well as our preparation for future armed conflict. Terrorist and insurgent organizations across the Middle East, Africa, Latin America, and Asia use violence and propaganda to excite historical grievances, magnify nationalist or sectarian identities, and pit communities against each other. Terrorist and insurgent organizations thrive in chaotic environments associated with communal conflict as they endeavor to control territory and populations. Some of the armed conflicts that fit this pattern today include those in Mali, Libya, Nigeria, Yemen, Somalia, Central African Republic, Syria, Iraq, Lebanon, Afghanistan, Pakistan, Thailand, and the Philippines. Understanding the special circumstances and recent experiences of the people among whom wars are fought is essential if military forces are to avoid mistakes, consolidate gains, and isolate enemies from popular support.

Understanding the human aspects of war prepares leaders, soldiers, and teams for operations in environments of complexity and persistent danger. Moral, ethical, and psychological preparation for combat is critical to building resilient soldiers and cohesive teams that are committed to the Army's professional ethic. Concepts or plans that neglect the human aspect of war are unlikely to achieve lasting favorable outcomes. Neglecting the political and human continuities of war can lead to confusing military activity with progress.

Third, War is Uncertain

Although advances in technology will continue to influence the character of warfare, the effect of technologies on land are often not as great as in other domains due to geography, the interaction with adaptive enemies, the presence of noncombatants, and other complexities associated with war's continuities.

—The U.S. Army Operating Concept (8)

The dominant assumption of the RMA was that knowledge would be the key to victory in future war. Near-perfect intelligence would enable precise military operations that, in turn, would deliver rapid victory. In Afghanistan and Iraq, planning based on linear projections did not anticipate enemy adaptations or the evolution of those conflicts in ways that were difficult to predict at the outset.

Army professionals recognize war's uncertainty because they are sensitive to war's political and human aspects, and they know from experience and history that war always involves a continuous interaction with determined, adaptive enemies. That continuous interaction with enemies and adversaries helped determine the course of events in the long wars in Iraq and Afghanistan. Coalition plans did not always keep pace with shifts in the character of those conflicts. In Afghanistan, planned reductions in troops continued even as the Taliban gained control of territory and populations in the south and east between 2004 and 2009. In Iraq, the strategy remained based on rapid transition to Iraqi Security Forces even as large percentages of those forces had become party to a sectarian civil war. Some aspects of the coalition military effort, such as the absence of operational reserves, or the practice of announcing changes in mission and force levels years in advance reveal a tendency to assume that our plans dictate the future course of events and that progress in war is linear and predictable.

The AOC emphasizes the tenet of adaptability and the need for leaders to "assess the situation continuously, develop innovative solutions to problems, and remain mentally and physically agile to capitalize on opportunities."9 The AOC also redefines the tenet of depth to highlight the need to "think ahead in time and determine how to connect tactical and operational objectives to strategic goals."10

Fourth, War is a Contest of Wills

While the ability to shape security environments through the threat of punitive action will remain important, Army forces conduct positive actions essential to reassuring allies, influencing neutrals, and dissuading adversaries.

—The U.S. Army Operating Concept (11)

Clausewitz defined strategy as a sustained act of will necessary to master war's terrible uncertainties. Strategy begins with establishing a clearly defined objective or goal. Strategic goals in Afghanistan and Iraq were, at times, ambiguous. Ambiguity was, in part, due to a belief that one can achieve acceptable outcomes in war without a commitment to win. Because war is a competition involving life and death, and in which each side tries to outdo the other, establishing objectives other than winning can be counterproductive and wasteful. Winning is psychological and moral, as well as physical. Ending war, as Clausewitz observed, requires persuading the enemy that he has been defeated. Winning in war, however, neither requires unconditional surrender nor a MacArthuresque lifting of restrictions on the amount of force applied. Rarely will winning be as simple as tracking the advance of forces across a map. What winning does require is a rational determination to achieve a sustainable outcome, usually a political outcome, consistent with vital interests.

In late 2001, the Taliban regime collapsed, in large measure because every Afghan was convinced of the inevitability of their defeat. The Taliban regenerated after 2004, not only because they were able to receive support from al-Qaida and foreign intelligence organizations in support bases in Pakistan, but also because they sowed doubts in the minds of Afghans, especially those in the south and east, about the Afghan government's and the coalition's ability and willingness to prevent their return. At times, in both Afghanistan and Iraq, doubts about U.S. and partner willingness to consolidate gains and sustain commitments for ample duration and in sufficient scale to win not only encouraged enemies but also sowed doubts among friends and neutrals.

Winning in war, of course, is not a military-only task. Achieving sustainable outcomes consistent with vital interests is an inherently civil-military task that requires integrated planning and execution of political, diplomatic, military, economic, informational, intelligence, and, increasingly, law enforcement and rule of law efforts. The AOC highlights the Army's role in providing foundational capabilities that permit the United States to project national power and "help integrate and synchronize the efforts of multiple partners."12

Members of the Afghan Uniformed Police, Naka District, including the local chief of police, point out an enemy combatant they have spotted on the ridgeline about 500 meters away to Brig. Gen. Gary Volesky, deputy commanding general–maneuver, 1st Cavalry Division, and members of Company B, Task Force 2-28, 172nd Infantry Brigade, 20 September 2013.

To cope with what Clausewitz described as the blind natural forces of "violence, hatred, and enmity" that challenge the will, professionalism, and moral character of soldiers and units, the AOC emphasizes the development of resilient soldiers, adaptive leaders, and cohesive teams capable of operating effectively and morally in environments of uncertainty and persistent danger.

The Four Fallacies of Future War

Thinking clearly about future armed conflict requires consideration of threats, enemies, and adversaries, anticipated missions, emerging technologies, opportunities to use existing capabilities in new ways, and historical observations and lessons learned.

—The U.S. Army Operating Concept (13)

What military and civilian leaders learn from recent experience is important because those lessons influence operational planning and force development. As historian Williamson Murray has observed:

It is a myth that military organizations tend to do badly in each new war because they have studied too closely the last one; nothing could be farther from the truth. The fact is that military organizations, for the most part, study what makes them feel comfortable about themselves, not the uncongenial lessons of past conflicts. The result is that more often than not, militaries have to relearn in combat—and usually at a heavy cost—lessons that were readily apparent at the end of the last conflict.14 Efforts to learn and apply lessons of recent armed conflict consistent with continuities in the nature of war will not go unchallenged. That is because four fallacies that portray future war as fundamentally different from even the most recent experiences have become widely accepted. Those fallacies are based in unrealistic expectations of technology and an associated belief that future wars will be fundamentally different from current and past wars.

These fallacies are dangerous because they threaten to consign the U.S. military to repeat mistakes and develop joint forces ill-prepared for future threats to national security.

The vampire fallacy. The first of these fallacies, like a vampire, seems impossible to kill. Reemerging about every decade, it was, in its last manifestation, the RMA in the 1990s. Concepts with catchy titles such as "shock and awe" and "rapid, decisive operations" promised fast, cheap, and efficient victories in future war. Information and communication technologies would deliver "dominant battlespace knowledge."15 Under the quality of firsts, Army forces would "see first, decide first, act first, and finish decisively" 16 Those who argued that these concepts were inconsistent with the nature of war were dismissed as unimaginative and wedded to old thinking.

The vampire fallacy is much older than the orthodoxy of the RMA. Earlier manifestations go back to strategic bombing theory in the 1920s. What is common across all that time is the belief that technology and firepower are sufficient to achieve lasting strategic results in war. Today, the vampire is back, promising victory delivered rapidly from standoff range, based on even better surveillance, information, communications, and precision strike technologies. Although the vampire fallacy is based on a suite of military capabilities vitally important to national defense, it is insufficient to solve the complex problem of future war.

This fallacy confuses targeting enemy organizations with strategy. Although targeting from standoff range can disrupt enemy organizations, strikes often embolden rather than dissuade enemies unless credible ground forces are available to compel an outcome.17

It is for these reasons that the AOC stresses that American military power is joint power. For example, Army forces make joint fires more effective because they compensate for enemy efforts to avoid detection (e.g., dispersion, concealment, intermingling with civilian populations, and deception). By placing valuable enemy assets at risk, Army forces may force enemies to reveal themselves as they concentrate to defend those assets. In short, Army forces, operating as part of joint teams, create multiple dilemmas for the enemy.

The Zero Dark 30 fallacy. The Zero Dark 30 fallacy, like the vampire fallacy, elevates an important military capability, raiding, to the level of strategy."18 The capability to conduct raids against networked terrorist or insurgent organizations is portrayed as a substitute for, rather than a complement to, conventional joint force capabilities. Because they are operations of short duration, limited purpose, and planned withdrawal, raids are often unable to affect the human and political drivers of armed conflict or make sufficient progress toward achieving sustainable outcomes consistent with vital interests. Like precision strikes, raids often embolden rather than dissuade the enemy and leave populations vulnerable not only to enemy action, but also to enemy propaganda and disinformation. It is for these reasons that the AOC calls for dynamic combinations of combined arms teams and special operations forces to provide multiple options to the joint force commander as well as Army forces capable of defeating enemy organizations and consolidating gains.

A line of Afghan policemen try to control a crowd during the celebration of Nowruz, the start of spring and the traditional new year celebrated in Afghanistan, Iran, and other countries of central Asia, from the hilltop at the Kart-e-Sakhi Shrine in Kabul, Afghanistan, 21 March 2010.

The Mutual of Omaha Wild Kingdom fallacy

The Mutual of Omaha Wild Kingdom fallacy requires explanation for those of younger generations. In the 1960s on Sunday nights, U.S. families with young children gathered to watch Mutual of Omaha's Wild Kingdom on television. The host, Marlin Perkins, introduced the topic of the show and provided commentary throughout, but he rarely placed himself in proximity to dangerous animals. He usually left close contact with the wildlife to his assistant, Jim Fowler. Under the Mutual of Omaha Wild Kingdom fallacy, western militaries assume the role of Marlin Perkins and rely on proxy forces in the role of Jim Fowler to do the fighting on land. There is no doubt that security force assistance, foreign internal defense, and combat advisory missions will increase in importance to national security; it is difficult to imagine future operations that will not require Army forces to operate with multiple partners. Primary reliance on proxies, however, is often problematic due to insufficient capabilities or lack of will based on incongruent interests.

Like the vampire and Zero Dark Thirty fallacies, the Mutual of Omaha fallacy confuses an important capability with defense strategy. While the AOC recognizes special operations as an Army core competency and identifies security force assistance as a first order capability, it also acknowledges that Army forces must not only operate with multiple partners but also be prepared to exert influence and convince those partners that actions or reforms are in their interest.19

The RSVP Fallacy. Finally, the fourth fallacy solves the problem of future war by opting out of armed conflict, or certain forms of armed conflict, such as fighting on land. The fundamental problem with this RSVP fallacy is that it fails to give due consideration to enemies in wars or adversaries in between wars. Wars often choose you rather than the other way around. And the application of exclusively standoff capabilities to complex land-based problems in war leaves decision making in the hands of the enemy. If Western militaries do not possess ready joint forces capable of operating in sufficient scale and in ample duration to win, adversaries are likely to become emboldened, and deterrence is likely to fail. As George Washington observed in his first State of the Union address: "To be prepared for war is one of the most effectual means of preserving peace."20

Ready Army forces play a vital role in preventing conflict because they communicate U.S. commitment and remain capable of compelling outcomes. Army forces are particularly valuable in deterring those who might be tempted to wage limited war to accomplish limited objectives. That is because the forward positioning of capable ground forces elevates the cost of aggression to a level that the aggressor is unwilling to pay and prevents the aggressor from doing what Russia has in Ukraine—posing to the international community a fait accompli and then portraying its reactions as escalatory.

Moreover, as joint force freedom of movement and action in the maritime, air, space, and cyber domains become more contested, the deterrent value of land forces will become more important. Land forces operating in areas such as the South China Sea or the Persian Gulf may have to control territory not only to deny its use to the enemy but also to project power from land across multiple domains to restrict enemy freedom of action and preserve the joint force's freedom of movement at sea, in the air, in space, and in cyberspace.

Thinking Clearly about War and the Future of Warfare

Shifts in the geopolitical landscape caused by competition for power and resources influence the character of armed conflict. These shifts, and violence associated with them, occur more rapidly than in the past due to advances in technology, the proliferation of information, and the associated increased momentum of human interaction.

Fallacies persist, in large measure, because they define war as one might like it to be. Preparing Army forces to operate as part of joint, interorganizational, and multinational teams to prevent conflict, shape security environments, and, if necessary, win in war requires clear thinking. Army professionals might begin by rejecting fallacies that are inconsistent with continuities in the nature of war. But Army professionals must also consider changes in the character of warfare.

To understand continuity and change, it is hard to improve on the approach found in historian Sir Michael Howard's 1961 seminal essay on how military professionals should develop what Clausewitz describes as their own "theory" of war." First, "study in width." Observe how "warfare has developed over a long historical period." Next, "study in depth" Study campaigns and explore them thoroughly, consulting original sources and applying various theories and interdisciplinary approaches. This is important, Howard observes, because as the "tidy outlines dissolve," we can "catch a glimpse of the confusion and horror of the real experience." And last, "study in context." Wars and warfare must be understood in context of their social, cultural, economic, human, moral, political, and psychological dimensions because "the roots of victory and defeat often have to be sought far from the battlefield." As we consider war and warfare in width, depth, and context, Army professionals might consider change and continuity in four areas: threats, missions, technology, and history and lessons learned during recent operations.

(U.S. Air Force photo by Master Sgt. Eric Petosky)

Personnel provide command and control information at the 612th Air and Space Operations Center, Hanscom Air Force Base, Mass.,16 February 2010.

* * * * * * * * * * * *

Army Operating Concept

First Principles for Technological Development

The Army works with joint partners, industry, allies, and other key stakeholders to develop future force capabilities with the following technological first principles in mind.

• Emphasize integration of technology with soldiers and teams

• Simplify systems and integrate soldier training into design

• Maximize reliability and reduce life cycle costs

• Design redundant systems that improve effectiveness under conditions of uncertainty

• Develop systems that degrade gracefully

• Maintain foundational knowledge to reduce the opportunity for surprise

• Reduce logistical demands

- Anticipate enemy countermeasures

- Ensure interoperability

- Consider scale and organizational implications

* * * * * * * * * * * *

Threats, Enemies, and Adversaries

Diverse enemies will employ traditional, unconventional, and hybrid strategies to threaten U.S. security and vital interests.

—The U.S. Army Operating Concept (23)

It is clear that Army leaders and units must be prepared to fight and win against state and nonstate actors. Due to what some have called the democratization of destructive power, nonstate actors, such as the Islamic State of Iraq and Syria (ISIS) and Hezbollah possess capabilities previously associated only with the fielded forces of nation-states. For example, nonstate organizations have unprecedented financial resources and access to sophisticated weapons. Moreover, nation-states such as Russia and Iran employ unconventional proxy forces, often in combination with their own special operations or conventional forces. As the historian Conrad Crane has observed, there are two ways to fight the U.S. military—asymmetrically and stupid.24 Future enemies will not be passive; they will make every effort to avoid U.S. strengths, emulate advanced U.S. capabilities, and disrupt U.S. advantages. They will expand operations to other battlegrounds such as those of perception, political subversion, and criminality.

The AOC acknowledges the continuous interaction with enemies in war and the interaction with adversaries between wars. That interaction requires the Army to be a learning organization. When engaged with determined enemies, Army leaders "think ahead in time to gain and maintain positions of relative advantage over the enemy." To defeat elusive and capable enemies, Army forces develop situational understanding through action in close contact with the enemy and civilian populations. In contrast to "rapid decisive operations," Army forces are capable of sustaining high-tempo operations while consolidating gains to seize, retain, and exploit the initiative and achieve "lasting outcomes in the shortest time span. 25 Future Army forces extend the "concept of combined arms from two or more arms or elements of one service to include the application of joint, interorganizational, and multinational capabilities in the conduct of joint combined arms operations.'26

Technology

The U.S. Army's differential advantage over enemies derives, in part, from the integration of advanced technologies with skilled soldiers and well-trained teams.

—The U.S. Army Operating Concept (27)

Science and technology will continue to influence the character of warfare. While the U.S. Army differential advantages over potential enemies will continue to depend in large measure on advanced technology, winning in a complex world requires powerful combinations of leadership, skilled soldiers, well-trained units, and technology. here are no technological silver bullets. he Army must integrate new technological capabilities with complementary changes in doctrine, organization, training, leader development, personnel, and other elements of combat effectiveness. 28 Army technological development emphasizes the need for all formations to possess the appropriate combination of mobility, protection, and lethality. And the Army places soldiers at the center of that effort, pursuing "advances in human sciences for cognitive, social, and physical development" while fitting weapons and machines to soldiers and units rather than the other way around.29

Missions

The complexity of future armed conflict, therefore, will require Army forces capable of conducting missions in the homeland or in foreign lands including defense support of civil authorities, international disaster relief and humanitarian assistance, security cooperation activities, crisis response, or large-scale operations.

—The U.S. Army Operating Concept (30)

The Army is not a boutique force. Soldiers and units must be prepared for a broad range of activities. The 2014 Quadrennial Defense Review identified 11 mission areas in which the Army plays a significant role. Army forces must be prepared to conduct operations successfully in the context of future enemy capabilities and technology. Missions will often overlap and place varied and simultaneous demands on the joint force. In future crises, demands on all components of the Army are likely to increase as threats overseas generate simultaneous threats to the homeland.

(U.S. Navy photo by Petty Officer 2nd Class Carlos M. Vazquez)

The guided-missile destroyer USS *Arleigh Burke* launches Tomahawk cruise missiles at ISIS targets 23 September 2014.

The Army's Missions and Contributions to Joint Operations

The 2014 Quadrennial Defense Review identified 11 enduring Armed Forces missions in which the Army plays a substantial role:

- Provide for military defense of the homeland

- Defeat an adversary

- Provide a global stabilizing presence

- Combat terrorism

- Counter weapons of mass destruction (WMD)

- Deny an adversary's objectives

- Respond to crisis and conduct limited contingency operations

- Conduct military engagement and security cooperation

- Conduct stability and counterinsurgency operations

- Provide support to civil authorities

- Conduct humanitarian assistance and disaster response

* * * * * * * * * * *

To shape security environments and prepare for a broad range of missions, Army "conventional and special operations forces contribute to a global land network of relationships resulting in early warning, indigenous solutions, and informed campaigns." The theater security cooperation activities of regionally aligned Army forces as well as the foundational capabilities that Army forces provide to the joint force set "favorable conditions for commitment of forces if diplomacy and deterrence fail".32 Because future enemies will attempt to deny access to the joint force, future Army forces must be prepared to conduct expeditionary maneuver, "the rapid deployment of task-organized combined arms forces able to transition quickly and conduct operations of sufficient scale and ample duration to achieve strategic objectives"33 Highly mobile combined arms air-ground formations will see and fight across wider areas, operating widely dispersed while maintaining mutual support and the ability to concentrate rapidly.

Regional engagement as well as the Army's ability to conduct expeditionary maneuver and joint combined arms operations are critical to demonstrating U.S. resolve, deterring adversaries, and encouraging allies and partners.

History and Lessons Learned

Sir Michael Howard warned that we should not study history to make us "clever for the next time," but instead to help make us "wise forever." 34 Similarly, Clausewitz, observed, the study of war and warfare "is meant to educate the mind of the future commander, or, more accurately, to guide him in his self-education, not to accompany him to the battlefield; just as a wise teacher guides and stimulates a young man's intellectual development, but is careful not to lead him by the hand for the rest of his life."35 In short, history can help military leaders ask the right questions, but leaders must consider the unique context and local realities of a particular conflict to develop answers. History does, however, amplify many of the lessons relearned in recent and ongoing conflicts.

On the need to consolidate gains or integrate efforts of multiple partners, for example, the father of the Army War College, former Secretary of War Elihu Root, commented in 1901 on "the wide range of responsibilities which we have seen devolving upon officers charged with the civil government of occupied territory; the delicate relations which constantly arise between military and civil authority" To cope with the complexity of war in the early twentieth century, Root highlighted the "manifest necessity that the soldier, above all others, should be familiar with history."36

Our Army pursues lessons of recent and ongoing operations enthusiastically but often has difficulty applying these lessons. It is for that reason that the AOC (Appendix B) establishes a framework for learning around the 20 first-order capabilities the Army must possess to win in a complex world. Lessons from recent armed conflicts, such as the need to put politics at the center of security force assistance, the growing importance of counterthreat finance, the increased overlaps between military and law enforcement operations, or the criticality of mobile protected firepower and combined arms capabilities in urban operations, can now inform interim solutions to warfighting challenges. 37

* * * * * * * * * * *

The Army Warfighting Challenges

The Army Warfighting Challenges provide an analytical framework to integrate efforts across warfighting functions while collaborating with key stakeholders in learning activities, modernization, and future force design.

TRADOC Publication 525-3-1, The U.S. Army Operating Concept: Winning in a Complex World

* * * * * * * * * * *

Defining the Future Army: Force 2025 and Beyond

As historians Williamson Murray and MacGregor Knox observed in a seminal book on military innovation, militaries that prepared successfully for the demands of future war took professional military education seriously. They cultivated in their leaders the ability to think clearly about war, considering continuities and changes.

"The military institutions that successfully innovated between 1919 and 1940 without exception examined recent military events in careful, thorough, and realistic fashion. Analysis of the past was the basis of successful innovation. The key technique of innovation was open-ended experiment and exercises that tested systems to breakdown rather than aiming at the validation of hopes or theories. Simple honesty and the free flow of ideas between superiors and subordinates—key components of all successful military cultures—were centrally important to the ability to learn from experience. And the overriding purpose of experiments and exercises was to improve the effectiveness of units and of the service as a whole, rather than singling out commanders who had allegedly failed."38

114

Our Army is innovating under Force 2025 Maneuvers, "the physical (experimentation, evaluations, exercises, modeling, simulations, and war games) and intellectual (studies, analysis, concept, and capabilities development) activities that help leaders integrate future capabilities and develop interim solutions to warfighting challenges."39 Successful innovation will require focused and sustained collaboration among Army professionals committed to reading, thinking, and learning about the problem of future armed conflict, and determining what capabilities our Army and joint force must develop to win in a complex world.

* * * * * * * * * * *

The author wishes to express gratitude to those who generously reviewed and provided helpful suggestions for this essay—in particular, Dr. Nadia Schadlow of the Smith Richardson Foundation and John Wiseman of the Army Capabilities Integration Center.

Lt. Gen. H. R. McMaster, U.S. Army, is the deputy commanding general, Futures, U.S. Army Training and Doctrine Command, and director of the Army Capabilities Integration Center. His previous assignments include commanding general, Maneuver Center of Excellence and Fort Penning, and commander, Combined Joint Inter-Agency Task Force Shafafiyat (Transparency) in Kabul, Afghanistan. He holds a Ph.D. in military history from the University of North Carolina at Chapel Hill. McMaster has served as a U.S. Army War College Fellow at the Hoover Institution on War, Revolution, and Peace, and as a senior consulting fellow at the International Institute of Strategic Studies in London.

Notes

Epigraph. U.S. Army Training and Doctrine Command (TRA-DOC) Pamphlet (TP) 525-3-1, The U.S. Army Operating Concept: Win in a Complex World (Fort Eustis, VA: TRADOC, 2014), 8.

1. Carl Von Clausewitz, On War, ed. and trans. Michael Howard and Peter Paret (Princeton, NJ: Princeton University Press, 1989), 30.

2. TP 525-3-1, 10.

3. Frederick W. Kagan, Finding the Target: The Transformation of American Military Policy (New York: Encounter Books, 2006) , 57-73, 144-175; see also H.R. McMaster, "Crack in the Foundation: Defense Transformation and the Underlying Assumption of Dominant Knowledge in Future War," Student Issues Paper, Center for Strategic Leadership, U.S. Army War College, November 2003, Vol. S09-03, 12-32.

4. TP 525-3-1, 16.

5. Ibid., 19.

6. Ibid.

7. Thucydides, The Landmark Thucydides: A Comprehensive Guide to the Peloponnesian War, ed. Robert B. Strassler (New York: Free Press, 1996), 43.

8. TP 525-3-1, 9.

9. Ibid., 21.

10. Ibid.

11. Ibid., 22.

12. Ibid., 17.

13. Ibid., 33.

14. Williamson Murray, "Thinking About Innovation," Naval College Review 54(2)(Spring 2001): 122-123.

15. William A. Owens, "Introduction," ed. Stuart E. Johnson and Martin C. Libicki, Dominant Battlespace Knowledge, (Washington, D.C.: National Defense University Press, 1996), 4; see also H.R. McMaster, "Crack in the Foundation," 1; and Janine Davidson, Lifting the Fog of Peace: How Americans Learned to Fight Modern War (Ann Arbor: The University of Michigan Press, 2010).

16. TP 525-7-1, The United States Army Concept Capability Plan for Unit Protection for the Future Modular Force, 20122024, Version 1.0 (Fort Eustis, VA: TRADOC, 28 February 2007) , 4.

17. Tom C. Schelling, Arms and Influence (New Haven, CT: Yale University Press, October 2008), 2-7.

18. Mark Boal, Zero Dark Thirty, Sony Pictures, 2012. The movie depicts the raid that resulted in the death of al-Q aida leader Osama bin Laden in May 2011.

19. TP 525-3-1, 19 and 46. Core competencies are those indispensable contributions in terms of capabilities and capacities beyond what other services and defense agencies provide and which are fundamental to the Army's ability to maneuver and secure land areas for the Nation.

20. George Washington, George Washington to the United States Senate and House of Representatives, 8 January 1790, National Archives Founders Online, http://founders.archives. gov/documents/Washington/05-04-02-0361 (accessed 23 January 2015).

21. TP 525-3-1, 8.

22. Michael Howard, "The Use and Abuse of Military History," in Michael Howard, The Causes of Wars, 2nd Edition (Cambridge, MA: Harvard University Press, 1983), 188.

23. TP 525-3-1, 10.

24. Conrad C. Crane, "The Lure of the Strike," Parameters 43(2)(Summer 2013): 5, http://www.strategicstudiesinstitute. army.mil/pubs/parameters/issues/Summer 2013/1 Crane SpecialCommentary.pdf (accessed 23 January 2015).

25. TP 525-3-1, 19.

26. Ibid., 18.

27. Ibid., 15.

28. Ibid., 36-41.

29. Ibid., 36.

30. Ibid., 16.

31. Ibid., 17.

32. Ibid.

33. Ibid.

34. Michael Howard, "The Use and Abuse of Military History," Parameters 11(1) (1981): 13, http://strategicstudies-institute.army.mil/pubs/parameters/Articles/1981/1981%20 howard.pdf (accessed 23 January 2015). Article was reprinted with permission of the Royal United Service Institute (R.U.S.I.) and originally appeared in R.U.S.I. Journal 107 (February 1962), 4-8.

35. Clausewitz, 141.

36. Elihu Root, Five Years of the War Department, Following the War with Spain, 1899-1903, as shown in the annual reports of the Secretary of War (Harvard, MA: Harvard University, 1904), 160. Digitized July 2008; available at https:// books.google.com/books?id=TuUpAAAAYAAJ&dq=Five+- Years+of+the+War+Department&source=gbs navlinks s (accessed 23 January 2015).

37. David E. Johnson, M. Wade Markel, and Brian Shannon,

The 2008 Battle for Sadr City (Santa Monica, CA: RAND Corporation, 2013); Juan C. Zarate, Treasury's War: The Unleashing of a New Era of Financial Warfare (New York: PublicAffairs, 2013).

38. Macgregor Knox and Williamson Murray, The Dynamics of Military Revolution, 1300-2050 (New York: Cambridge University Press, 2001), 188.

39. TP 525-3-1, 33.

* * * * * * * * * * * *

Studying War and Warfare

Major General H.R. McMaster - Modern War Institute

This essay was originally published on January 13, 2014.

Submitted by Major General H.R. McMaster, Commanding General of the U.S. Army Maneuver Center of Excellence:

I would like to thank MAJ Matt Cavanaugh for extending an opportunity to participate in this forum. As WarCouncil.org gets off the ground, I thought that we might consider how to develop our understanding of war and warfare and prepare ourselves intellectually for future armed conflict.

Approaching the Study of War and Warfare

It is hard to improve on the approach to studying war and warfare found in historian Sir Michael Howard's 1961 seminal essay on how military professionals should develop what

Clausewitz described as their own "theory" of war. First, to study in width: To observe how warfare has developed over a long historical period. Next to study in depth: To study campaigns and explore them thoroughly, consulting original sources and applying various theories and interdisciplinary approaches. This is important, Sir Michael observed, because as the "tidy outline dissolves," we "catch a glimpse of the confusion and horror of real experience." And lastly to study in context. Wars and warfare must be understood in context of their social, cultural, economic, human, moral, political, and psychological dimensions because "the roots of victory and defeat often have to be sought far from the battlefield."

To develop understanding in "width, depth, and context," we must be active learners dedicated to self-study and self-critique. Discussion and debate with others exposes us to different perspectives and helps us consider how what we learn applies to our responsibilities. Participative intellectual activity is critical to the "Self-Development Domain" of our Army's leader development efforts. And the self-development domain is as important as the Operational Domain (unit training and operational experience) and the Institutional Domain (official Army schools) in helping leaders prepare for the challenges of future war. This is why forums such as the WarCoucil.org are important. Discussions on this site should challenge our assumptions and refine our thinking.

Understanding the Context — and the Continuities — of War

Successful American military leaders supplemented their formal learning through active reading, study, and reflection. In 1901, the father of the Army War College, Secretary of War Elihu Root, commented on "the great importance of a thorough and broad education for military officers," due to the "rapid advance of military science; changes of tactics required by the changes in weapons; our own experience in the difficulty of working out problems of transportation, supply, and hygiene; the wide range of responsibilities which we have seen devolving upon officers charged with the civil government of occupied territory; the delicate relations which constantly arise between military and civil authority." Thus, Root wrote, there was a "manifest necessity that the soldier, above all others, should be familiar with history."[1]

Self-study and professional discussions help leaders understand the character of particular conflicts, inform ideas of how armed conflict is likely to evolve, and help leaders understand the complex interactions between military, political, and social factors that influence the situation in war. Because leaders cannot turn back time once war occurs; they must develop an understanding of war and warfare before they enter the field of battle. As nineteenth century Prussian philosopher of war, Carl von Clausewitz, observed, the study of war and warfare "is meant to educate the mind of the future commander, or, more accurately, to guide him in his self education, not to accompany him to the battlefield; just as a wise teacher guides and stimulates a young man's intellectual development, but is careful not to lead him by the hand for the rest of his life."[2] Clausewitz continued, emphasizing that leaders should use their knowledge of military history "to analyze the constituent elements of war, to distinguish precisely what at first sight seems fused, to explain in full the properties of the means employed and to show their probable effects, to define clearly the nature of the ends in view, and to illuminate all phases of warfare in a thorough critical inquiry."[3]

Many of the recent difficulties we have encountered in strategic decision-making, operational planning, and force development have stemmed, at least in part, from the neglect of critical continuities in the nature of war. Military professionals, through their study of war and warfare in width, depth, and context as well as through discussion and debate in a variety of forums can help identify changes in the character of conflict as well as underscore important continuities in the nature of war. Consider these continuities, for example:

First, war is political. As von Clausewitz observed, "war should never be thought of as something autonomous but always as an instrument of policy." In the aftermath of the 1991 Gulf War, defense thinking was hijacked by a fantastical theory that considered military operations as ends in and of themselves rather than just one of several instruments of power that must be aligned to achieve sustainable strategic goals. Advocates of the "Revolution in Military Affairs" (RMA) predicted that advances in surveillance, communications and information technologies, along with precision strike weapons, would overwhelm any opponent. Experience in Afghanistan and Iraq revealed the flawed nature of this thinking. Professionals should be skeptical of ideas and concepts that divorce war from its political nature. And skepticism is particularly appropriate concerning theories that promise fast, cheap, and efficient victories through the application of advanced military technologies.

Second, war is human. People fight today for the same fundamental reasons that the Greek historian Thucydides identified nearly 2500 years ago: fear, honor, and interest. Thinking associated with the RMA dehumanized as well as depoliticized the nature of war. The cultural, social, economic, religious, and historical considerations that comprise the human dimension of war must inform wartime planning as well as our preparation for future armed conflict. In Iraq and Afghanistan, gaining an appreciation of the fears, interests, and sense of honor among their internal communities was critical to move those communities toward political accommodations.

Third, war is an uncertain contest of wills. War's political and human nature place armed conflict squarely in the realm of uncertainty. The dominant assumption of the RMA, however, was that that knowledge would be the key to victory in future war. Near-perfect intelligence would enable precise military operations within a realm of certainty. In Afghanistan and Iraq, planning was sometimes based on linear projections that did not account for enemy adaptations or the evolution of those conflicts in ways that were difficult to predict at the outset. War remains fundamentally uncertain due to factors that lie outside the reach of information and surveillance technologies. Moreover, war's uncertainty and non-linearity are results of war's political and human dimensions as well as the continuous interaction with determined, adaptive enemies. And wars are uncertain because they are contests of wills that unleash unpredictable psychological dynamics.

Conclusion

While a student at the German staff college between the World Wars, General Albert C. Wedemeyer noted that "an indomitable will and broad military knowledge, combined with a strong character, are attributes of the successful leader." Wedermeyer continued, stating that leaders "must have a clear conception of tactical principles and their application," and "only by continual study of military history and of the conduct of war with careful attention

119

to current developments can the officer acquire the above stated attributes of leadership."[4] As professional Soldiers, we share a moral and professional obligation to read, think critically, and engage in professional discussions. Forums such as WarCouncil.org are critical because junior leaders must develop an appreciation for leadership at the operational, joint, and strategic levels so they can place the actions of their units in context of war aims and develop an ability to advise senior military and civilian leaders on matters of policy and strategy.

To help develop professional expertise, the Maneuver Center of Excellence has developed the Maneuver Leader Self-Study Program (MSSP). The MSSP consists of books, articles, doctrine, film, lectures, practical application exercises, and on-line discussion forums to educate maneuver leaders about the nature of war and the character of warfare, as well as to emphasize their responsibilities to prepare their Soldiers for combat, lead them in battle, and accomplish the mission. The broader intent of the of the MSSP is to enhance understanding of the complex interaction between war and politics in "width, depth, and context." The program is also meant to foster a commitment to lifelong learning and career-long development to ensure that our leaders are prepared for increased responsibilities. Each MSSP topic contains a brief summary of the chosen topic, its relevance to maneuver leaders, and several study questions for reflection. Topics also contain annotated bibliographies as well as a link to an on-line discussion forum.

1. Elihu Root, General Correspondence to the United States Congress, 1901 (Manuscript Division, Library of Congress), Washington D.C., 2011, available at http://www.loc.gov/rr/mss/address.html

2. Carl Von Clausewitz, On War, Edited and Translated by Michael Howard and Peter Paret, Princeton University Press, 1989. pg. 141

3. Ibid.

4. Albert C. Wedemeyer - Wedemeyer on War and Peace, Edited by Keith E. Eiler, Hoover Press, 1987, 5.

* * * * * * * * * * * *

The Role of the Judge Advocate in Contemporary Operations: Ensuring Moral and Ethical Conduct During War

Lecture to the U.S. Army 58th Judge Advocate Officer Graduate Course

Brigadier General H.R. McMaster

MAY 2011

THE ARMY LAWYER • DA PAM 27-50-456

The strength of any Army unit and across our military is, as you know, our junior officers and our noncommissioned officers. A great example of junior officer leadership was Dylan Reeves, the brother of your fellow JAG officer Shane Reeves. Dylan was an incredibly courageous and effective combat platoon leader that I served with while commanding 3rd ACR. General Harmon, one of my personal heroes, while commanding the 2nd Armored Division in World War II, stated that his division would succeed only if the platoon succeeded. Dylan showed me that this statement remains true and the importance of resiliency in combat units. Therefore, one of the things I would like to talk with you about today is the importance of building resiliency among your Soldiers and creating cohesive, tough teams that can stand up to the demands of any mission. As judge advocates you play a big part helping prepare our units for the extreme demands of combat and understanding how to do that holistically is really important.

I was not sure what I was going to talk about today as there are numerous relevant areas in which judge advocates play a significant role in contemporary operations. Judge advocates, as you know, have taken on a broad range of responsibilities, far beyond what anybody would have anticipated prior to the current wars. I believe that our judge advocates, more than anybody else, have adapted extraordinarily well to these increased demands. I personally know the value of a good legal advisor as I benefited tremendously from Lieutenant Colonel Neoma White's efforts and counsel. Major Mike Martinez, our Deputy, who was killed in action in Tal Afar, was an awesome officer as well. There is so much we have taken on in terms of assistance, training host nation security forces, rule of law missions, detention operations, and working within an indigenous law system that relies upon legal expertise. Who would have thought that our military would be at this nexus of war fighting and the law? I believe our judge advocates have done a brilliant job adapting to this reality and have been a primary reason for the successes we have had in Iraq as well as in Afghanistan.

Before I go on with our discussion, I want to take a moment and really thank you for your service. Thank you for what you are doing in this time of war. I know it has placed great strains on you and your families. I hope you take time during this course to reflect, to share varying perspectives with fellow officers, and to think broadly about our profession and how we can improve the combat effectiveness of our forces. As you all know, we are engaged with enemies that pose a grave threat to all civilized peoples. Just as previous generations defeated Nazi fascism, Japanese imperialism, communism, and totalitarianism, we will defeat these enemies. We all remember the murder of thousands of our fellow Americans on September 11th. Since those attacks, our nation has been at war and it is you who stand between them and those who they would murder—not just in our country, but also in places like Afghanistan, Iraq, Pakistan, Somalia, and Yemen.

As the attempt to commit mass murder on a flight bound for Detroit reminds us, security and the operations we are conducting overseas are naturally connected to our own security. Our enemies seek to enlist masses of ignorant, disenfranchised young people with a sophisticated campaign of propaganda and disinformation. They work within and across borders, posing a new kind of threat due to their ability to communicate and mobilize resources globally. Moreover, the enemy employs mass murder of innocents as their principal tactic within this war. I think all of us recognize that if these terrorists were to gain access to weapons of mass destruction, attacks such as those on September 11 and those against innocents elsewhere would pale in comparison.

As President Obama observed in Oslo, to say that force is sometimes necessary is not called cynicism, but a recognition of history, imperfections of man and the limits of reason. He observed that a nonviolent movement could not have stopped Hitler's armies. Negotiations cannot convince Al Qaeda's leaders to lay down their arms. The President also observed that the use of military power—for example our humanitarian mission in the

Balkans—can be used to help others to live in freedom and prosperity and this, in turn, secures a better future for our children and grandchildren. So I firmly believe the service women and men who are serving in our armed forces today are both warriors and humanitarians, and it falls on you in large measure as judge advocates to help your commanders communicate that message and to inculcate that belief into our institutional culture. So, again thank you for your service.

What I would like to talk about today is the need for us, as an institution, to build cohesive teams and create resilient Soldiers capable of overcoming the enduring psychological and moral challenges of combat. My idea for this discussion came from a book I was reading about a week ago called Black Hearts. It is a book about a platoon that essentially disintegrates under the pressures of operations in South Baghdad. In the platoon, discipline and cohesion breaks down for a number of different reasons resulting in the rape and murder of an Iraqi family. This of course raises the question: How could this happen? Today, I want to address this troubling question by picking out a few themes from the book.

More specifically, I would like to focus my remarks on our connected responsibilities of ensuring moral and ethical conduct in war, while also preparing Soldiers psychologically for the extraordinary demands of combat. It is likely you will be called on to advise commanders on these issues, and I want to share some thoughts on how we can prepare our Soldiers and our units for these challenges.

Prior to the wars in Afghanistan and Iraq, the debate over future armed conflicts focused on the importance of emerging technologies. Many believed that technology would completely transform war, calling this the revolution in military affairs. The consensus was that technologically advanced U.S. Forces would be able to overwhelm inferior enemy forces with superior communication capabilities, precision munitions, and perfect surveillance of the battlefield. Simply put, we were seduced by technology. You remember some of the language, right? No pure competitor until 2020, we are going to achieve full spectrum dominance and so forth. However, this definition of armed conflict divorced war from its political nature. It tried to simplify war into a targeting exercise where all we had to do was target the enemies' conventional forces which conveniently look just like ours. As we now know, this approach did little to prepare us for the challenges we subsequently faced in Iraq and Afghanistan.

As British Lieutenant General, Sir John Kisley observed, for many military professionals, warfare, the practice of war, war fighting and combat were synonymous. Thus, these military professionals misled themselves into believing that there was no more to the practice of war than combat. Despite many armed forces finding themselves involved in other types of operations, like we did in Somalia and the Balkans, these missions were largely considered by many in the military establishment to be aberrations. Operations other than war, as they came to be known in British and American doctrine, were viewed as distractions from the real thing; more specifically, large-scale, high-tech intrastate conflict. The lack of intellectual preparation for the wars we are in clearly limited our military effectiveness at the beginning of our operations in Afghanistan and in Iraq.

But our military is a learning institution, and we adapted to the demands of the conflicts by undertaking a broad range of adaptations, including improving our military education and training; refining our tactics; and investigating abuses and other failures. These adaptations derived in part from a better appreciation of the political complexity of the wars we were in and the complexity of war in general. Many of these lessons were formalized in the December 2006 publication of the counterinsurgency manual. The manual is meant to provide a doctrinal foundation for education, training, and operations. Our forces have adapted, our leaders have emphasized ethical conduct, and every day our Soldiers take risks and make sacrifices to protect innocents.

However, as I mentioned, there are at times breakdowns within units. It is our responsibility to steel our Soldiers and our units against these breakdowns. The blind faith in technology that I discussed earlier, essentially dehumanized our understanding of war. It ignored critical continuities in war and exaggerated the effect of technology on the nature of armed conflict. As John Keegan observed in The Face of Battle, a 1974 classic study of combat across five centuries, the human dimension of war exhibits a very high degree of continuity. He said, "What battles have in common is human, the behavior of men struggling to reconcile their instinct for self-preservation, their sense of honor, and the achievement of some aim over which other men are ready to kill them. The study of battle is, therefore, always the study of fear and usually of courage; always of leadership, usually of obedience; always of compulsion, sometimes of insubordination; always of anxiety, sometimes of elation or catharsis; always of uncertainty and doubt misinformation and misapprehension, usually also of faith and sometimes of vision; always of violence, sometimes also of cruelty, self-sacrifice, compassion. Above all, it is always a study of solidarity, and it is usually also the study of disintegration. For it is the disintegration of human groups that battle is directed."

Keegan was obviously sensitive to the social and psychological dimensions of combat. He argued though against turning the study of war over to sociologists or psychologists. He contended that understanding war and warriors required an interdisciplinary approach and a long perspective. If you take away one thing from our discussion today, I ask you to embrace your duty to study warfare in order to form your own vision of war and to use that vision to help prepare yourself and your fellow Soldiers, Airmen, Marines, and Sailors for the challenges that they are going to face in combat. Additionally, it is imperative that you help your commanders ensure Soldiers are ethical in how they conduct warfare. Commanders must not allow their units to disintegrate. Keegan observes that units disintegrate under the extraordinary physical and psychological demands of combat.

Because our enemies are unscrupulous, some argue for relaxation of ethical and moral standards. I would guess you have talked a lot about this in connection with interrogation techniques or targeting. Some argue that the ends—the ends of defeating this nihilistic, brutal enemy—justify the means employed. But to think this way would be a grave mistake as the war in which we are engaged demands that we retain the moral high ground regardless of the depravity of our enemies. Ensuring ethical conduct goes beyond the law of war and must include a consideration of our values, our ethos.

Prior to the experiences of Iraq and Afghanistan, ethical training in preparation for combat was centered almost exclusively on the law of war. Training covered the Geneva Conventions and the relevant articles of our Uniform Code of Military Justice. However, as Christopher Coker observed in a great book called The Warrior Ethos, individual and institutional values are more important than legal constraints on moral behavior. This is because legal contracts are often observed only as long as others honor them or as long as they are enforced. Experience in Iraq and in Afghanistan have inspired our military to emphasize values training as the principle means, along with law of war training, of ensuring moral and ethical conduct in combat. So let's talk about philosophy for a little bit.

In particular, utilitarianism, associated with the thinking of John Stuart Mill, would have us focus on achieving good consequences from the conflicts we are in. As the counterinsurgency manual points out, the insurgent often tries to provoke excessive or indiscriminate use of force. Therefore, we are fighting these wars really on two battlegrounds: a battleground of intelligence and a battleground of perception. We have to, both locally in Afghanistan and in Iraq and more broadly in the war on terror, be able to separate insurgents and terrorists from the population. This means treating the local population with respect and building relationships with the people, as trust leads to intelligence. We have to counter what is a very sophisticated enemy propaganda disinformation campaign, and we have to clarify our true intentions, not just with words or messages, but with our deeds and our actions. This is particularly difficult because the enemy seeks to place the onus on us for their indiscriminate type of warfare. They try to deny us positive contact with the population and blame us for their own murderous acts.

Immanuel Kant would say that it is our duty to ensure ethical and moral conduct in this war. Kant would have us treat the people as the ends, not simply the means that we manipulate in order to achieve our own ends. In essence this is the ethics of respect. Where there is a contest for the trust and allegiance of the people, moral and ethical conduct permits us to defeat our enemies, whose primary sources of strength are coercion and intimidation. This might sound a bit theoretical, so I would like to talk to you about specific components of ensuring moral and ethical conduct despite the uncertain and dangerous environments in which our forces are operating. Breakdowns in discipline will result in immoral or unethical conduct in war. These breakdowns can be traced to four factors.

The first factor is ignorance: ignorance concerning the mission, the environment, or failure to understand or internalize the warrior ethos or a professional military ethic. This results in breaking the bond that binds Soldiers to our society, and more importantly, Soldiers to each other. The second factor is uncertainty. Ignorance causes uncertainty, and uncertainty can lead to mistakes—mistakes that can harm civilians unnecessarily. Warfare will always have a component of uncertainty, but leaders must strive to reduce uncertainty for their troopers and for their units.

The third factor is fear. Uncertainty combines with the persistent danger inherent in combat to incite fear in individuals and units. Leaders must strive not only to reduce uncertainty for their troopers, but also must build confident units, because it is confidence that serves as our firewall against fear, and it is fear that has a disintegrating effect on organizations. The final factor is combat trauma. Fear experienced over time, or caused by a traumatic experience, can lead to combat trauma. Combat trauma often manifests itself in actions that compromise the mission and in actions that violate our professional military ethic and our ethos.

The Army and Marine Corps counterinsurgency manual (COIN) recognizes that strong moral conduct during counterinsurgency operations is particularly difficult because in a counterinsurgency, violence, immorality, distrust, and deceit are intentionally used by the insurgent. So the COIN manual directs leaders to work proactively to establish and maintain the proper ethical climate in their organizations and to ensure violence does not undermine our institutional values. For us to be successful in counterinsurgent operations, servicemembers must remain faithful to the basic American military standards of proper behavior and respect for the sanctity of life. To inculcate Soldiers in units against the four aforementioned causes of moral and ethical breakdowns, leaders should make a concerted effort in four parallel areas.

The first of these areas, and this is an area that I think you will advise commanders on, is applied ethics or values-based instruction. The second area is training: training that replicates as closely as possible the situations that Soldiers, as well as units, are likely to encounter in combat. The third area is education: education about the cultures and the historical experiences of the people for whom these wars are being fought. The fourth area is leadership: leadership that strives to set the example, keep Soldiers informed, and manage combat stress. Let me talk about each of these in more detail.

First, applied ethics and values-based education. Our Army's values aim in part to inform Soldiers about the covenant between them, our institution, and our society. The seven U.S. Army values of loyalty, duty, respect, selfless service, honor, integrity, and personal courage are consistent with philosophy, and, in particular, the Aristotelian virtue as well as the Asian philosophy of Cicero and modern philosophy of Immanuel Kant. It is easy, for example, to identify the similarity between our Army's definition of respect as beginning "with the fundamental understanding that all people possess worth as human beings" and Cicero's exhortation that "we must exercise a respectfulness towards men, both towards the best of them and also towards the rest."2 The U.S. Army's values have obvious implications for moral conduct in counterinsurgency, especially in connection with the treatment of civilians and captured enemies. Applied ethics indoctrination for new Soldiers is perhaps even more important today than in the past because of the need to differentiate between societal and military professional views on the use of violence. Young Soldiers, Airmen, Marines, and Sailors are exposed to video games, action films, and gangster rap music which make violence appear justifiable as a demonstration of prose or as a way to advance personal interest.

We need to make sure that our servicemen and women understand that the law of war, as well as our Code of Military Justice, justifies violence only against combatants. The way to offset these sources of societal pressures can be found in the collective nature of Army ethics training. It is important to do it in basic training; it is important to do it in officer basic courses; and it is important that Soldiers understand that our Army and their fellow Soldiers expect them to exhibit a higher sense of honor than that to which they are exposed to in popular culture. As again, Coker observes, in a world of honor, the individual who discovers his or her true identity and his or her role, and then turns away from the role, is turning away from themselves. Particularly important is the Soldiers recognition that he or she is expected to take risks and make sacrifices to accomplish the mission, to protect fellow Soldiers, or to safeguard innocents. Use of force that reduces risk to the Soldier, but threatens the mission or puts innocents at risk, must be seen as inconsistent with the military's code of honor and our professional ethic.

However, values education of this kind can seem hollow unless it is pursued in a way that provides context and demonstrates relevance. While we assume the ethical behavior as an end, we also should stress the utilitarian basis for sustaining the highest moral standards. Showing Soldiers enemy propaganda and saying "Okay your behavior can either support their propaganda, or it can counter their propaganda" is a powerful tool. Respectful treatment, addressing grievances, and building trust with the population ought to be viewed as essential to achieving success in counterinsurgency operations. Historical examples and case studies that point out how excesses or abuse in the pursuit of tactical expediency corrupted the moral character of units and undermines strategic objectives are also powerful tools. You might consider using films such as The Battle of Algiers to inspire discussions on topics such as torture, insurgent strategy, terrorist tactics, and propaganda. Applied ethics education by itself, however, cannot steel Soldiers and units against the disintegration that can occur under stressful combat. Training Army troopers and integrating them into cohesive, confident teams must also remain a priority for us as leaders.

Tough realistic training builds confidence and cohesion that serves as psychological protection against fear and psychological stress. As Keegan observed, much of the stress Soldiers experience in combat stems from uncertainty and doubt. Training must endeavor to replicate the conditions of combat as closely as possible and thereby reduce Soldiers' uncertainty and fear about the situations they are likely to encounter. Uncertainty and fear can cause inaction, or in a counterinsurgency environment, may lead to an overreaction that harms innocents and undermines the counterinsurgency mission. For example, how many times have we seen warning shots used against approaching vehicles? But how helpful are these shots when those on the receiving end of a warning shot most likely cannot even hear the shot? The warning shot is simply a way for a Soldier feeling fear to address uncertainty while possibly causing innocents to be harmed unnecessarily.

In Nancy Sherman's great book titled Stoic Warriors, she quotes Seneca to emphasize the importance of training as a form of bulletproofing Soldiers against the debilitating effects of fear and combat stress. Seneca said, "A large part of the evil consists in its novelty, but if evil has been pondered before that, the blow is gentle when it comes."[3] We must base training scenarios directly on recent experiences of the units in Afghanistan and Iraq, and conduct training consistent with Aristotle's observation that virtues are formed by repetition.

Repetitive training under challenging and realistic conditions prepares units to respond immediately and together to any situation that they encounter by using battle drills or rehearsed responses to a predictable set of circumstances. Demonstrating their ability to fight together as a team will build the confidence and cohesion necessary to suppress fear and help Soldiers and units cope with combat stress while preserving their professionalism and preserving their ethos. Further, Soldiers trained exclusively for conventional combat operations may be predisposed to over respond with disproportionate fire power upon contact with the enemy. Such reaction in a counterinsurgency environment might result in the unnecessary loss of innocent life and thus counter the overall aim of the operation. Now I am not saying that in training we should avoid evaluating units on the ability to overwhelm the enemy because it is to our advantage to not have a fair fight! What I am talking about is overwhelming the enemy in tactical situations while simultaneously applying firepower with discipline and discrimination. To help support this difficult balance, our training should include civilian role players, and it should also replicate as closely as possible ethnic religious tribal landscapes in the areas in which units operate. When role players are not available, we should train our own Soldiers to play those roles. Using Soldiers as role players can have a very positive effect by allowing them the opportunity to view our operations through the perspective of the civilian population.

Cultural and historical training and understanding is also extremely important. Unfamiliar cultures can compound the stress associated with physical danger. Ensuring that Soldiers are familiar with the history and culture of the region in which they are operating is critical for sustaining combat effectiveness and promoting respectful treatment of the population. I recommend using professional reading programs as well as lectures and films to educate your Soldiers on their area of operations. For example, there are excellent documentaries that are available on the history of Islam as well as the history of Iraq and Afghanistan. Understanding the ethnic cultural tribal dynamics will allow Soldiers to evaluate sources of information and also allow them to understand the second and third order effects of their actions. Additionally, leaders who have a basic understanding of the history of the culture will recognize and counter the enemy's misrepresentation of history for propaganda purposes.

But perhaps most importantly, education and training that includes history of culture promotes moral conduct by generating empathy for the population. The COIN manual describes genuine compassion and empathy for the populace as an effective weapon against insurgents. If Soldiers understand the population's experience, feelings of confusion and frustration might be supplanted by concern and compassion. As Roman Emperor and Stoic philosopher Marcus Aurelius observed, respect becomes concrete through empathy. As Cicero reminds us, a Soldier's respect must extend to the enemy and civilians as "we must exercise respectfulness towards all men." As I mentioned before, this respect must be universal as we "ought to revere and to guard and to preserve the common affectionate and fellowship of the whole of humankind."

Let me digress for a minute. There are some people who say that we cannot really connect with "these people." They ask, "How can you connect to people in Iraq and Afghanistan?" They believe that our cultures are so different that we can never really connect as human beings. I believe there is a tendency among some people to cloak bigotry with the language of cultural sensitivity. If you think about, in late 2006, when we were deciding whether or not to reinforce the security effort in Iraq in order to stop what was at that time a humanitarian crisis of a colossal scale and a violent sectarian civil war, many who were against the idea justified their position by stating that "those Arabs have been killing each other for many years and there is nothing we can do about it." This is bigotry cloaked in a language of cultural sensitivity. To combat this mentality, you must truly try to understand the culture, and thus I would recommend a good book on this called Military Orientalism which discusses Western military perspective on Eastern militaries over the centuries.

It is also important for us as leaders to study history in order to evaluate ourselves and help us understand others. Examining previous counterinsurgency experiences allows our leaders to ask the right questions, avoid some of the mistakes of the past, recognize opportunities, and identify effective techniques. A critical examination of history also allows Soldiers to understand the fundamentals of counterinsurgency theory and thereby equips them to make better decisions in what are highly decentralized operations. We must continually ask, what are we doing to prepare junior leaders to take on those additional responsibilities?

Soldiers need to recognize that the population must be the focus of the counterinsurgency effort and that the population's perceptions of their government, of counterinsurgent forces, and of the insurgents, are of paramount importance. This highlights the need for Soldiers to treat the population respectfully and to clarify our intentions with our deeds and with our conduct. While it is important that all Soldier possess basic cultural knowledge, it is also important that leaders and units have access to cultural expertise. Soldiers often tend to share what they learn with other members of their team, so if you send just a few Soldiers to language training or to take college courses in the history of the area, you are going to see that knowledge spread throughout your organization. Everybody should get a base of education and a base of training but I would recommend trying to develop some depth across your organization as well. Greater cultural expertise helps units to distinguish between reconcilable and irreconcilable groups, which ultimately reduces violence and achieves enduring security by mediating between factions that are willing to resolve differences in politics rather than in violence. Cultural expertise also contributes to the ethical conduct of war by helping Soldiers and units understand their environment. This richer understanding can help them determine how to apply force discriminately and to identify opportunities to resolve conflict short of force.

Finally, I would like to talk about combat stress. Education or indoctrination in professional military ethics and tough realistic training are important; however, they are insufficient in preserving moral character when confronted by the intense emotional and psychological pressures of combat. Soldiers in units must be prepared to cope with the stress of continuous operations in a counterinsurgent environment. An example is a unit like Dylan Reeves's platoon. Dylan's platoon took over fifty percent casualties in the city of Tal Afar, but had the resiliency to continue highly successful combat operations. So how do you get a unit to be able to handle such extreme combat stress without disintegrating into unprofessional or immoral conduct?

The answer is that control of stress is a command responsibility. Leaders must be familiar with grief counseling and grief work. Grieving our losses must be valued, not stigmatized. We have to understand how to communalize grief so we can get through difficult times together. We have to watch Soldier behavior carefully and identify warning signs. These include social disconnection, distractibility, suspiciousness of friends, irrationality, and inconsistency. If units experience losses, get them to stress counseling. Watch for Soldiers who become vindictive, as the pursuit of revenge can break down discipline of the unit and do significant damage to the mission. Commitment to fellow troopers and the mission must be the motivating factors in battle, not rage. Additionally, developing and maintaining unit cohesion is critical in preventing disorders associated with combat stress and combat trauma. As Jonathan Shay notes in a great book called Achilles in Vietnam, subtitled Combat Trauma and the Undoing of Character, what a returning Soldier needs most when leaving war is not a mental health professional, but a living community to whom his experience matters. Military education is thin on the psychological dynamics of combat. This is something as a judge advocate and an advisor to a commander that you can emphasize. Some of the books you might read and discuss include J. Glenn Gray's The

Warriors: Reflections of Men in Battle, Jonathan Shay's book that I mentioned, Achilles in Vietnam, Dave Grossman's and Loren Christensen's book On Combat, The Psychology and Physiology of Deadly Conflict in War and in Peace.

But the factor that cuts across all of these areas is leadership. Common to all of these efforts to preserve the moral character of Soldiers in units is leadership. Lack of effective leadership has often caused combat trauma. Sun Tzu had it right 2500 years ago. Leadership is a matter of intelligence, trustworthiness, humaneness, courage, and sternness. Humaneness in the face of the ambiguous, difficult situations that we are facing today, and will face tomorrow, will permit Soldiers to remain psychologically ready and must be an area that our Soldiers and leaders focus on. Sternness involves ensuring that leaders are in positions of leadership—as well as not hesitating to remove those who do not enjoy the trust or confidence or do not deserve the trust and confidence of their troopers. Effective communication as a leader is important, vitally important. Leaders have to explain to troopers the importance of their mission, mistakes that are involved, and to make sure that they understand the higher commander's intent and concept for defeating the enemy and accomplishing the mission.

A key part to ensuring psychological well being, which is so critical to preserving discipline and moral conduct in combat, depends in large measure on preserving the Soldiers' sense of control. It is vital that troopers understand how the risks they are taking and how the sacrifices they and their comrades are making contribute to a mission worthy of those risks and sacrifices. Senior commanders must establish the right climate, and they have to send a simple and clear message to their troopers: every time you treat a civilian disrespectfully, you are working for the enemy. A command must have some basic standards of conduct, something along the enduring lines of Standing Orders, Rogers Rangers, given by Major Robert Rogers to his Rangers in 1759, that lets the unit know that they will overwhelm the enemy in every tactical engagement, but only apply firepower with discipline and discrimination. Other clear and simple messages important to impart to the unit include, treat Iraqis with respect; do not tolerate abusive behavior; and treat detainees humanely. Simple messages are important to set out the command's expectations and to establish the right climate. However, we must recognize that junior officers and noncommissioned officers enforce those standards of moral conduct in what are very highly decentralized operations. Preparing those leaders at the squad, platoon, and company levels for that responsibility is vitally important.

In the book I mentioned at the beginning, Black Hearts, the Headquarters and Headquarters Company commander within this battalion commented on the cause of the horrible rape and murders of civilians south of Baghdad. He said the following, "Clearly a lot of what happened can be attributed to a leadership failure, and I'm not talking about just at the platoon level. I'm talking about platoon, company, and battalion. Even I feel in some way indirectly responsible for what happened out there. I mean, we were all part of the team. We just let it go, and we let it go and go and go. We failed those guys by leaving them out there like that without a plan."4

It is a warrior ethos that permits Soldiers to see themselves as part of an ongoing historical community, a community that sustains itself across our armed forces through bonds of sacred trust, and a covenant that binds up to one another and then binds us to the society that we serve. The warrior ethos forms the basis for this covenant. It is comprised of

129

values such as honor, duty, courage, loyalty and self-sacrifice. The warrior ethos is important because it makes military units effective and because it makes war less inhumane, as our Commander-in-Chief observed in Oslo. Make no mistake: evil does exist in the world, but it is your advice as a judge advocate and it is your leadership as an officer that helps our forces remain true to our values as we fight these brutal and murderous enemies. I am proud to serve alongside of you, and thanks very much for the opportunity to visit here with you today.

* * * * * * * * * * *

Brigadier General McMaster is serving as Commander, Combined Joint Task Force Shafafiyat (Transparency) at International Security Assistance Force (ISAF) Headquarters in Kabul, Afghanistan. General McMaster, a native of Philadelphia, Pennsylvania, was commissioned as an officer in the U.S. Army upon graduation from the U.S. Military Academy in 1984. His military education includes the Airborne Course, Ranger School, Armor Officer Basic and Career Courses, Cavalry Leader's Course, Combined Armed Service Staff School, Command and General Staff College, and a U.S. Army War College fellowship at the Hoover Institution on War, Revolution, and Peace. General McMaster holds a Ph.D. in military history from the University of North Carolina, Chapel Hill.

General McMaster served in numerous command and staff positions in the United States and overseas. His initial duty assignment was to the Second Armored Division at Fort Hood, Texas, where he served as a support platoon leader, tank platoon leader, tank company executive officer, and scout platoon leader in 1st Battalion, 66th Armor Regiment. In 1989, he was assigned to the Second Armored Cavalry Regiment in Nuremberg, Germany where he served as regimental plans officer. In March 1990, he assumed command of Eagle Troop, Second Squadron which he commanded in Bamberg, Germany and Southwest Asis during operations Desert Shield and Desert Storm. After the squadron returned to Germany, he assumed duties as squadron operations officer. In the summer of 1992, General McMaster began graduate study in history at the University of North Carolina, Chapel Hill. In 1994, he reported to the Department of History at the U.S. Military Academy where he served as an assistant professor. He was assigned to the National Training Center in June of 1997 and joined the 11th Armored Cavalry Regiment where he served as executive officer of 1st Squadron and regimental operations officer. In October 1989, Brigadier General McMaster joined the 1st Squadron, 4th Cavalry in Schweinfurt, Germany and commanded the "Quarterhorse" until June of 2002. From May 2003 to May 2004, he served as Director, Commander's Advisory Group at U.S. Central Command. General McMaster assumed command as the 71st colonel of the Third Armored Cavalry Regiment at Fort Carson, Colorado in June 2004. His command tour included a one-year combat mission in Iraq from 2005 to 2006. From July 2006 until June 2008, he was assigned to U.S. Central Command with duty in London as a Senior Research Associate at the International Institute for Strategic Studies and duty in Iraq as Special Assistant to Commander, Multi-National Force-Iraq. From August 2008 until July 2010 Brigadier General McMaster served as the Director, Concept Development and Learning in the Army Capabilities Integration Center, Training and Doctrine Command at Fort Monroe, Virginia.

* * * * * * * * * * *

FOOTNOTES

1 Jim Frederick, Black Hearts (Harmony Books 2010).

2 Nancy Sherman, Stoic Warriors, The Ancient Philosophy Behind the Military Mind 56 (Oxford Univ. Press 2005).

3 Id. at 117.

4 Frederick, supra note 1, at 9.

* * * * * * * * * * * *

Book Review: DERELICTION OF DUTY: Lyndon Johnson, Robert McNamara, The Joint Chiefs of Staff, and the Lies that Led to Vietnam

MILITARY LAW REVIEW

Vol. 160

Reviewed by Major Robert K. Fricke 2

"Vietnam was not forced on the United States by a tidal wave of Cold War ideology. It slunk in on cat's feet."3

I. Introduction

In his book, Dereliction of Duty (1), H. R. McMaster vigorously argues that neither the American entry into the war in vietnam, nor the manner in which it was conducted was inevitable.4 Instead, he reasons that the escalation of U.S. military intervention "grew out of a complicated chain of events and a complex web of decisions that slowly transformed the conflict in Vietnam into an American war."5

After his own experiences in the Persian Gulf War as the commander of an armored cavalry troop, McMaster wondered how and why Vietnam had become an American war. As the full title of the book suggests, the author answers these two questions by focusing primarily on the personalities of, and the interactions between, Lyndon Johnson, Robert McNamara, and the Joint Chiefs of Staff.

Ultimately, McMaster argues that American policy on Vietnam was arrived at by default-there was no strategic vision or planning. It was instead, the by-product of the dynamic that existed between these individuals, the advice they gave or failed to give, and the conflicts that Vietnam posed to Lyndon Johnson's primary goals of reelection in 1964 and the passing of his "Great Society" legislation during his second term. McMaster supports his thesis through extensive research that relies primarily on personal papers, oral histories, and tape-recorded interviews of the people named in the book's title and others who worked closely with them.

McMaster's thorough analysis of the personalities of these essential figures, their selfish goals, and the policy-making structure in which they operated helps to answer how we fought in Vietnam. Dereliction of Duty is not nearly as probative as he would have us believe in answering why we fought there. To use his metaphor, while Vietnam may have "slunk in on cat's feet,"6 the feet of this "cat" were the feet of a wild, hungry tiger that had escaped from its cage long before the Johnson administration. This "cat" remained on the prowl until it was returned to its cage during the Reagan administration.

Sprinkled throughout Dereliction of Duty are isolated references to the events of the Cold War. Among some of the crises and Cold War doctrine mentioned within the book are Truman's "Domino Theory;" Korea; the Bay of Pigs; the Cuban missile crisis; the Laotian crisis; the Congo from 1961-1963; confrontation with the Kremlin over a divided Berlin; Kruschev's support for communist insurgents fighting wars of national liberation in the countries of the developing world; and Kennedy's inaugural speech where he exhorted America's youth to "pay any price" and "bear any burden" to extend the virtues of their country to the rest of the world. Johnson, McNamara, and the Joint Chiefs of Staff lived through these events as adults.

McMaster's sparse treatment of these events helps to lessen their impact on his theory of the why of Vietnam. He uses these events not to explain a Cold War mentality that led to Vietnam, but rather to explain the relationships that were formed based on the advice given during these crises. He argues that it is the nature of these advisory relationships that ultimately led to the Americanization of Vietnam.

It is his attempt to use the interaction of these personalities to explain the why of Vietnam that causes McMaster's work to fall short. He offhandedly discounts, and all but ignores, the cumulative affect these Cold War events had on the "inevitability theory" of why Vietnam. In fact, McMaster waits until a footnote in his epilogue to acknowledge the argument of a large majority who believe the war in Vietnam was inevitable due to this "Cold War mentality."7 McMaster's view of this theory is that the Cold War crises, particularly those that occurred during the Kennedy years, shaped advisory relationships that carried over into the Johnson administration.

McMaster, however, betrays his why theory early on in his book. "November 1963 marked a turning point in the Vietnam War. The U.S. role in fomenting a change in the South Vietnamese government saddled the United States with responsibility for its successor."8 By his own words then, the author acknowledges the "inevitability theory" of Vietnam that he builds a case against throughout the remainder of his book.

Perhaps the best evidence of the Cold War theory of the inevitability of American involvement in Vietnam is provided unwittingly by McMaster. He uses the Dominican Republic crisis to illustrate Johnson's political "gimmick" to overcome opposition to his Vietnam policy. More telling is the introduction of 20,000 troops to prevent a Communist takeover that would result in another "Cuba" in the Caribbean. "Although he was aware that the intervention would expose him to charges of gunboat diplomacy, Johnson thought that the public and congressional criticism would be 'nothing compared to what I'd be called if the Dominican Republic went down the drain.'"9 The Dominican Republic crisis was not "bequeathed" from Kennedy. It best illustrates the cultural milieu of our nation at the time, and our unthinking, knee-jerk reaction to the potential spread of Communism. The battle between the "Free World" and "Communism" is the correct answer to the why of Vietnam.

McMaster's analysis is brilliant, however, in explaining the how of Vietnam. Johnson, McNamara, and the Joint Chiefs of Staff each get their chance in the McMaster spotlight. He illuminates throughout the book the improper functioning of staffs, the very deep consequences that are paid in failing to exercise moral courage to voice one's true beliefs, and how those bent on political gain can distort the policy making process to achieve their own selfish goals.

II. Lyndon Johnson

Lyndon Johnson's dereliction in the how of American involvement in Vietnam was primarily fourfold. First, he accepted and ratified a method of doing business that limited the source of advice and displaced the role of the Joint Chiefs of Staff on military issues. Second, his insecurity in having "inherited" the presidency caused him to crave consensus. As such, he was so obsessed with validating himself in the 1964 election that he neglected to develop a coherent policy on Vietnam. Third, after the election, his focus became his legacy. Passage of his "Great Society" legislation was the mechanism by which he would achieve it, again, to the exclusion of a coherent policy on Vietnam.10 Fourth, he was willing to lie for political purposes, and did so when it served his need.

McMaster uses the Kennedy administration as the backdrop for the flawed policy-making process that Lyndon Johnson adopted when confronted with issues on Vietnam. Kennedy had dismantled the National Security Council apparatus in favor of "task forces" and "inner clubs" of most trusted advisors to weigh the advantages and disadvantages of proposed policy actions. McMaster makes a compelling argument that an assassin's bullet thrust Johnson into a job he was not yet ready to assume,11 and that Kennedy's flawed method of doing business carried over into Johnson's administration.12

McMaster's use of the word "bequeathed"13 is correct. While Kennedy certainly felt free to change his predecessor's method of doing business to a leadership/management style that Kennedy was more comfortable with, his assassination did not afford Johnson that luxury - at least not initially. Continuity and status quo were the guiding principles after Johnson initially assumed his duties as President. At some point, however, Johnson adopted the policy-making apparatus that he inherited from Kennedy, and it reflected his own leadership style.

McMaster provides no evidence that Johnson was ever privy to Kennedy's "task forces" and "inner clubs."14 For all the reader knows, Johnson the vice-president was busy attending state funerals, as had been the experience of most vice-presidents until the very recent modern era. If anything, Johnson's exclusion from these groups as a vice-president arguably should have made him more resentful of such groups as President. At some point, presumably after the mandate he received in the 1964 election, Johnson could have refused this "inheritance." Instead, he made it his own.

III. Robert McNamara

Robert McNamara's dereliction in relation to the how of American involvement in Vietnam was threefold. First, he believed that geopolitical and technological changes of the last fifteen years had rendered advice based on military experience irrelevant and, in fact, dangerous.15 Second, and related to the first point, he overused the "success" of the Cuban missile crisis, and the policy of "graduated pressure" as the model for a solution to the Vietnam situation. Third, instead of assuming the role of "honest broker," he tried to live up to the label given to him by Johnson as a "can do fellow." He would make Johnson's wishes come true.

McMaster paints McNamara, through the comments of uniformed military personnel, as a statistician who believed that statistics and the Harvard business-school solution would be the answer to all problems.16 Yet it was the uniformed services' parochialism that alienated McNamara and prompted him to centralize power in the Office of the Secretary of Defense. In light of "Goldwater-Nichols" and the emphasis on "jointness" in our services today, McNamara seemed visionary in this regard.

McMaster's criticism of McNamara is misplaced as to his perceived over-reliance on the Cuban missile crisis as a model for the graduated use of force. McNamara had concluded that the principal lesson of the Cuban missile crisis was that graduated pressure provided a "firebreak between conventional conflict and that situation of low probability but highly adverse consequences" that could lead to nuclear war.17 This "success" (with the caveat of the under-the-table negotiation of the removal of Jupiter missiles brokered between Robert Kennedy and Anatoli Dobrynin) is a concrete example of a real life, military "lesson learned." These "lessons" are what our uniformed military is so anxious to collect, catalogue, and apply as guiding principles to ensure the success of future operations. It is easy for the author to criticize applying this "lesson learned" to Vietnam based upon its subsequent failure. The proper question is whether it was reasonable at the time to apply this lesson. Given the "Cold War" mentality that existed at the time and that the author chooses to minimize, criticism of McNamara on this point is unjustified.

McMaster asserts that the collective lack of military experience among McNamara and his "whiz kids" caused them to "fail to consider that Hanoi's commitment to revolutionary war made losses that seemed unconscionable to American white-collar professionals of little consequence to Ho's government."18 McMaster properly charges McNamara with trying to do the enemy's thinking for him and validates the advice of the uniformed services based upon the war gaming results of the Joint Chiefs of Staff. In the same vein, however, McMaster seems unwilling to give any credence to McNamara's concern over possible Russian or Chinese involvement based upon the United States' recent experience in Korea.

McMaster's greatest criticism of McNamara is the "can do" label that was placed on him by Johnson, and McNamara's zealous efforts to live up to it.

McNamara knew that Johnson wanted advisors who would tell him what he wanted to hear, who would find solutions even if there were none to be found. Bearers of bad new or those who expressed views that ran counter to his priorities would hold little sway. McNamara could sense the president's desires and determined to do all that he could to fulfill them. He would become Lyndon Johnson's "oracle" for Vietnam.19

McNamara and others had witnessed Johnson's exclusion of Vice President Humphrey from future deliberations on Vietnam after he had offered advice that questioned the direction of Johnson's policy. It was this blind loyalty and personal desire to hold sway over the President that was the most destructive.

When Johnson "wanted to conceal from the American public and Congress the costs of deepening American involvement in Vietnam, McNamara's can-do attitude and talent for manipulating numbers and people would prove indispensable."20 This point goes a long way toward answering the how of Vietnam.

IV. The Joint Chiefs of Staff

The dereliction of the Joint Chiefs of Staff in relation to the how of American involvement in Vietnam is Dereliction of Duty's greatest revelation. McMaster unmasks the service parochialism that virtually paralyzed the Joint Chiefs of Staff in carrying out their role as principal military advisor to the President. In sum, because of their inability to put their rivalries and own self-interests aside, they were relegated to the role of technicians for planners in the Office of the Secretary of Defense, rather than as strategic planners in their own rite.

Dereliction of Duty is full of concrete examples of how each service elevated its own interest at the expense of the common good. McMaster makes a very strong case for the proposition that the Joint Chiefs determined their own fate and shared in the complicity for how we fought in Vietnam, principally due to their own inaction.

McMaster tempers this argument slightly with some sympathy for their plight by listing the unique restraints that encumbered them as military professionals. McMaster reminds the reader of the Truman-Mac-Arthur controversy during the Korean War and the dangers of overstepping the bounds of civilian control. He also points out that the professional code of the military officer prevents political activity.

In the same breath, McMaster posits that action that could have undermined the administration's credibility and derailed its Vietnam policy could not have been taken lightly. This is an excellent point. Where a civilian advisor might "leak to the press"[21] that he opposed a policy course in an effort to derail it, the leadership trait of loyalty is most certainly burned into the psyche of the military officer by the time he attains flag rank. The true mark of a military professional is the ability to execute lawful orders that you do not agree with personally without blaming the "old man." The same traits that make military officers "professionals" also serve to inhibit their role and influence in a political setting.

V. Vitality for Today

The reader need look no farther than the present presidential administration to find many of McMaster's observations relevant today. The political use of the military can still occur. Johnson's use of the "Gulf of Tonkin" incident and his desire for action "in time for the seven o'clock news" might be an interesting case study for analyzing President Clinton's decision to use retaliatory missile strikes against Sudan and Afghanistan during the Monica Lewinsky grand jury testimony.[22]

McMaster makes a telling reference to General Westmoreland's complaint to General Wheeler, Chairman of the Joint Chiefs of Staff, about Washington's control of the Vietnam air campaign. General Westmoreland relayed that "experience indicated that the more remote the authority which directs how a mission is to be accomplished, the more we are vulnerable to mishaps resulting from such things as incomplete briefings and preparation, loss of tactical flexibility and lack of tactical coordination."[23] These appear to be prophetic words in light of the criticism of President Clinton and then Secretary of Defense Les Aspin for their role in the massacre of U.S. Army rangers in Somalia.[24]

Dereliction of Duty is highly recommended reading for any young military staff officer and should be mandatory reading for general officers. Senior military leaders must be prepared to deal with the tension between the restraint on political activity of the military officer and his concomitant duty in a democratic society to propose military solutions that take into account political viability. Senior military leaders must also be able to properly balance their loyalty to their service branch with the welfare of the nation. Future officers who aspire to such positions owe their country no less.

Those senior level policy advisors whose uniform consists of a civilian coat and tie should also read it. The lack of prior military experience in the staff of the present presidential administration, and the likelihood that the trend will continue in the future based upon military downsizing, makes the "lessons learned" in Dereliction of Duty even more relevant today.

FOOTNOTES

1. H.R. McMaster,Dereliction of Duty:Lyndon Johnson,Robert McNamara, the Joint Chiefs of Staff, and the Lies that Led to Vietnam (2d ed., HarperPerrennial 1998) (1997).

2. United States Marine Corps. Written while assigned as a student, 47th Judge Advocate Officer Graduate Course, The Judge Advocate General's School, United States Army, Charlottesville, Virginia.

3. McMaster, supra note 1, at 323.

4. Id.

5. Id.

6. Id.

7. Id. at 323.

8. Id. at 41 (emphasis added).

9. Id. at 282.

10. Id. at 317 ("Thirty years later McNamara admitted that the Great Society had dominated the president's desire to conceal the cost and scale of American intervention in Vietnam.").

11. Id. at 50 ("He later told a biographer that he felt as if he was "illegitimate, a naked man with no presidential covering, a pretender to the throne, an illegal usurper.").

12. Id. at 41 ("John Kennedy bequeathed to Lyndon Johnson an advisory system that limited real influence to his inner circle and treated others, particularly the Joint Chiefs of Staff, more like a source of potential opposition than of useful advice.").

13. Id. at 41.

14. Id. at 26. For example, membership of the Executive Committee (EXCOM) of the National Security Council during the Cuban missile crisis did not include Vice-president Johnson.

15. Id. at 328.

16. Id. at 20.

17. Id. at 73.

18. Id. at 163.

19. Id. at 61.

20. Id. at 54.

21. Howell Raines, Reagan Defends Policies to Curb New Disclosures, N.Y. Times, Dec. 10, 1983, at B1.

22. Russell Watson & John Barry, Our Target Was Terror, Newsweek, Aug. 31, 1998, at 24.

23. McMaster, supra note 1, at 233.

24. Steven A. Holmes, The Somalia Mission: Clinton Defends Aspin on Action Regarding Request for U.S. Tanks, N.Y. Times, Oct. 9, 1993, at sec. 1-7.

* * * * * * * * * * * *

Thinking Clearly About the Future of Warfare

Posted on July 1, 2015 by RDECOM Public Affairs

Lt. Gen. H.R. McMaster is the deputy commanding general, Futures, U.S. Army Training and Doctrine Command, and director of the Army Capabilities Integration Center.

By Lt. Gen. H.R. McMaster, U.S. Army

Anticipating the demands of future armed conflict requires an understanding of continuities in the nature of war as well as an appreciation for changes in the character for armed conflict. —The U.S. Army Operating Concept

Expert knowledge is a pillar of our military profession, and the ability to think clearly about war is fundamental to developing expert knowledge across a career of service. Junior leaders must understand war to explain to their Soldiers how their unit's actions contribute to the accomplishment of campaign objectives. Senior officers draw on their understanding of war to provide the best military advice to civilian leaders. Every Army leader uses his or her vision of future conflict as a basis for how he or she trains soldiers and units. Every commander understands, visualizes, describes, directs, leads and assesses operations based, in part, on his or her understanding of continuities in the nature of war and of changes in the character of warfare.

A failure to understand war through a consideration of continuity and change risks what nineteenth century Prussian philosopher Carl von Clausewitz warned against: regarding war as "something autonomous" rather than "an instrument of policy," misunderstanding "the kind of war on which we are embarking," and trying to turn war into "something that is alien to its nature."

In recent years, many of the difficulties encountered in strategic decision making, operational planning, training and force development stemmed from neglect of continuities in the nature of war. The best way to guard against the tendency to try to turn war into something alien to its nature is to understand four key continuities in the nature of war and how the U.S. experience in Afghanistan and Iraq validated their importance.

In the aftermath of the 1991 Gulf War, defense thinking was dominated by theories that considered military operations as ends in and of themselves rather than essential components of campaigns that integrate the broad range of efforts necessary to achieve campaign objectives. Advocates of what became the orthodoxy of the "revolution in military affairs," or RMA, predicted that advances in surveillance, communications, and information technologies, combined with precision strike weapons, would overwhelm any opponent and deliver fast, cheap, and efficient victories. War was reduced to a targeting exercise. These conceits complicated efforts in Afghanistan and Iraq as unrealistic and underdeveloped war plans confronted unanticipated and underappreciated political realities.

War is Uncertain

Although advances in technology will continue to influence the character of warfare, the effect of technologies on land are often not as great as in other domains due to geography, the interaction with adaptive enemies, the presence of noncombatants, and other complexities associated with war's continuities. —The U.S. Army Operating Concept

The dominant assumption of the RMA was that knowledge would be the key to victory in future war. Near-perfect intelligence would enable precise military operations that, in turn, would deliver rapid victory. In Afghanistan and Iraq, planning based on linear projections did not anticipate enemy adaptations or the evolution of those conflicts in ways that were difficult to predict at the outset.

Army professionals recognize war's uncertainty because they are sensitive to war's political and human aspects, and they know from experience and history that war always involves a continuous interaction with determined, adaptive enemies.

The Army Operating Concept, or AOC, emphasizes the tenet of adaptability and the need for leaders to "assess the situation continuously, develop innovative solutions to problems, and remain mentally and physically agile to capitalize on opportunities." The AOC also redefines the tenet of depth to highlight the need to "think ahead in time and determine how to connect tactical and operational objectives to strategic goals."

Technology

The U.S. Army's differential advantage over enemies derives, in part, from the integration of advanced technologies with skilled soldiers and well-trained teams. —The U.S. Army Operating Concept

Science and technology will continue to influence the character of warfare. While the U.S. Army differential advantages over potential enemies will continue to depend in large measure on advanced technology, winning in a complex world requires powerful combinations of leadership, skilled soldiers, well-trained units and technology. There are no technological silver bullets. The Army must integrate new technological capabilities with complementary changes in doctrine, organization, training, leader development, personnel and other elements of combat effectiveness.

Army technological development emphasizes the need for all formations to possess the appropriate combination of mobility, protection and lethality. And the Army places Soldiers at the center of that effort, pursuing "advances in human sciences for cognitive, social, and physical development" while fitting weapons and machines to soldiers and units rather than the other way around.

Our Army is innovating under Force 2025

Maneuvers, "the physical (experimentation, evaluations, exercises, modeling, simulations, and war games) and intellectual (studies, analysis, concept, and capabilities development) activities that help leaders integrate future capabilities and develop interim solutions to warfighting challenges."

Successful innovation will require focused and sustained collaboration among Army professionals committed to reading, thinking and learning about the problem of future armed conflict, and determining what capabilities our Army and joint force must develop to win in a complex world.

Editor's note: This article is an excerpt from "Continuity and Change," a March/April 2015 Military Review article by Lt. Gen. H. R. McMaster. McMaster is the deputy commanding general, Futures, U.S. Army Training and Doctrine Command, and director of the Army Capabilities Integration Center. He has a doctorate in military history from the University of North Carolina at Chapel Hill. McMaster has served as a U.S. Army War College Fellow at the Hoover Institution on War, Revolution, and Peace and as a senior consulting fellow at the International Institute of Strategic Studies in London.

This article appears in the July/August 2015 issue of Army Technology Magazine, which focuses on innovation.

* * * * * * * * * * * *

McMaster: We Will Unleash Power of Combined Arms

FORT BENNING, Ga. (Nov. 7, 2012) -- Now 21 weeks into his tenure as commanding general of the Maneuver Center of Excellence, Maj. Gen. H. R. McMaster shared how combined arms is the foundation of the effective Army training that takes place at Fort Benning.

"The power of combined arms is what we need to unleash across our Army," he said. "There is so much power here now with Infantry, Armor, and Cavalry together. We now have the opportunity across our programs of instruction to ensure that all our leaders get a combined arms experience -- that they remain grounded in the fundamentals of their branch competencies, but that they (also) understand the power of combined arms."

Combined arms training and education is already in place at the Maneuver Center, but Soldiers will experience even more, McMaster said.

In addition to expanding combined arms experience within courses, the Maneuver Center is also integrating training and education across courses.

"What our leaders are doing now already is integrating the portions of those courses that make sense to integrate," he said. "So why not have a new lieutenant issue an operations order to sergeants first class in the Senior Leader Course and get feedback directly from those sergeants? We're doing that. Why not have captains work on troop leading procedures, planning operations with lieutenants? We're doing that. Why not have officer candidates leading our basic training Soldiers on patrol? That's happening."

The growth of combined arms training and integration of courses doesn't mean what's integral to Armor or Infantry or the Maneuver Center's focus on fundamental skills will fall by the wayside, the general said.

"We're not going to dilute -- ever -- Infantry culture or Armor or Cavalry culture," he said, "or really in any way dilute the branch proficiencies in those critical tasks: for our Infantry to cover that last 100 yards, for our Armor formations to bear the brunt of the battle and our Cavalry formations to develop the situation, gain and maintain contact with the enemy. We have this tremendous opportunity to work together on problems in a sustained manner and come up with solutions that are combined arms solutions. We've got to take advantage of this gift."

McMaster defined combined arms as Infantry, Armor and reconnaissance elements working together with artillery, aviation and engineers as well as joint capabilities such as close air support.

To put it simply, he compared combined arms to "the kids' game of rock, scissors, paper."

"If you have a rock and the enemy has paper, you better have scissors ready. When you mess with the U.S. Army Infantry squad, you should be messing with the whole combined arms package."

Capabilities Must Match Future Threats, Army Leader Says

By Jim Garamone DoD News, Defense Media Activity

WASHINGTON, Feb. 24, 2015 — Success in future armed conflict boils down to ensuring the capabilities put in place today can match the threats of the future, deputy commanding general for futures, U.S. Army Training and Doctrine Command, said here today.

Army Lt. Gen. H.R. McMaster, who also serves as director of Army Capabilities Integration Center, told the audience at International Security's "Future of War" conference that because threats have changed, American responses must change as well.

Nations were the source of threats in the past, he said. Today, they also come from nonstate actors and the confluence of networked insurgent and terrorist organizations bridging over into transnational organized crime networks and having access to capabilities they didn't have in the past.

The capabilities include communications, mobilized resources and access to destructive technologies. The Islamic State of Iraq and the Levant is one such group, the general said, and Russia's use of special operations forces under cover from regular forces in Ukraine also serves as an example of why the U.S. military must balance continuity in the nature of war with change in the character of warfare.

Width, Depth, Context - Officials should look at war "in width, depth and in context," McMaster said. Width means looking at war over time to understand how war and warfare have changed, and to understand the possibilities and limitations of the future. By depth, he said, he means looking at a campaign and examining all aspects of it, "so you see war as it is: chaotic and profoundly human."

Finally, he said, officials should consider war in the context of what the United States wants to achieve politically in armed conflict, what the military's role is in American society, and what needs to happen for societies to generate and sustain the will to engage in armed conflicts.

America's Differential Advantage - American military power is joint power, the general noted, as the military uses land, air, maritime, space and cyber capabilities together, with each dependent on the other. "America's differential advantage over the enemy has to do with skilled soldiers, sailors, airmen, Marines and teams with multiple technologies that give us the advantage," McMaster said.

Capitalizing on that is the way forward for the military, he added.

In Ukraine, Russian President Vladimir Putin is engaged in a limited war for limited objectives, McMaster said. "Go into Ukraine, take some territory at very low cost and very low risk, and then portray the international community's reaction as escalatory. How do you cope with that?" he asked.

One of the ways to do it is forward deterrence, which entails ratcheting up the price of such actions, the general said. "We undervalue deterrent capabilities at our own peril," he added.

Countering Anti-access Technologies - Being able to operate in contested areas will be a problem for the future, McMaster said, and all services must be concerned about countering anti-access technologies and strategies, including in cyberspace.

"From the Army perspective, we are going to have to project power outward from land into the maritime, air, space and cyber domains to ensure our freedom of movement and action in those domains and restrict the enemy's use of them," he said.

Enemies will increasingly use urban areas as terrorist safe havens or as launching points for missiles or other long-range strikes, McMaster said.

"For the Army, we're going to have to conduct what I call expeditionary maneuver," he added. "That's rapidly deploying forces to unexpected locations to bypass anti-access. But that can't just be a force that gets there. It has to be a force that has the mobility, protection and have lethality to operate."

* * * * * * * * * * *

Honoring Ramadan, Celebrating Diversity

By Maj. Gen. H. R. McMaster July 10, 2013

FORT BENNING, Ga., (July 10,2013) -- This week marks the beginning of Ramadan, Islam's holiest month. During Ramadan, Muslims fast from food and drink during daylight hours, observing one of the five pillars of Islam. Each day, Muslims break the fast after sunset, at or about 8:40 p.m. Eid-Ul-Fitr, a three-day festival of thanksgiving and rejoicing, takes place at the end of Ramadan, beginning Aug. 8 this year.

Please make accommodations for personnel observing Ramadan. Adjust physical training schedules and duty release times when possible. Do your best to ensure our Muslim Soldiers, civilians and international students are able to break the fast each day and celebrate Eid-Ul-Fitr.

Our Muslim Soldiers as well as our international students are a tremendous source of strength for our Army and our Maneuver Center. Ramadan is an opportunity to celebrate with our Muslim brothers and sisters our common commitment to service and humanity.

One Force, One Fight!

* * * * * * * * * * *

Sustaining Balance in the Future Force, the goal of Unified Quest 09

John Harlow/TRADOC News Service May 1,2009

FORT MONROE, Va. (May 1,2009) - Unified Quest is the not just a future game that concludes with a week-long exercise at the Army War College. It is a year-long campaign of learning with the theme in 2009 of Sustaining Balance in the Future Force.

Throughout the year, participants in the exercise have conducted small working group seminars in preparation for the final game in May.

"The demands of the wars in Iraq and Afghanistan have placed a significant strain on our force," said Col. H.R. McMaster, Director, Concept Development and Experimentation with the Army Capabilities Integration Center (ARCIC). "It is important for us to not only win the wars that we are in, but to ensure that in doing so, we preserve our ability to sustain the Army's effort in the long term in those wars but to remain prepared for future conflict."

Unified Quest is just one of the contributing tools that help devise the Army Capstone Concept.

"I think we have a great opportunity to contribute significantly to the Capstone Concept," said Col. Cecil Lewis, Future Warfare Division Chief for ARCIC. "We have an opportunity to contribute to the way the generating force supports the operating force. We can figure out ways and methods to make that support more efficient."

In the current conflicts in Iraq and Afghanistan and also in future conflicts, it takes more than the Army to win our Nations wars. It takes a multi-service, multi-national and whole of government approach to effectively win the battles between armed enemies, but also win the hearts and minds of the citizens of the country in which our troops are engaged in.

Unified Quest brings many minds together. Soldiers who have served in Iraq and Afghanistan, members from many branches of the government, from think tanks, academia and former senior leaders, to collectively look at the problems and try to find solutions.

"We have put together a tremendous team to look at the key questions we are examining," said McMaster. "We need to be able to study recent and ongoing conflicts and understand their implications. To understand the broad range of experience, we need to be able to look at problems, challenges and opportunities in depth to really understand some of the details associated with those conflicts. We also need to study them in context. The expertise we bring in provides that context. We need to make sure the Army is integrated into the Joint force, multi-national and whole of government approach to the problems ahead. The all-star cast that is coming to Unified Quest helps put our thinking into the context of a wide ranging career of service experience for many of them and also a context through the different perspectives of national security that they bring to the game."

Through the experiences of OIF and OEF, the Army is competent in confronting irregular adversaries, a competency that must be maintained for the foreseeable future. In FM 3-0 Operations, the Army is expecting its Soldiers to be able to operate across the full-spectrum of conflict and Unified Quest is helping the Army achieve the appropriate balance of capabilities to do so.

Through the expertise assembled at Unified Quest, the study hopes to be able to examine the following issues.

Determine how to enhance the expeditionary quality of the generating force-the institutional component of the Army - so that it can lend its unique skills and expertise to the fight.

Determine how the Army can enhance unity of effort with its interagency partners (with a special emphasis on interagency planning at the JTF-country team level).

Determine how the Army can best enable, sustain and support diverse military and civilian partners without a large, conventional force footprint.

"The work at Unified Quest is immensely important," said McMaster. "A solid conceptual foundation for thinking about the future wars and identifying the problem sets that are associated with future armed conflict is important because it drives so much of what our Army does to prepare for future wars. Through UQ, we're getting it right. We are making a grounded projection into the near future and taking a step back from what we are doing today so we have time to think about the future."

Because of the work done in the Unified Quest campaign of learning, Army leaders will have the ability to make hard choices about the commitment of resources. The insights gained through Unified Quest enable policymakers to provide full-spectrum capabilities in a resource constrained ambiguous environment.

Unified Quest 09 concludes next week at the Army War College, in Carlisle, Pa.

* * * * * * * * * * *

The Myths We Soldiers Tell Ourselves (and the Harm These Myths Do)

Lt. Col. Peter Fromm, U.S. Army, Retired; Lt. Col. Douglas Pryer, U.S. Army; and Lt. Col. Kevin Cutright, U.S. Army

When a man has so far corrupted and prostituted the chastity of his mind as to subscribe his professional belief to things he does not believe, he has prepared himself for the commission of every other crime. Can we conceive of anything more destructive to morality than this?1

Thomas Paine, The Age of Reason

A man who lies to himself, and believes his own lies, becomes unable to recognize truth, either in himself or in anyone else.2

Fyodor Dostoevsky, The Brothers Karamazov

* * * * * * * * * * *

Lt. Col. Peter Fromm, U.S. Army, Retired, is the deputy G1 for U.S. Army, Japan and I Corps (Forward). He is a former infantryman who taught ethics at the U.S. Military Academy (USMA).

Lt. Col. Douglas Pryer is the IEWTD technical support division chief at Fort Huachuca, Ariz., has an MMAS (military history) from CGSC, and is the author of The Fight for the High Ground: The U.S. Army and Interrogation during Operation Iraqi Freedom, May 2003 - April 2004.

Lt. Col. Kevin Cutright is serving in Korea as strategy and plans branch chief for Eighth Army. Lt. Col. Cutright holds an M.A. in pilosophy and an M.M.A.S. from the School for Advanced Military Studies. He also taught ethics at USMA.

* * * * * * * * * * *

MILITARY REVIEW

September-October 2013

The Army espouses admirable values, and it is justifiably proud of its traditions of service. Today, America's Army is arguably the best-trained, most disciplined force in the nation's history, one that strives to fight effectively, legally, and ethically. However, while this self-image is certainly something we strive to fulfill, we have not always been as successful as we might wish. Regrettably, dishonesty and related trust problems plague the American Profession of Arms, human endeavor that it is. In the authors' 70-plus years of military experience, the root of this dishonesty is self-deception, something in which everyone indulges.

Illustrative of this malady was the Vietnam War, where self-deception and disillusionment watered America's loss of will at home and contributed to eventual defeat.3

In Dereliction of Duty, H.R. McMaster describes the lies from the National Command Authority that led to the war.4 The Joint Chiefs of Staff (JCS) supported these machinations with their silence. As McMaster describes it—

The president was lying, and he expected the Chiefs to lie as well or, at least to withhold the whole truth. Although the president should not have placed the Chiefs in that position, the flag officers should not have tolerated it when he had.5

Such lies set the conditions. In December 1964, Gen. William Westmoreland directed optimistic outlooks from senior military advisors, telling them: "As advisors we must accentuate the positive and bring best thought to bear to work out solutions to problems in a dynamic way."6 Consequently, reports rarely reflected reality.7 Lt. Gen. William Peers, the lead investigator for the My Lai atrocity, reported a massive cover-up: "Efforts were made at every level of command from company to division to withhold and suppress information."8 In a 1974 report that surveyed officers from six service schools, close to half admitted they had submitted false reports to higher, including inaccurate officer efficiency reports, body counts, and numbers of soldiers going absent without leave.9

When in command, Westmoreland not only believed he could control the media's message but also fell victim to the upbeat propaganda he had directed: "The stubborn commitment of the high command to error defies belief," the historian John Gates later said, referring to Westmoreland and other Vietnam War generals, "but the evidence of it would seem to be overwhelming."10 Those leaders who lied to investigators about what had happened at My Lai or who, serving on juries, refused to punish the indicted had convinced themselves they were doing the right thing, protecting good Americans driven temporarily insane by the horrors of war.

To military leaders serving today, this analysis of the Vietnam War may strike uncomfortably close to home. A decade ago, the nation went to war in Iraq, ostensibly over weapons of mass destruction that the administration had convinced themselves were there. For media engagements in Iraq and Afghanistan, commanders have typically directed their subordinates to adhere to scripted talking points that may ignore some facts on the ground. There has also been little accountability exercised in the cases of officers and soldiers who have abused—or contributed to the abuse of—civilians and prisoners.

As before, there remains a huge gap between who we soldiers say we are and who we actually are, and this gap is often due to institutionally reinforced self-deception.11

The worst aspect of indulging in inaccurate self-assessments is the erosion of trust that accompanies it. When an institution adopts false beliefs about itself, it corrodes itself. Our institution's unwitting promotion of self-deception remains not only the biggest obstacle to meaningfully professionalizing our military, but also remains a significant impediment to our Army's fulfilling its core mission—defending the nation by winning favorable, enduring outcomes from our nation's wars.

The Siren Song of Self-Deception

The impulse to self-deception calls to mind Nietzsche's claim that the will to untruth is stronger than the will to truth.12 Perhaps more accurately, we are sometimes driven by a "will to limited truth" to meet our selfish aims. People honestly calculate and, with good intentions, recalculate what reality is until they find a place where they are comfortable with their moral myths, where they can sit complacent. Soldiers cannot afford moral complacency.

The problem of "American exceptionalism."

A prevalent form of this complacency involves rationalizing one's own superiority above others. The myth of American exceptionalism permeating the U.S. military's ranks is an example. It usually occurs when Americans apprehend the empirical fact that they enjoy remarkable freedoms and prosperity and transfer those accomplishments of their forebears into feelings of personal superiority. Instead of perceiving their heritage as a lucky accident, they irrationally perceive it as a personal virtue and a sign of their own superiority.

We can use the imagined racial superiority of the anti-Semite as a straw man to evaluate this sense of exceptionalism. Using this approach is not the same as saying that self-deceived soldiers dehumanize others to the degree that, say, German Nazis dehumanized Jews. Instead, it illuminates the psychological process underlying our own forms of exceptionalism by stretching this process to its logical extreme.

In Anti-Semite and Jew, Jean Paul Sartre says that by localizing all the evil in the world in the Jew, the anti-Semite objectifies himself as the Jew's virtuous antagonist. He objectifies the Jew as the embodiment of evil and sees himself as an elite human being.13 The anti-Semite is perhaps at first conscious of his fallibility, but finally rejects it through his hatreds. He lifts himself up by simply "being," in this case by being non-Jew, rather than by "doing," by acting in a manner that would in fact elevate himself.

As Sartre points out, if the Jew did not exist, the anti-Semite would create him. Sartre concludes, "Anti-Semitism is thus seen to be at bottom a form of Manichaeism."14 By this he means the extreme, dehumanizing black-and-white outlook that led to pogroms against Jews and the Holocaust of World War II. Such attitudes are not entirely unfamiliar to some American service members. There is, for example, the American soldier in Iraq who said, "A lot of guys really supported the whole concept that if they don't speak English and they have darker skin, they're not as human as us, so we can do what we want."15

There is the soldier at Abu Ghraib who, while forcing a detainee to masturbate above the face of another detainee, remarked, "Look at what these animals do when you leave them alone for two seconds."16 And then there is the Army chief of staff who compared Fallujah to "a huge rat's nest" that was "festering" and needed to be "dealt with"—a metaphor that may be more unconsidered machismo than willful dehumanization, but that is still unsettlingly reminiscent of the depiction of Jews as a scurrying horde of rats in the infamous Nazi propaganda film, "The Eternal Jew."17

Such extreme, dehumanizing words about the "other" is today the exception rather than the rule within our ranks. More commonly, this form of self-deception asserts itself as half-hearted applications of the ethic of reciprocity (what is more commonly known as "The Golden Rule"). That is, to some American "exceptionalists," a restriction that applies to other nations and militaries does not necessarily or fully apply to the United States if, by applying it, an apparent American advantage is taken away.

U.S. Army official SHARP poster. The Army's problems with sexual harrassment illustrate the efforts to overcome objectification of others.

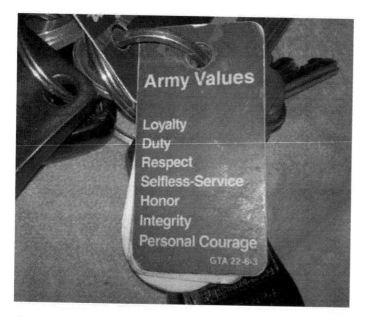

U.S. Army Values Tag. In the view of the authors, the implementation of Army values needs a review.

The slippery slope of dehumanization.

Failure to fully consider the ethic of reciprocity is apparent in the ongoing debate on torture. Nearly all American service members would call it "torture" if they were subjected to waterboarding, forced nudity, waterdousing, extreme hot and cold temperatures, sleep deprivation, or any one of the so-called "enhanced interrogation techniques" (EITs). After all, the goal of these EITs is to inflict suffering so great that it overcomes the subject's will to resist without physically marking or injuring the subject. Many of these same service members, though, become offended when any description of Americans applying these techniques refers to "torture."18

Hazing, sexual harassment, sadistic "corrective training," detainee abuse, torture, and murder usually derive from the similar delusion that other people are commodities and that it is okay to treat them as such. The difference is one of degree, rather than quality. This is why serious crimes often have small beginnings, and people refer to a "slippery moral slope" when discussing right and wrong. For the soldier at war, objectifying oneself as superior and the "other" as inferior can rapidly transform even minor abuses into very serious crimes.

At the heart of this delusion is self-interested self-deception. There is not only the desire to feel superior, but also there is the wish to make one's core task—the killing of one's enemies—as easy as possible. Soldiers tell themselves that the enemy is an inhuman "kraut," "Jap," "gook," "dink," or "rag-head," and, by doing so, hope to remove all natural empathy toward those they aim to kill.

Leaders often condone this self-deception because they believe they are helping themselves and their troops to do what "must be done." Unfortunately, while attempts at dehumanizing the enemy may make killing easier for some (at least in the short-term), these attempts can be the first steps on the road toward atrocities—acts that cannot occur without such dehumanization. Such attitudes cause unjustifiable harm to others, inspire the enemy to fight while hurting morale at home, and often inflict upon the perpetrators cognitive dissonance, deep regret, and "moral injury" (a condition that can lead to severe psychiatric problems and even suicide).19

An abundance of absolute princes. Reinforcing and strengthening self-deception within the ranks is what John Stuart Mill termed the "unlimited deference" accorded the powerful:

[W]hile everyone well knows himself to be fallible, few think it necessary to take any precautions against their own fallibility, or admit the supposition that any opinion, of which they feel very certain, may be one of the examples of the error to which they acknowledge themselves to be liable. Absolute princes, or others who are accustomed to unlimited deference, usually feel this complete conidence in their own opinions on nearly all subjects. . . .20

The U.S. military often suffers from virtual "absolute princes" in the form of command authority gone awry. Though not a general condition, it remains common enough among senior military leaders and commanders. Even popular culture makes fun of this tendency at the Army's expense. In the satirical film Little Big Man, there is a scene where Lt. Col. George Armstrong Custer (played by Richard Mulligan) announces his ability to tell a man's profession just by his appearance.21 All of his subordinates assent to the truth of his special perceptive power. When he pronounces Dustin Hoffman's character, Jack Crabb, to be "a muleskinner"—contrary to fact—even Jack himself assents to it so that he can get a job with the Army. Custer rides off satisfied with his powers of perspicuity. Such self-deception of course catches up with him at the Little Big Horn. The satire is funny because it evokes a truth we all recognize.

Those who assent to everything the "prince" says encourage further erosion of his ability to see error. The cycle toward incoherence becomes ever more pernicious as blind spots become entrenched. Leader and led immerse themselves in self-deception. The authors call this the "unlimited deference syndrome," a condition that leads to real problems with managing agreement toward the best outcomes.

Even in the formal process of studying operational options, anticipating what will please the boss (via doctrine and built-in assumptions) is often the main shaper of proposed courses of action. In the authors' experience, the courses of action a staff presents the commander are usually just shades of the anticipated. In going through formal motions of "analysis," everyone loses track of the fact that foregone, unacknowledged conclusions are driving the process. Thus, lawed discourse yields lawed options. The rise of "design" in U.S. military planning is a tacit acknowledgement that this problem exists. Design methodology is an attempt to correct an institutional inability to properly frame problems, but it probably will not change the underlying problem of unlimited deference.22

Enshrining self-deception. Military doctrine encourages self-deception via key articulations within each service's codified ethos. Consider the Army's well-worn leadership rubric "Be— Know— Do," which was recently revamped as "attributes" (who leaders are and what they know) and "competencies" (what leaders do, because of their attributes).23 The sequence of concepts in both of these frameworks leads people to think that "being" something precedes "doing" anything to achieve it. It reverses Aristotle's virtue ethics, from which this approach was originally derived.24 Aristotle wrote: "The virtues arise in us neither by nature nor against nature, but we are by nature able to acquire them, and reach our complete perfection through habit."25 Acquiring virtues is how character develops. Only when one develops the knowing habit of right action, does one become good. One learns, one does, and one becomes. Habit eventually forms the person one has educated oneself to become. So, for instance, one cannot simply pronounce oneself a "warrior" or "professional" and reasonably believe it must thus be so. Whether one is a philosopher, mason, physician, muleskinner, or machinist, only training and habit lead to the realization of what one becomes, to being.

One expression of the pervasive be-do philosophy is the Army Values rubric. This rubric contributes to self-deception by convincing people that they are good, an ethical member of a values-based organization, even though it does very little to actually encourage right action. For example, before the Detainee Treatment Act of 2005 made "enhanced interrogation" illegal, one could employ Army Values to endorse harsh treatment of detainees. Those who used torture could argue they displayed "loyalty" to their nation and fellow troops by helping extract intelligence that might save lives. They could display "duty" to country and "selfless service" by their hard, dirty work for good ends. They could show proper "respect" for detainees, since they treated detainees like evil terrorists should be treated (meaning, with no respect). They could show "integrity" through the use of only approved techniques. They could embody "honor" by fulfilling the other Army values, especially the "personal courage" needed to deliberately agitate dangerous detainees.26 Indeed, it is difficult to think of any tough ethical problem that this paradigm could help a soldier solve. For example, does one lie in service to one's country? To protect one's fellow soldiers?

The biggest problem with the Army Values is how they are sloganeered. By simply saying them, we soldiers frequently delude ourselves into thinking they make us more ethical, like they are a talisman. Indeed, they can actually set the stage for unethical action by inspiring moral complacency and allowing us to justify nearly any action that appears legal.27

Another expression of the be-do philosophy is the enshrinement of key policies and programs, thereby stymieing honest debate. Such stultification is fairly common in large institutions, where the tendency is to create a narrative that makes assent to form fashionable, demonizes the naysayers, and then enforces buy-in with rewards and punishments. Those who possess the proper faith are righteous, those who do not are unrighteous. The result is groupthink rather than a helpful, continuous, living dialectic concerning the problem at hand. Thanks to the unlimited deference associated with rank and command authority, the U.S. military is especially prone to this tendency.

Some examples of Army projects that have been susceptible to this dynamic include worthy endeavors like counterinsurgency, mission command, the "warrior project," and the Profession of Arms campaign. All of these programs have suffered from various degrees of debilitating dogmatism, of which some advocates and participants may be blissfully unaware. The recent fall from grace of counterinsurgency, for instance, seems to have stemmed primarily from its over-zealous execution as the new religion.28

Self-Deception Goes to War

Recent wars have brought moral issues into focus, which is a normal outcome. Acknowledging the good with the bad, we can gauge the force's professionalism by how openly it addresses failures and takes steps to limit them.

Valuing form over substance.

Unfortunately, our Army has suffered from mediocre, narcissistic, appearance-obsessed leaders too frequently. As an extreme instance, the book Black Hearts by Jim Frederick documents the downward spiral of one platoon in Iraq, its members so distraught by the deaths of comrades that they became increasingly abusive of Iraqis. Meanwhile, its brigade and battalion leadership remained completely ignorant of the moral cancer spreading within this platoon, focusing its attention instead on soldier appearances and by-the-book solutions to tactical problems. For example:

A lieutenant colonel down from brigade headquarters asked the platoon leader, Lieutenant Paul Fisher, why none of his men had shaved. Fisher, after the Alamo bridge incident, after all of the work and all of the loss, couldn't hide his exasperation. "We drink all the water we have, sir, so that we don't dehydrate," he said. "We have been running nonstop since our guys got abducted. We are not really concerned about our looks right now." "I am just trying to keep the heat off of you, Lieutenant," the lieutenant colonel said. "You guys are not looked upon too favorably these days."29

Members of this platoon eventually gang-raped a young Iraqi girl, then shot and immolated her, her little sister, and her parents. Months later, senior leaders were shocked at the revelations. However, the reader is left questioning whether this horrendous crime could even have occurred if these leaders and their subordinates had cared less about haircuts and shaves and more about what was really going on inside their soldiers' heads.

Manipulating and ignoring the truth.

Probably the most futile, quixotic endeavor in an age of the Internet and ubiquitous hand-held information devices are the attempts by many commanders to control what the media reports. In the authors' experience, "controlling the narrative" has emerged as the hallmark of Army public relations. Via talking points and feel-good, often unsustainable public relations projects, commanders and their staffs vainly expend energy trying to convince everyone (sometimes themselves included) that, thanks to their efforts, progress is being made. They appear to believe that, if they trumpet something as "true" loudly and frequently enough, this thing will actually become reality. Leading the way in this regard, former Secretary of Defense Donald Rumsfeld vehemently denied there was an insurgency in Iraq, something he maintained for more than three years as he called insurgents everything but insurgents.30 In such cases, the leader thinks he is right, and if he has a momentary moral epiphany that he is being dishonest, he tells himself how complicated things are and that the end justifies the means. If he has to manipulate appearances of reality to make his narrative "true," so be it. Of course, such manipulation nearly always backfires, taking away the leader's credibility and whatever strategic or tactical benefit that may have been at stake.

Frustrated by the media's tendency to emphasize "bad news" rather than "good news" stories ("good news is no news," we soldiers like to say), we tend in turn to dismiss all media and nongovernmental organization reporting as biased and unworthy of consideration. This is a grossly counterproductive response: just because the media may have a bias to focus on sensational "bad news" does not make such news untrue.

The soldier and torture.

As discussed above, objectifying others and treating them as commodities, as less than human, can lead to serious abuse. Compounding this problem is another delusion— the belief of leaders that such dehumanization can be controlled.

Consider the role that "enhanced interrogation techniques" and military Survival, Escape, Resistance, and Evasion (SERE) schools played in the abuse of prisoners in Iraq and Afghanistan. When EITs were formally promulgated via policy memoranda, one assumption was that they would be used only under strict supervision. After Rumsfeld approved EITs for use at Guantanamo Bay ("Gitmo") in December 2002, this assumption largely held true at that location. There, the relatively high interrogator-to-detainee ratio and the presence of supervisory psychologists and, even more importantly, of large numbers of law enforcement personnel all helped limit occurrences of EITs evolving into worse crimes.

Tragically, this was far from the whole story. Soon after their approval at Gitmo, EITs migrated via formal policy memoranda to Afghanistan and then, shortly after, to Iraq.31 At places like Bagram, Abu Ghraib, Mosul, and al Qaim, relatively minor detainee abuse turned into horrific crimes that shocked the world.

However, more widespread and just as damaging was the informal, unsanctioned promulgation of harsh detainee treatment that grew from the set conditions. This occurred via the transfer of interrogators from one facility to another. Also, service members applied tactics they had learned or heard about at SERE schools.32 Most commonly, soldiers applied the same physical "corrective training" they themselves sometimes received to their prisoners.33 Such informal promulgation occurred despite SERE cadre regularly briefing their trainees that they were not to treat detainees like they themselves were being treated and despite the assumption of some noncommissioned officers that their subordinates would realize that corrective training was only intended as a disciplinary measure for soldiers, not prisoners.

It seems that, once the impulse to dehumanize and degrade the other is set free, putting the genie back in the bottle is nearly impossible. The result in the ongoing conflicts has been a steady boon for recruiters of America's enemies.34 Thus it is that another form of self-deception—the idea that we can control how, where, and when we dehumanize others—has greatly damaged our nation's recent war efforts. Better to completely avoid the self-deception and insist detainees and adversaries be considered the human beings that they are.

A failure of accountability.

The scale at which detainee abuse took place during the first few years of our conflicts in Afghanistan and Iraq is disturbing. The military's abject failure to hold offenders accountable for their crimes is almost as bad. Of the 100 detainees who died in U.S. custody between 2002 and 2006, 45 are confirmed or suspected murder victims.35 Of these, eight are known to have been tortured to death.36 Only half of these eight cases resulted in punishment for U.S. service members, with five months in jail being the harshest punishment meted out.37

This is only a summary of the most extreme cases. During the last decade, the military opened hundreds of investigations concerning detainee abuse. Investigators closed most of these quickly, not because there was nothing to them, but because investigators lacked the resources, command support, or willpower to meaningfully investigate them.38 Even in those cases where investigators found criminal negligence, military juries and commanders consistently chose not to punish wrongdoers. Of the hundreds of cases of alleged abuse the under-resourced "Detainee Abuse Task Force" investigated in Iraq, not one went to court martial: "It didn't accomplish anything," John Renaud, the warrant oficer who led the task force later said. "It was a whitewash."39

A 2006 report by three human rights organizations found, "Of the hundreds of personnel implicated in detainee abuse, only ten people have been sentenced to a year or more in prison"—four of these as a result of the highly publicized crimes they had committed at Abu Ghraib.40 More worrying still, strong anecdotal evidence suggests that reported crimes were only the small, visible portion of the massive iceberg of detainee abuse, the vast bulk of which is impossible to accurately measure because it went unreported.41

Mental Health Advisory Teams conducted two surveys in Iraq and Afghanistan that support this conclusion. At the request of Gen. David Petraeus, the Multinational Forces-Iraq commander, the fourth iteration of their survey included questions pertaining to battlefield conduct—the first time since World War II the ethics of service members had been systematically surveyed during combat.42 The results of this 2006 survey were distressing: The survey found that only 47 percent of soldiers and 38 percent of marines agreed that noncombatants should be treated with dignity and respect. More than one-third of all soldiers and marines reported that torture should be allowed to save the life of a fellow soldier or marine, and less than half of marines said they would report a team member for unethical behavior. Also, 10 percent of soldiers and marines reported mistreating noncombatants or damaging property when it was not necessary.43 A fifth survey reported a similar percentage of service members saying they had mistreated non-combatants and unnecessarily damaged locals' property. 44 However, for this 2007 survey, the particularly troublesome, previously highly publicized attitudinal questions were not asked.45 Worse, although this 2007 report concluded that "soldiers who screened positive for mental health problems of depression, anxiety, or acute stress were significantly more likely to report engaging in unethical behaviors," subsequent surveys did not pose any questions pertaining to U.S. battlefield conduct—thus avoiding potentially problematic findings.46

Likely underlying much of this dismal, self-deceptive lack of accountability is the aforementioned myth of exceptionalism. A sense of American superiority makes it easier to tolerate and forgive offenses that we would decry if committed by the enemy. How can we hope to curtail such abuse when we systematically fail to punish it? How can we hope to be trusted by local nationals and the international community when we so grossly fail to live up to our own proclaimed principles? The obvious answer to non-Americans is that

Americans cannot be counted upon to curtail this abuse in the future, nor can we be trusted to keep any population's best interests in mind but our own.47

What is also obvious is that the mistrust stemming from our failure to punish criminals in our ranks works against the legitimacy of U.S. military actions abroad. For instance, U.S. forces withdrew from Iraq earlier than desired because the Iraqi government insisted on jurisdiction over major crimes committed by American service members.48 After the previous ten years, most Iraqi leaders had concluded that the American system of accountability was unjust.

Poor stewardship.

One of the authors recently served in Afghanistan as the chief of intelligence for Task Force 2010, a joint, interagency unit consisting largely of law enforcement, intelligence, forensic accounting, and contract specialists. This unit is charged with reducing the flow of American taxpayer dollars via pilferage and U.S.-contracted insurgent front companies to the enemy.

During his deployment, the task force uncovered a massive criminal enterprise that, over the previous year, had stolen tens of millions of dollars of U.S. goods. Task Force 2010 needed the help of two tactical units to shut this operation down. The author and two of his analysts briefed a small group of staff officers from these units, hoping to persuade them to help. He prefaced this brief by saying, "I know counter-pilferage isn't sexy, but we'll get to the sexy stuff shortly." One of his analysts gave the background to the investigation, then his other analyst described how profits from the sale of these stolen goods were supporting transnational terrorist and insurgent groups operating out of Pakistan.

The brief finished, one of the officers in the small audience said, "Ok, now where is the sexy stuff?" The author's jaw dropped: "What do you mean? The American taxpayer is giving millions of dollars to bad guys who are killing our troops. What's not important about that?" The officer asked, "Where are the guys planting IEDs? Where are the suicide bombers?" The author responded, "These guys provide bad guys with enough funding to buy tens of thousands of IEDs, not to mention pay the salary of thousands of recruits. That's a helluva lot more important than killing someone planting an IED every night." Despite his impassioned plea, the staff officers ultimately left the brief unconvinced, promising to provide only limited support.

These staff officers clearly had a blind spot. Even if convinced that stopping this criminal enterprise would impact the insurgency far more than, say, removing 10 Taliban foot soldiers, they would not have cared. The root cause of their shortsightedness lay, not in ignorance or a lack of common sense, but in the lies we soldiers tell ourselves. We idealize ourselves as warriors, as noble killers, and we produce metrics of success to reinforce this objectification. For combat troops, preventing an IED network from receiving the support it needs to operate may seem unimportant—even if this support is indirectly, unknowingly, and shamefully provided by American taxpayers.49

Although "body count" fell from favor long ago as an acceptable measure of effectiveness, our military is not all that far removed from this metric culturally. Most daily command briefs in combat zones begin with a roll-up of "SIGACTS" (significant acts) tallying friendly versus enemy casualties, and much reporting is likewise dominated by such SIGACTS—text that implicitly evaluates only friendly and enemy casualties as "significant." Combat support troops suffer from similarly flawed metrics. Logisticians, for example, love to report that supported combat troops are "green" on ammo, fuel, and food, but they rarely report or reliably track how many supplies were stolen enroute to the troops (even when these stolen supplies support the enemy). Losses of 10, 20, or a much higher percentage are acceptable, as long as combat troops are "green" on all supplies.

Becoming Who We Say We Are

We reap the fruits of our actions in ways too many military leaders simply fail to see, let alone acknowledge. This strategic sowing and harvesting is a pattern the Army has to break.

For example, when we fail to hold adequately accountable those soldiers who have abused locals, we are repeating a pattern within the history of expeditionary warfare. The Roman Empire's troubled experience in the Middle East illustrated this problem. In Palestine, the lack of soldier accountability contributed heavily to the revolts the Romans suppressed there. Roman satirist Juvenal complained that Roman military courts in the provinces would rarely serve justice to soldiers abusing the inhabitants:

Military law: no soldier, it's stated, may sue or be tried except in camp, by court-martial. "But still, when an officer's trying a guardsman, surely the proceedings must be conducted with exemplary Justice? So if my complaint is legitimate I'm sure to get satisfaction." . . . Easier [to] find a witness to perjure himself against a civilian than one who'll tell the truth, if the truth's against a soldier's honor or interest . . . And it's in any commander's interest to see the bravest soldiers obtain the best recompense . . .50 The U.S. military has to learn this lesson if we expect to achieve any success in the future from counterinsurgencies.

The authors argued in a previous essay, "War is a Moral Force," that the most critical considerations of human conflict are moral ones.51 These considerations were as important to the Romans as they are now to us, not something new to modern war. However, the information age has amplified the effects. There may have been a time when self-mythologizing served a useful purpose in war, but only ignorance could make it work. Today, in an age in which information flies around the world at the speed of light, immediately bringing great coherency and power to moral opinion, we can no longer assume such ignorance will last. We cannot long hope to be allowed to say we are one thing while actually being something else. Our spoken words (and values) must be indicative of our actions.

Within war's "moral domain," especially critical are judgments of right and wrong actions and the impact such judgments have on the fighting spirit of nations, communities, and warfighters. Self-deception, however, encourages an orientation toward the world that is antithetical to success in this domain. Believing the myth that we are prima facie better than others leaves us vulnerable to committing acts of strategically grave moral error that sustains our enemies' will to fight while sapping the fighting spirit of Americans and America's allies.

Today, getting out of the self-mythologizing business as much as we humanly can has become a mission essential task. All human beings deceive themselves about why they do the things they do. The difference is one of degree. Officers and soldiers who practice real moral leadership are those who resist their own self-deceptive tendencies toward superiority, who genuinely care about others and their opinions, who judge people (themselves included) in accordance with their actions, and who actively search for ways that they could be wrong in order to correct their own courses. In John Stuart Mill's words, these leaders treat their own fallibility seriously. Humility needs to be an Army Value.

Specifics. The following are some steps the modern Army should take to become a true, more effective profession:

• Transform the "be-do" misapprehension at the heart of Army doctrine to "Learn-Do-Become."

• Give more serious attention to virtue education, to include reidentifying and redefining our selected values. Is it really necessary that we confine ourselves to virtues that it the "LDRSHP" rubric? Should we not instead choose virtues based on meaning and mutual compatibility?52

• Actively seek, and frankly acknowledge, truth from subordinates and external, disinterested sources (such as journalists), even when it contradicts earnestly desired narratives about events and ourselves.

• Actively fight the impulse to dehumanize our enemies and the populations in which they hide via doctrine, education, and leader-exemplars. Real honor comes from honoring humanity.

• Educate soldiers more thoroughly on the circumstances under which killing is justified and hold leaders more accountable than their subordinates

• Develop a written professional ethic reinforced with a robust education and training program that actually prepares soldiers for tough ethical choices.

• Make leader efficiency reports more honest by ensuring text from 360-degree feedback is incorporated into these reports (especially critical for the evaluations of senior leaders).

• Make indicators that a unit is a learning organization an important element of leader evaluations.

• Always integrate moral with operational concerns when teaching military leaders how to successfully "manage violence."53 Simply avoiding what is clearly illegal should not be the point; striving to do what warring parties and allies will deem "the most just alternative" should be the point.

• Make operational leaders the moral "subject matter experts."

What the Army values. Answering these issues of unlimited deference, self-serving idealizations, exceptionalism, valuing form over substance, manipulative communication, and poor accountability must grow out of leadership. Serious accountability among the leadership and more honesty at the top could go a long way to shoring up self-deception in the force at large. Gauging the force's opinions on these matters through data may help, but the stewards of the Army Profession should have the wisdom to see further than those they lead. They should seek a better integrity for the force at large.

In an organization as large as our military, one expects the institution to be vulnerable to myth making and to moral errors. The fact that these errors have already contributed to gross and counterproductive outrages at home and abroad, while greatly disturbing, is not what is most troubling. What is most troubling is that we can do far better than we have been doing but remain too blind, complacent, and self-deceived. Earning lasting success in war and the full trust of all will be impossible to achieve until we soldiers challenge, head on, the myths we tell ourselves.

1. Thomas Paine, The Age of Reason, available at <http://www.deism.com/images/theageofreason1794.pdf> (15 January 2013).

2. Fyodor Dostoevsky, The Brothers Karamazov, translated by Andrew R. MacAn-drew (New York: Bantam Books, 1970).

3. The literature regarding U.S. military and political deception during the Vietnam War and its profoundly disillusioning effect on veterans and the American public is voluminous. Three of the best books are Neil Sheehan, A Bright Shining Lie: John Paul Vann and America in Vietnam (New York: Vintage Books, 1988), Arnold Isaac's Vietnam Shadows: the War, Its Ghosts, and Its Legacy (New York: Modern Library, 2009); and H.R. McMaster, Dereliction of Duty (New York: HarperCollins, 1998). The treatment of this subject in movies is also vast, of which Francis Ford Coppola's Apocalypse Now is probably the best known.

4. McMaster, 329-31.

5. Ibid., 331.

6. Lewis Sorley, Westmoreland: The General Who Lost Vietnam (New York: Houghton Mifflin Harcourt, 2011), 74.

7. Ibid.

8. William R. Peers, "Summary of Peers Report," The University of Missouri-Kansas City, March 1970, <http://law2.umkc.edu/faculty/projects/ftrials/mylai/sum-mary rpt.html> (16 February 2013).

9. Thomas E. Ricks, The Generals (New York: The Penguin Press, 2012), 312; U.S. Army War College, Study on Military Professionalism, 30 June 1970, B-31 through B-34.

10. John Gates, "American Military Leadership in the Vietnam War," in Military Leadership and Command: The John Biggs Cincinnati Lectures, 1987, edited by Henry S. Bausum, 185-209, Lexington, VA: The VMI Foundation, Inc., 1987, 198.

11. This statement, which is this essay's thesis, is supported by the 16 December 2011, "Army Profession Campaign Overview," <http://cape.army.mil/Army%20Profes-sion/AP%20Campaign%20Briefing.pdf>. The Center for the Army Profession and Ethic (CAPE) produced this brief, slide 8 of which says that "corrosive effects [exist] of [our] not always practicing what we espouse."

12. Friedrich Nietzsche, Aphorism no. 4 in "Prejudices of Philosophers," Beyond Good and Evil (Project Gutenberg: The Complete Works of Friedrich Nietzsche), available at:

<http://www.marxists.org/reference/archive/nietzsche/1886/beyond-good-evil/index.htm> (10 October 2012).

13. Jean-Paul Sartre, Anti-Semite and Jew (New York: Schocken Books, 1965), 40.

14. Ibid.,15. Leonard Doyle, "'A Dead Iraqi is Just Another Dead Iraqi': You Know, So What?" The Independent, 12 July 2007.

16. Seymour M. Hersh, "Torture at Abu Ghraib," New York Times, 10 May 2004.

17. Richard Myers, "Perspectives," Newsweek, 3 May 2004; David Livingstone Smith, Less Than Human: Why We Demean, Enslave, and Exterminate Others (New York: St. Martin's Press, 2011), 254-55.

18. A completely different problem is the number of service members who would precisely call it torture and consider it legitimate. This essay addresses only the problem of soldiers who consider torture wrong but deceive themselves about American instances of it.

19. Moral injury is the cognitive dissonance that occurs when people see or do things that conflict with their own deeply held values: when a transgression is great enough to lead to serious inner conflict, it is the source of the moral injury. The notion that moral injury can lead to suicide is anecdotally but compellingly and poignantly explored in two recent books by journalists, Joshua E.S.Phillips, None of Us Were Like This Before: American Soldiers and Torture (New York: Verso, 2012) and Justine Sharrock, Tortured: When Good Soldiers Do Bad Things (New York: Verso, 2012).

20. John Stuart Mill, On Liberty, available at <http://www.constitution.org/jsm/ liberty.htm> (17 September 2012).

21. Little Big Man, available at <http://www.imdb.com/title/tt0065988/> (14 February 2013).

22. Design methodology is the Army's version of Systemic Operational Design developed by the Israeli Defense Forces under Brig Gen. Shimon Naveh as a means for developing better analysis of emergent conditions in framing complex situations. See U.S. Army Field Manual (FM) 5-0, The Operations Process (Washington DC: U.S. Government Printing Office [GPO], 26 March 2010), 3-1.

23. U.S. Army, Army Doctrine Reference Publication (ADRP) 6-22, Leadership (Washington DC: GPO, August 2012), 1-5; FM 6-22, Leadership (Washington DC: GPO, October 2006) 2. In the Foreword to FM 6-22, GEN Peter Schoomaker, the Chief of the Staff of the Army at the time of publication, describes Be-Know-Do as the doctrine's foundation, stating that the rubric expresses "what is required of leaders."

24. FM 22-100, Leadership (Washington DC: GPO, August 1999) 1-6. This statement is testament to Aristotelian virtue ethics at the foundation of the Be-Know-Do rubric: "Character describes a person's inner strength."

25. Aristotle, "Habit and Virtue," in Nichomachean Ethics, translated by Terence Irwin (Indianapolis, Hackett, 1985), 33-40.

26. Both ADRP 6-22, Leadership, and the field manual it recently replaced, FM 6-22, Leadership, define the Army Value of "respect" as treating someone as they deserve. This

definition does little to promote the humane treatment of prisoners, when captors believe that prisoners are "evil terrorists" and deserve to be treated like inhuman monsters or animals.

27. James R. Schlesinger, Harold Brown, Tillie K. Fowler, Charles A. Horner, James A. Blackwell Jr., "Final Report of the Independent Panel to Review DOD Detention Operations," FindLaw, August 2004, <http:news.findlaw.com/wp/docs/dod/abughraibrpt.pdf> (16 February 2012), 124-5. The Schlesinger Panel's independent investigation into the scale and causes of U.S. detainee abuse recognized that core values programs like the Army Values do more to promote self-deception than ethical behavior, concluding: "Core-values programs are grounded in organizational

efficacy rather than the moral good. They do not address humane treatment of the enemy and noncombatants, leaving military leaders and educators an incomplete tool box with which to deal with 'real-world' ethical problems. A professional ethics program addressing these situations would help equip them with a sharper moral compass for guidance in situations often riven with conflicting moral obligations."

28. T.X. Hammes, for example, states: "Counterinsurgency is not a strategy but rather a range of possible ways in the ends, ways, and means formulation of strategy. Furthermore, population-centric counterinsurgency, as documented in Field Manual 3-24, Counterinsurgency, is only one possible approach to counterinsurgency." From "Counterinsurgency: Not a Strategy, but a Necessary Capability," Joint Force Quarterly 65 (April 2012): 49.

29. Jim Frederick, Black Hearts: One Platoon's Descent into Madness in Iraq's Triangle of Death (New York: Random House, 2010), 323-24.

30. Paul Richter, "Rumsfeld Hasn't Hit a Dead End in Forging Terms for Foe in Iraq," Los Angeles Times, 30 November 2005. Rather than call insurgents what they were, Rumsfeld used such terms as "Former Regime Loyalists," "Former Regime Elements," "Anti-Iraq Forces," "Deadenders," and "Enemies of the Legitimate Iraqi Government." He also denied there even was an insurgency.

31. Carl Levin, U.S. Senator Michigan, Senate Armed Services Committee, "Inquiry into the Treatment of Detainees in U.S. Custody," 2009, <http://www.levin.senate.gov/issues/treatment-of-detainees-in-us-custody> (16 November 2012), xvii-xxiv.

32. Douglas A. Pryer, The Fight for the High Ground: The U.S. Army and Interrogation During Operation Iraqi Freedom, May 2003-April 2004 (Fort Leavenworth, KS: Command and General Staff College Foundation Press, 2009), 27, 54, 58-60. As described in these cited pages, key leaders and/or other personnel of at least four of the facilities most notorious for employing torture during the irst year of Operation Iraqi Freedom had previously attended Survival, Escape, Resistance, and Evasion (SERE) school. One interrogation chief had even been a SERE instructor.

33. Phillips, 58-62; Scott Ewing, "Discipline, Punishment, and Counterinsurgency," Military Review (Special Edition, Center for the Army Profession and Ethic) (September 2010): 27-37.

34. Matthew Alexander, "I'm Still Tortured by What I Saw in Iraq," The Washington Post, 30 November 2008, <http://www.washingtonpost.com/wp-dyn/content/ article/2008/11/28/AR2008112802242.html> (22 April 2009). The interrogator Matthew Alexander is one of many who have testified to the recruitment boon that detainee abuse scandals provided anti-U.S. jihadist groups. During his in-brief at a special operations interrogation facility in Iraq, he was told that "the number one reason foreign fighters flocked there to fight were the abuses carried out at Abu Ghraib and Guantanamo."

35. Hina Shamsi, "Command's Responsibility: Detainee Deaths in U.S. Custody in Iraq and Afghanistan," Human Rights First, edited by Deborah Pearlstein, February 2006, <http://www.humanrightsirst.org/wp-content/uploads/pdf/06221-etn-hrf-dic-rep-web.pdf> (16 February 2012), 1.

36. Ibid.

37. Ibid.

38. Phillips, None of Us Were Like This Before, 110-29. This chapter ("Crimes of Omission") is a well-researched summary of both the inadequacies of U.S. military investigations into detainee abuse and the causes of these inadequacies.

39. Phillips, "Inside the Detainee Abuse Task Force," The Nation, May 2011, 26-31, 26.

40. Center for Human Rights and Global Justice, Human Rights First, Human Rights Watch, "By the Numbers: Findings of the Detainee Abuse and Accountability Project," Human Rights First, 22 February 2006, <http://www.humanrightsirst.org/ wp-content/uploads/pdf/06425-etn-by-the-numbers.pdf> (16 November 2012), 2.

41. Phillips, None of Us Were Like This Before, 50-67, 179-201; Tony Lagouranis and Allen Mikaelian, Fear Up Harsh: An Army Interrogator's Dark Journey through Iraq (New York: New American Library, 2008), 57-140. Phillips describes waterboarding and other tortures at a facility run by an armor battalion that was never investigated for abuse. Tony Lagouranis describes abuse at a facility that was investigated and that an investigator conirmed as abusive of detainees. However, despite the investigator's recommending punishment, no punishment was delivered, and when Lagouranis later interrogated at this facility, the abuse seems to have gotten even worse—abuse which subsequently went uninvestigated. See also Jim Frederick's Black Hearts: One Platoon's Descent into Madness in Iraq's Triangle of Death (UK: Pan MacMillan, 2010),which describes abuses of both locals and detainees that went uninvestigated. Such evidence, while anecdotal rather than conclusive, indicates that publicized detainee abuse may have only been the tip of the iceberg of what actually occurred.

42. Office of the Surgeon Multinational Force-Iraq and Office of the Surgeon United States Army Medical Command, "Mental Health Advisory Team (MHAT) IV, Operation Iraqi Freedom 05-07, Final Report," Army Medicine, 7 November 2006, <http://www.armymedicine.army.mil/reports/mhat/mhat iv/MHAT IV Report 17NOV06.pdf> (3 June 2013).

43. Sara Wood, "Petraeus Urges Troops to Adhere to Ethical Standards," U.S. Department of Defense News, 11 May 2007, <http://www.defense.gov/News/NewsArticle.aspx?ID=45983> (3 June 2013).

44. Ofice of the Surgeon Multinational Force-Iraq and Ofice of the Command Surgeon and Ofice of the Surgeon General United States Army Medical Command, "Mental Health Advisory Team (MHAT) V, Operation Iraqi Freedom 06-08: Iraq; Operation Enduring Freedom 8: Afghanistan," Army Medicine, February 2008, 14, <http://www.armymedicine.army.mil/reports/mhat/mhat v/mhat-v.cfm> (3 June 2013).

45. Ibid.

46. The 2008 and 2009 surveys can be found at <http://www.armymedicine.army. mil/reports/reports.html>.

47. A 2008 Pew Report based on a survey of 23 countries described growing anti-Americanism across the world, concluding, "In the view of much of the world, the United States has played the role of bully in the school yard, throwing its weight around with little regard for others' interests," <http://www.pewglobal.org/2008/12/18/ global-public-opinion-in-the-bush-years-2001-2008/>.

48. Tim Arango and Michael S. Schmidt, "Iraq Denies Legal Immunity to U.S. Troops After 2011," 4 October 2011, <http://www.nytimes.com/2011/10/05/world/ middleeast/iraqis-say-no-to-immunity-for-remaining-american-troops.html? r=1&partner=rss&emc=rss> (15 October 2011).

49. Douglas A. Wissing, Funding the Enemy: How US Taxpayers Bankroll the Taliban (Amherst, NY: Prometheus Books, 2012). Wissing's book is probably the best researched, most comprehensive open-source account of the extent to which American taxpayers unknowingly fund Afghanistan's insurgents.

50. Juvenal, XVI, translated by P. Green, quoted in Michael Grant's The Army of the Caesars (New York: M. Evans and Company, 1974), xxv.

51. Peter Fromm, Douglas Pryer, and Kevin Cutright, "War is a Moral Force," Joint Force Quarterly 64 (1st Quarter 2012).

52. For a philosopher's deconstruction of the Army Values and a more rational alternative, see Timothy Challans, Awakening Warrior: Revolution in the Ethics of Warfare (Albany, NY: State University of New York Press), 2007, 85-91.

53. Samuel P. Huntington, The Soldier and the State: The Theory and Politics of Civil-Military Relations (Cambridge: Harvard College, 1957). Samuel Huntington famously described the peculiar skill of the military oficer as being the successful "management of violence."

* * * * * * * * * * *

Deputy Secretary of Defense Speech

Remarks to the Association of the U.S. Army Annual Convention

As Delivered by Deputy Secretary of Defense Bob Work, Washington, D.C. , Oct. 4, 2016

(contains reference to the work of McMaster on Russian issues)

Thank you. Well, I would just like to start by saying, and with apologies to the CNO who wrote an article on this today that Washington traffic is the most effective A2/AD network in the world.

I very much apologize for keeping you waiting. And so I want to just dive right in. I want to thank the AUSA, Secretary Fanning, General Milley, General Perkins for this opportunity. I am honored to be invited here and speak with this important forum and with an organization that has done so much to support our remarkable American Army.

Now, in talking to General Perkins about what he wanted me to try to do today, he just asked me to kind of set the stage for the future operating environment as we see it and talk in terms of the reconceptualization and concept development that is occurring right now within the joint force and throughout the joint force.

Over 27 years since the Cold War's ended, and as demonstrated convincingly in Operation Desert Storm, Operation Allied force, the conventional campaign and Operation Iraqi Freedom, the United States has enjoyed a remarkable run of unparalleled conventional dominance at both the tactical and operational levels of war. During this period, we have had generally unimpeded freedom of action, access on the land, in the air, on the sea.

But now, competitors such as big competitors, like Russia and China, medium-sized regional powers like Iran and North Korea, they're developing capabilities and challenges and they contest us in all domains now; cyberspace, space, air, land, sea, under seas. And this threatens to erode not only our operational advantage, but in some cases, our technological superiority and overmatch, which then impacts our ability to project powers over trans-oceanic distances.

Now, addressing this challenge is, in my view, one of the most if not the most important challenges facing the Department of Defense, and that is why Secretary Carter has directed us to take concrete steps to remain at the forefront of operational and tactical excellence, and changing the way we plan, changing the way we innovate, changing the way we invest and most importantly changing the way we fight.

Now, I don't have to convince this crowd among all the crowds that I talk to that war is won by humans and not technology, but at least since World War II, it is incontrovertible that our national security strategy and our national defense strategy has assumed that we will enter the battle with superior technology, or at least technology that is better than our competitors, and we will be better trained and our individuals will be higher caliber.

And you don't have to take my word for this. This started in World War II with General George C. Marshall, who said after the war, the vastly superior industrial establishment of the United States eventually overcame the initial advantages of the enemy. We dared to mount operations all over the world with a strategic inferiority and troops through superiority and mobility and firepower.

Now, for the historians in this group, what he was referring to was his famous 90 division gamble. Right after the war started, planners said how big of an army are we going to need to fight this global war? The answer came back 213 divisions and 273 air groups, but Marshall bet, and he admitted this was a gamble, that he thought the material superiority as well as the mobility, the superior mobility, coupled with far-reaching heavy fisted air arm would allow the United States to fight the war with 90 divisions instead of 213.

In the end, he approved the air -- the goal of the 273 air groups. Now, this gamble was a close-run thing. As all -- as you most probably know, in the winter of 1944 in the European theater of operations, we literally ran out of infantrymen. But in the end, the superior training, leadership, skill, tactical ingenuity and tenaciousness of the American soldier made this gamble pay off.

The same thinking animated President Eisenhower in his "New Look" strategy, where he basically said, I will invest in a smaller army armed with battlefield nuclear weapons and backed up by tactical fighters that would deliver tactical nukes against deep targets.

Now, we can debate today on whether that was the same strategy. The Army debated throughout the '50s that it was not, and in the end, President Kennedy agreed with the Army and introduced the strategy of flexible response which called for a larger army, and not so much, you know, use of tactical nuclear weapons. But without question, through the 1970's, our conventional defense of Europe assumed that we would -- might have to go to tactical nukes early in the fight, especially once the United States became tied down in Vietnam.

But coming out of Vietnam, we had three problems, and these three problems are exactly -- not exactly, never exactly -- but pretty darn close to analogous to what we face today.

First, the Soviets had achieved nuclear parity at the time and had developed new operational concepts specifically designed to upset the new look strategy. They would attack by successive echelons against the NATO frontline. At that time, I think it is called people so the FEBA, so the forward edge of the battle area. They'd effect a penetration, an operational maneuver group would pound through, go deep in NATO's rear, and the judgment was the Soviets could do that faster than NATO leaders could agree on the use of nuclear weapons.

So our conventional deterrent was completely undermined. It just was no longer credible.

Second, throughout the 1960s, the Soviets had spent a lot of money on improving their tactical equipment, and the 1973 war showed that the character of war was changing, exactly what Chief Milley is saying. In '73, the T-62 was pretty darn close to the M-60 that we were using, the SA-6 surface-to-air missiles wrested air superiority from one of the finest air forces in the world for three days, until a ground maneuver was able to break open up that network and wire guided antitank missiles really, really were a problem for Israeli armor.

U.S. Army sent teams over to the deserts and they said, wow, the lethality of the modern battlefield is far above anything that we are used to. In fact, retired general Bob Scales said the '73 war was the first evidence of the precision revolution in warfare applied to ground combat. The message was pretty clear, the character of war, had changed significantly, and if we got into a fight in the European front, it could be a big, big problem for us.

Third, we didn't have a lot of money. We were coming out of Vietnam, so there were -- we didn't have a lot of freedom of action when it comes to budgets. So again, parity at the nuclear level, new operational concepts which start to upend the way we -- our operational design, tactical, kind of equivalence, and then finally low resources. So the response really bears remembering because I'm going to come back to it really quickly.

We concluded that a smaller ground force backed by technology and honed by training could still form the foundation of a credible conventional deterrent. This smaller force would be all volunteer, and would be guided by a doctrinal renaissance with a focus at the operational level of war. Tactical superiority would be restored by fielding the big five: the M1 tank, the Bradley infantry fighting vehicle, the Black Hawk helicopter, the Apache attack helicopter, and the Patriot missile, and by owning the night.

And we would hone the skills of the smaller force through hard, realistic training in places like a national training center and red flag. Now meanwhile up at OSD, Secretary of Defense Harold Brown and his AT&L, is what is now called the Undersecretary Defense for AT&L -- it wasn't then -- but they were going to focus on the operational level of war also, and they envisioned an operational level battle network: a sensor grid, a C3I Grid, and an affects grid, all interconnected.

And that operational level battle network would allow us to solve the problem of the successive echelons. We would look deep and shoot deep, and we would rely upon the tactical ingenuity, skill, and tenaciousness of the American soldier on the FEBA.

We demonstrated this in a demonstration called "Assault Breaker" in 1982, but here is the key, and it is directly associated with this panel. Long before the assault breaker demonstrated the technology, the Army was creating a new operational construct focused again at the campaign level, the operational level of war. They took the lessons of the Yom Kippur war in they said, you're right, the character of war is changing.

And they were driven by the imperative to find outnumbered and win. TRADOC Commander Donn Starry, teamed with Air Force General Bill Creech, to develop what we now look back upon and called AirLand Battle, integrating fires and maneuvers at both the operational and the tactical level of war. And when meshed with the technologies that came out of the assault breaker demonstration, the result was an astounding increase in combat effectiveness that has served us well to this day.

Now we demonstrated this at Desert Storm in a very nascent state, and it was a wake-up call for all of our competitors. This crowd knows warfare is a dynamic interactive endeavor, that's warfare 101. We shouldn't have expected her adversaries to sit still and they certainly haven't. So now we are faced with much of the same situation that the U.S. Army in the joint force faced in 1973. This is what we need to now offset once again.

Most of our combat power resides now in the continental United States or on U.S. territory. We can no longer assume that we will have large forces in theaters, they are expected to fight, and this will give a potential adversary an advantage in the initiative time and forces initially.

Second, our largest state adversaries will have achieved rough parity in battle networks and guided munitions. This will make movement to the theater and movement within the theater more difficult; not impossible, just much more difficult than we're used to. And third, because our adversaries know the fearsome power of our battle networks, they have invested a lot of money in counter network technologies like electronic warfare and cyber. And so these are changing, once again, I could not agree more with the chief. The character of war is changing once again.

And as I said, make no mistake about it, this is a big strategic issue because it threatens our ability to project power across the oceans, which is the very foundation of our conventional deterrent.

Now, like the 1973 war, Russian operations in both Ukraine and Syria have given us a glimpse of how this might play out on the tactical battlefield. I want to make absolutely clear to everyone here, we are not planning to fight a war against Russia, but it would be foolish not to pay attention to their operations because they are quite frankly, a pacing competitor that tells us where we need to go to make sure that we have operational and tactical superiority.

And I know General Perkins, **HR McMaster** and his team are looking at these lessons very, very carefully. The Russians have effectively employed cross domain fires using a variety of long-range guided munitions from the air, sea, and under the sea. They have improved the accuracy and responsiveness of their already formidable indirect fire skills, using artillery and rockets guided by UAVs, cyber, Sigint and ELINT right on the forward line of troops.

Russian-backed separatists have jammed GPS frequencies, communications and imaging radars, so not only will our future Army have to fight on the battlefield swept by precision munitions, but it's going to be swept by persistent and very effective VW and cyber threats.

The old adage was back in the second offset, if you can be seen, you can be hit and if you can hit, you can be killed. The new adage is, if you emit, you die. So during the last 15 years of war, the greatest threat that we have really faced was from below, the IED, a simple but very devastating weapon. But in this future battlefield, we will be faced with precision guided fire from above and a direct line of sight, and all sorts of different capabilities that we haven't faced. And we still have the Big Five.

We don't have enough money to replace the Big Five. We're spending money to update them but we're going to have to keep them a while. So we find ourselves in this very similar broken terrain. Our adversaries are close to parody at the operational level.

They've demonstrated, at the tactical level, new capabilities we have to be aware of and there's not a lot to be enthusiastic about, our resources at this point. So it's time to get busy and I'm proud to say that the army has really been getting after it. I went up to the army work college last year and I said look, technology is one thing and there's all sorts of technological advances we can do. But if that technology is not guided and shaped by good, operational constructs, concepts and organizational constructs, it just isn't going to work.

And I challenged the army at that time, would you please start thinking about Air-Land battle 2.0. But thankfully, **General Perkins and General McMaster didn't listen to me, they knew that I was barking up the wrong tree. They looked beyond Air-Land Battle to envision war in what General Perkins called multi-domain battle with cross-**

domain fires. On a battlefield swept by precision guided munitions, you've got about two options.

You can dig in and immobilize yourself hoping you survive or you disperse, stay mobile and fire and maneuver to gain advantage. And you're going to have to do that maneuver across all operational domains. Multi-domain battle chooses maneuver in all these domains. Both the service and create windows of opportunity to enable the joint force freedom of maneuver and to allow them to achieve effects on the battlefield. Past campaign plans have called for an extensive roll back campaign against A2AD type technologies so that we could get the rest of the Joint Force in.

But Multi-Domain Battle envisions a future where you synchronize cross-domain fires and maneuver in all the domains to achieve physical, temporal and positional advantages. So as the CNO often says, it allows us to look at A2AD networks, or whatever we will call them in the future, not as a solid block of cheddar cheese but a block of Swiss cheese with a lot of discrete holes that we can exploit. Adversaries think they can keep us out, I'm here to tell you they are absolutely wrong.

We will mass effects from the air, from the sea, from the ground, from under the sea and we will quite frankly pound the snot out of them from range and in the close fight. Now Multi-Domain Battle and cross-domain fires get at the very heart of the changing character of war and how ground forces will be central, as they always have been, in the joint war fight. They will operate within what we call joint collaborative human machine battle networks at the operational level of war that will provide us an enormous advantage there.

We hope that all of the focus on readiness and training on the high end and the advances are the improvements we can make to the Big Five, well, we're not hoping, we're counting on it and we're absolutely confident that at the tactical level of war, our soldiers are going to outmatch anybody they face.

But we're going to move what this does, what **General Perkins and General McMaster have been talking about**, is that we're going to move beyond a mere synchronization of joint capabilities to the complete integration of capabilities where anti-air capabilities might be coming from a surge submarine or anti-ship cruise missiles might be coming from an army unit on the ground.

There are so many different ways that we can create dilemmas for our adversaries that if we seize the opportunity, we will be just fine. I also see another grand alliance, I'm glad to see that General Goldfein is here sitting next to General Perkins. General Goldfein has said that we have to have a new conception of command and control in these joint collaborative human machine battle networks because command and control must be multi-domain, multi-functional, coalition friendly and often trans-regional and he's taken that on as one of his top three priorities as a chief to think that through.

And just like the Army and the Air Force came together for Air-Land Battle, I think it's absolutely critical that the Army and the Air Force and the Navy by the way that has really advanced thinking about tactical battle networks et cetera and the Marines who are still thinking innovatively about operational maneuver from the sea, multi-domain battle really is where we need to go. So it's time to get after this. I'm not certain that multi-domain battle, as it's expressed today, is going to be the final solution.

I can look back in the 1985, 1985, the Army adopted Active Defense but within two years they said, look Air-Land Battle is a better way to do this. That's the signature of the U.S. Army. Doctrinal innovation and if they don't think that's going to work, they're going to go to something that does. And once they have that doctrinal innovation, they train, train, train, and they train better and they field capabilities faster than our opponents.

Look, anybody could have bought night vision goggles in 1977, 1978. But the Army said, we're going to own the night and it was all the TTP's, the tactics, techniques and procedures and the training that allowed them to own the night. So when people say, oh somebody might get technology faster than us, I say, OK but will they be able to employ it in an operational, effective way? And I bet on the U.S. Army and the U.S. Joint Force, we will get there faster than them.

Now the Army has a long history of war gaming and experimentation, whether it's the famous Louisiana maneuvers of the 1940's, the 11th AASLT division of the 60's, the light infantry division experiments of the 80's, the fourth I.D. and the digitization experiments in the 90's, the Army after next program, look we're confident the Army can get after it but we also know that resources are tight. So we've established a war fighting lab incentives fund so if the Army comes up and says, we'd like to do this demonstration, we can come up with maybe 2 million. If we could use another two, that fund is designed to let the Army get after it.

So let me say a millionth time, I say it all the time, the third offset is not about technology per say. It is about the operational concepts and organizational constructs that will shape the way we use technology. And there is no better organization in the world that thinks about this than the United States Army.

And let me say that Secretary Carter and I have absolute confidence that we can do this for one reason, and that is because one thing that never changes, whether it's in World War II, the Korean War, the Vietnam War, Desert Storm, Operation Iraqi Freedom, it doesn't matter, it's the quality of our people. Look, this force does things that Second Lieutenant Work in 1975 couldn't even conceive of and the Army is now conceiving what that next great leap will be.

And I am extremely excited to hear this because nothing gets me more energized than advancements at the operational level of war, which is, as the Army has always said, that's where you have to keep your eyeballs on.

So Amy, General Perkins, all I can say is drive on. This is exciting time. Just like we own the night, I want you to tell us how we're going to own the electromagnetic night. I want to know how we do multi-domain battle. I want to understand how command-and-control has to change because those things -- when those questions are answered, we will -- you will start to see investments flow that way because of force imbued with Army values, trained hard and allowed to operate under the widest latitude possible, will always outperform a force tied to a rigid command structure in an authoritarian dogma.

Our training and professional development must be tailored to empower our people, exploit the technology, but most importantly achieve operational and tactical effects using really smart thinking.

So I'm really looking forward to this panel. I won't be able to stay for the entire time, but I'd like to commend AUSA for having the panel. I'd like to commend the Army for their far-reaching thinking. I'd like to commend all of the services because I'm telling you right now, there hasn't been a situation like this in quite some time, where every one of the services are involved in such deep thought about operational and tactical innovation.

So again, thank you all to you here -- those here in the audience and I can't wait to hear what comes out of the panel. Thank you.

Now, because I may have to leave, General Perkins has asked me to answer just one or two questions because I already arrived a little late. I will be happy to do so. If there are no questions, I am happy to sit down. So if anybody has a question, I have time for one or maybe two.

Yes, sir?

Q: You didn't mention about autonomous systems. In light of the third off-set strategy, what is your thinking about letting in the future autonomous systems make lethality decisions without a human in the loop?

MR. WORK: I purposely didn't talk a lot about the technology behind the third off-set because in a audience like this, you get that the most important thing is the operational concepts and the organizational constructs that employ that technology.

But let me state this -- state it this way. There will be some instances where operations are happening at machine speeds and we will have to rely upon A.I. and autonomy to actually fight. Three of them come immediately to mind; cyber attacks, electronic warfare attacks and heavy guided missile salvo attacks. In each of those three cases, we will have to delegate authority to the machines to make the final decisions.

In every case that I can think of in terms of offensive operations, we will use machines to empower the human and not vice versa. Our competitors may go in a different way. Authoritarian regimes see every single person inside their organization as a potential liability, because if the supreme commander says take this hill and if the squad leader on the ground says I can achieve better affects by taking that hill, that is not something they would want. And we know this because the conception of the Soviet reconnaissance strike complex was ultimately to be totally automated.

Our battle networks will empower humans. Humans will make the decisions on lethality, humans will make the decision on campaign design, humans will make the decision on tactical courses of action. So this is not about Skynet and Terminator.

This is about Iron Man. Really, think about Iron Man. This is human. This is machines helping the human achieve effects.

One last question and then I have got to cede the field. Did you have a question there? You were standing by the mic. Why don't you ask a question?

Q: I'm good, sir. Thank you.

MR. WORK: Okay. Well, again -- yes. One more real quick.

Q: Sydney Freedberg from Breaking Defense.

MR. WORK: Hi, Sydney.

Q: You've mentioned the importance of the operational level of war, which is certainly crucial. But one critique we've had -- well, from Vietnam on, but particularly with Iraq and Afghanistan -- is that we've actually fallen down -- (inaudible) -- strategic level that we've, you know, kind of like the Germans in World War II, have been really, really good at the military parts but terrible at the pol-mil parts.

Is there a way to make sure that in our focus on multi-domain that we don't create a very effective military machine that once again has terrible strategic direction?

MR. WORK: Listen, the Department of Defense focuses on conventional and strategic deterrence. That's what we focus on. And conventional deterrence is based on making sure our adversaries understand that we do have an advantage at both the operational and tactical level of war, and if they decide to take us on, they are most likely, and in my case I would say they are certain, to lose.

The decision about how you employ the military is far beyond what this panel is about. I want them focused on one thing and one thing only; multi-domain battle, electromagnetic maneuver, operational maneuver from the sea, what is EABO --I really like that one, but I can't remember what it is -- expeditionary advanced basing operations where Marine and Army soldiers control the sea from the land. I mean, that's what this focus is about.

So I am going to dodge the questions --

And say I'm looking forward to the panels.

And thank you again.

* * * * * * * * * * * *

Deputy Secretary Discusses Third Offset, First Organizational Construct

By Cheryl Pellerin DoD News, Defense Media Activity

WASHINGTON, Sept. 21, 2016 — The Defense Department's technological and organizational leaps over the decades have been characterized as strategies to offset or overcome the conventional strengths of potential adversaries.

DoD is now in the throes of the Third Offset Strategy, according to defense officials, and today Deputy Defense Secretary Bob Work explained the offset's main elements -- and discussed its first organizational construct -- to an audience at the Air Force Association's Air, Space and Cyber conference in National Harbor, Maryland.

"Offset strategies are not about technology per se," Work said. "... [They're] about technologically enabled operational and organizational constructs that [give] the joint force an advantage -- primarily at the operational level of war, but also the tactical -- thereby strengthening conventional deterrence. And we're starting to see examples of both."

The Joint Interagency Combined Space Operations Center, or JICSpOC, at Schriever Air Force Base in Colorado went live in October 2015 as collaboration among the U.S.

Strategic Command, the National Reconnaissance Office, the Air Force Space Command, the Air Force Research Laboratory, the intelligence community and commercial data providers.

The Third Offset's first organizational construct is the Air Force's Joint Interagency Combined Space Operations Center, or JICSpOC, he said, at Schriever Air Force Base in Colorado.

JICSpOC went live in October 2015 as collaboration among U.S. Strategic Command, the National Reconnaissance Office, the Air Force Space Command, the Air Force Research Laboratory, the intelligence community and commercial data providers, according to the Stratcom website.

In January the center held a tour for distinguished visitors who included Stratcom Commander Navy Adm. Cecil D. Haney and senior defense officials. Defense Secretary Ash Carter visited the center in May.

Work said JICSpOC "is designed to perform battle management and command and control of a space constellation under threat of attack. It has to fight through those attacks and provide the space support that the joint force relies upon."

He added, "We've never had something like that before because we've never needed something like that before but it is the first step in the Third Offset to start to readdress and to extend our margin of operational superiority."

After his visit, Carter described space as a domain that must be the province of warfighters and not just engineers.

"JICSpOC is about combining the operators with the space community -- the DoD space community and the intelligence community, which operates very important space systems," Carter said. "… What the JICSpOC is doing is asking itself how we would change the way [the Global Positioning System] operated if the GPS constellation came under threat or attack, electromagnetic or physical attack."

Offsetting What?

As early as 2012, Work said, DoD started thinking about a Third Offset Strategy simply to restore the margin of operational and tactical advantage that underwrites conventional deterrence.

In response to the question, "Offsetting what?" the deputy secretary makes a list.

"Most of our combat power is in the United States. We no longer have large concentrations of forces in theaters [where] they might fight [giving] our potential adversaries an initial advantage in time and space and probably numbers," he said.

Second, great-power competitors now have achieved rough guided-munitions parity with the United States, something the nation hasn't had to deal with in quite some time, Work added.

Third, he said, adversaries "know how important and how powerful our networks are so they spend an awful lot of money to pay for counter-network technologies such as electronic warfare, cyber and counter-space because they know how central the space constellation was to the second offset" in the 1970s to the 1990s.

AI and Autonomy

Achieving the Third Offset depends on taking the advice of the Defense Science Board, whose members surveyed a range of technologies and determined that improving the battle network's performance meant exploiting advances in artificial intelligence and autonomy, allowing the joint force to assemble and operate advanced joint collaborative human-machine battle networks of even greater power, Work said.

"We believe strongly that this will help restore the margin of operational superiority and strengthen conventional deterrence," he added.

The five key technologies described by the deputy defense secretary are as follows:

-- Learning machines;

-- Human-machine collaboration, which Work said means using advanced computers and visualization to help people make faster, better and more relevant decisions;

-- Assisted human operations, which means plugging every pilot, soldier, sailor and Marine into the battle network;

-- Human-machine combat teaming, creating new ways for manned and unmanned platforms to operate; and

-- Network-enabled autonomous weapons, he said, all connected on a learning command, control, communications and intelligence, or C3I, network.

"We believe this vision is very well-matched for an evolving era of technological dynamism as well as warfare where challenges are multidomain and multifunctional and operations -- especially cyber, electronic warfare and guided-munition salvos -- move at high speeds," Work said.

"These speeds are going to shrink the human-based [observe, orient, decide and act] loop and we're going to have to go after these technologies to fight fire with fire and buy back the time for our [people] to make decisions that will allow us to prevail at the tactical and operational levels of war," he added.

Emerging Constructs

Work said that new operational constructs are emerging not only from the Air Force but from the Army and the Navy.

The Army's new operational construct is the concept of multidomain battle, he said, and the Navy has introduced an idea called electromagnetic maneuver.

In an introduction to a 2016 Naval War College Review reading posted to the Army Capabilities Integration Center website, **Army Lt. Gen. H.R. McMaster**, deputy commanding general-futures at the Army's Training and Doctrine Command, wrote that multidomain battle is cross-domain operations in the context of joint combined arms maneuver that creates temporary windows of superiority across multiple domains, and allows joint forces to seize, retain and exploit the initiative.

An unclassified briefing called A Cooperative Strategy for 21st Century Seapower presented in March 2015 characterized electromagnetic maneuver as the Navy's warfighting approach to gaining military advantage in the electromagnetic spectrum, or EMS, to enable freedom of action across all Navy mission areas.

The approach would let the Navy understand and control signatures, command the EMS as critical maneuver space, and use the EMS to deliver integrated fires, according to the briefing.

To the Air Force, the deputy secretary described a specific area where airmen could naturally help advance third offset thinking and serve the joint force.

"We need ideas about how to connect sensing and effect grids through a command and control grid that is multidomain, multifunctional and coalition friendly," Work said.

"We need Air Force thinkers to expand the idea of the [combined air operations center] and think in terms of building a joint learning C3I network that can mesh operations across domains, across functions, with allies and sometimes across regions," he added.

"All have the potential to once again transform the way the joint force fights," Work said.

* * * * * * * * * * * *

Deputy Secretary of Defense Speech

Army War College Strategy Conference

As Delivered by Deputy Secretary of Defense Bob Work, U.S. Army War College, Carlisle, PA, April 8, 2015

It's great to be here this beautiful Susquehanna Valley – and visiting Carlisle Barracks, which is the cradle, in my view, of Army strategic thought, the Army War College.

Now, the theme of this year's conference is exactly the right one, "First Principles for 21st Century Defense." It's especially apt. That's exactly what the entire Department right now is trying to do. We're wrestling to try to figure out what the future shape and structure of our Joint Force is going to be because we want to make sure that we get those principles right that will shape what our force will look like.

And one of the first principles of successful innovation for any military organization is correctly identifying those specific future challenges that demand solving today, and then making the right adjustments and changes to get after it. Hopefully, he's right. Sometimes, he'll choose wrong. But if we do choose right, then you've set yourselves up to be among the best competitors in the future landscape.

So I want to begin today by discussing some of the trends we're seeing on today's battlefield. And I'd like to focus my comments this morning, especially as they pertain to our ground forces. Because as we go about developing new operational concepts and new capabilities, it's important to understand what our future ground forces may be up against.

Now, it's also important for everyone in this room to know and everyone in the Department of Defense to know that the pace of strategic change that we see right now, which Gen. Odierno calls the velocity of instability, and the pace of technological innovation that's going on, primarily in the commercial sector, will not allow us to simply graft incremental changes upon our existing operational and organizational constructs with which we are familiar and comfortable with.

I cannot overstate the sense of urgency that our new Secretary of Defense, Ashton Carter, has right now. There is a clock in his head. It's ticking down. And he shares the sense of urgency, and he is determined to really try to make some significant and lasting changes over the next two years. And he is intent on talking about the big strategic issues that face us and make the big changes necessary to prepare ourselves for them.

Now, one of the big strategic issues facing us is going to be the nature and character of future ground warfare. Now, as you all know too well, in the last 13 years, the United States military has focused intensely on fighting an irregular warfare campaign and counterterrorism operation in both Iraq and Afghanistan and now back to Iraq and Syria.

And our ground forces undoubtedly have honed their skills in these two particular areas. And it's important that all of us retain these skills because it is certainly possible, as has just been demonstrated in Iraq and Syria, and even probable that we are going to fight similar campaigns in the future.

But if the streets of Baghdad and the valleys of Afghanistan were a laboratory for irregular warfare, I believe that ground forces will increasingly need to prepare for future hybrid war, which my good friend Frank Hoffman, who I see in the audience today, defines as combat operations characterized by the simultaneous and adaptive employment of a complex combination of conventional weapons, irregular warfare, terrorism and criminal behavior to achieve political objectives.

Now, we all caught a vivid glimpse of what hybrid warfare is all about in 2006, when the Israeli Defense Forces (IDF) battled Hezbollah. Now, Hezbollah had gone to school on the IDF, without question. They transformed themselves from a purely guerrilla organization to a formidable quasi-conventional righting force that for a short period of time was able to fight the IDF to a standstill.

In earlier wars, the IDF had demonstrated their mastery of high-tempo combined arms operations. In the 1973 Yom Kippur War, in the face of swarms of anti-tank guided munitions and advanced air defenses, they countered those threats by combining artillery suppression with mechanized infantry and armored forces, and they unhinged the entire Egyptian integrated air defense system through combined arms maneuvers.

But as many of you know, especially here in the Army in our heavy forces, in our mechanized forces, these skills are very perishable. And over the course of the Second Intifada which lasted from 2000 to 2006, the Israeli army started to focus almost exclusively on irregular warfare. Dave Johnson from RAND in a study, estimated that in the years leading up to the 2006 Lebanese war, the IDF trained for high-intensity combat only about 25 percent of the time. The remainder of their time, they focused on irregular warfare and counterterrorism operations.

As a result, when the IDF crossed swords with Hezbollah, they were caught by surprise. Hezbollah – fighters were armed with advanced anti-tank missiles, thousands of long-range rockets, Chinese-made Silkworm anti-ship missiles, advanced man-portable anti-air missiles, and unmanned aerial vehicles (UAVs). They had very simplistic, but very effective battle networks to employ them. They practiced irregular warfare, but at the same time maneuvered effectively against Israeli armored columns, proved proficient in indirect fire, and they used swarms of heavy anti-tank missiles to great effect.

In the future, without question, hybrid adversaries will pose a qualitative and quantitative challenge. But they probably will be smaller, but like Hezbollah, they will be disciplined, organized, have effective command and control, and will be equipped with standoff weapons with large quantities. As Gen. McMaster has described it, "These state-sponsored adversaries are small in number, moderately trained, and often decentralized. But what they lack in manpower, they make up for in fire power." Hezbollah showed us that defeating hybrid adversaries will demand entirely different skills than those needed for counterinsurgency. It is important that we do not forget that.

Now, being prepped for irregular warfare and hybrid warfare will be challenging enough for our nation's ground forces. But there is no rest for the weary, I fear, because our land warriors must now also consider the operational and organizational constructs to fight wars like we have seen in Crimea and Ukraine.

In both places, the Russians have unleashed what their chief of the general staff called "non-linear warfare," which evolves from covert actions by special operations forces, to sustained unconventional combat waged under an umbrella of denial. And then ultimately escalating to high-end force-on-force proxy warfare with the state actively involved in combat operations.

What's so challenging about this type of war is that in a straight up conventional fight that we all are kind of familiar with, the avenues of approach are often very well understood. Think of the Fulda Gap on the inter-German border. By contrast, non-linear adversaries make those avenues harder to detect, using agents, paramilitaries, deception, infiltration, and persistent denial to make those avenues of approach very hard to detect, operating in what some people have called "the gray zone."

Now, that's the zone in which our ground forces have not traditionally had to operate, but one in which they must now become more proficient. But as difficult and challenging as the gray zone will be, it will pale in comparison when that type of conflict then escalates from the shadowy actions of "fifth-columnists" and "little green men," to state-sponsored and state-directed hybrid proxy war.

Now, as we saw in Ukraine, the state-backed proxy separatists have access to advanced capabilities, provided in some cases by the state to the separatists, and in some cases operated by the state itself, can quickly ratchet up a conflict's intensity to a point that is largely indistinguishable from high end warfare. Today in Ukraine, Russian-backed separatists resemble Hezbollah on steroids. They're backed by modern fire and counter-fire capability that the Army and the Marine Corps simply has not had to consider since the end of the Cold War.

Historically, as you all know, artillery has been the biggest killer on the battlefield, and that is proving once again to be the case in Ukraine. Separatist forces use advanced counter-battery radar to accurately pinpoint Ukrainian fires capability and command and control. They use UAVs to identify targets Ukrainian commanders are telling us that within minutes of coming up on the radio, they were targeted by precise artillery strikes. As Lt. Gen. Ben Hodges, commander of U.S. Army Europe, told an Army audience last week, none of us have ever been under -- as massive as a Russian artillery attack in the way that Ukraine -- the Ukrainians have.

Now, making matters much worse. In addition to this new era of precision and guided fires, Russian-backed separatists and their state sponsors were very definitely using advanced electronic warfare equipment, which we were just trying to understand how effective they were in jamming GPS frequencies, command and control networks. And these technologies are proliferating as widely as conventional guided munitions.

So in the future, U.S. Army and U.S. Marine forces and our allies that fight with us, are going to have to fight on a battlefield that is swept by precision-guided munitions, but also one that is swept by persistent and effective cyber and electronic warfare attacks.

So how's that for a daunting list of challenges? Irregular warfare, hybrid warfare, non-linear warfare, state-sponsored hybrid warfare, and high-end combined arms warfare, like we might see on the Korean peninsula.

But how do we best prepare for all of these threats? Well, first thing is to get down first principles. Now, one is in my view that future ground warfare, regardless of type, is going to see a proliferation of guided munitions and advanced weaponry. We should just assume that is the case.

If we're wrong – so much the better. If we're right, we better be prepared for it. And this proliferation of precision will continue because we see it continuing today. So our ground forces are going to be faced with what many people call G-RAMM -- guided rockets, artillery, mortars and missiles, with GPS and laser guidance, infrared homing, anti-radiation weapons and fire-and-forget anti-armor weapons.

We're not too far away from guided .50 caliber rounds – we're not too far away from a sensor-fused weapon, and instead of going after tanks, we'll go after the biometric signature of human beings. Now, our air and naval forces have been faced with fighting and a guided-munitions regime for decades. Our ground forces will now have their chance to do so, and it is a formidable challenge that we have to prepare for.

Second principle of the future as a ground combat on the front lines is going to have to contend with what the Chinese call "informationalized warfare". This is the combination of cyber, electronic warfare, information ops, deception and denial to disrupt our command and control to give the enemy an advantage in the decision cycle.

At the National Training Center (NTC), if our decisive-action rotations are not being faced by a sophisticated EW and cyber threat, then we are shortchanging the men and women that are going to have to fight on future battlefields.

So the third principle, this is the combination of guided munitions and informationalized warfare, will span all types of ground combat, a regular, hybrid, nonlinear, state proxy and high-end combined-arms warfare. And that means, like the Israelis found out, that the foundation for ground force excellence is going to be combined-arms operational skill. It's no wonder right now that the IDF has flipped the script, and 80 percent of their training time is now spent on combined-arms warfare, because it is proven to be effective against all the different types of adversaries that the IDF has had to face.

It's also why we applaud the fact that the U.S. Army will not declare its BCTs full-spectrum combat-ready until they have completed two decisive-action rotations at the National Training Center. Now, I believe that the threats that we portray to our forces going through the NTC rotations has to change and has to more reflect what we think they might see on the battlefield. But as the IDF experience tells us, we simply cannot let our excellence and combined-arms operations slip away.

Now, training is only going to take us so far, using the operational and organizational constructs that we are familiar with. We are going to have to go about identifying these new operational and organizational constructs and technological capabilities in a deliberate fashion. And that is what the Defense Innovation Initiative is all about. Now, although it was announced in November, Secretary Carter has expanded it, and he wants the Department focused on three things.

He wants us to focus on increasing our competitiveness by attracting talent. And this is a broad idea, talking about the future of the all-volunteer force, the way we train our people, the way we train our leaders, as well as the future civilian and contractor force that supports us. He wants to improve our competitiveness through technological superiority and operational excellence. And that's what we're talking about primarily here today. And the third thing he wants to do is increase our competitiveness through accountability and efficiency throughout the Department and the way we going about doing our business, finding new technologies, fielding them and using them.

And a key part of the DII, the Defense Innovation Initiative, is what you might've heard a lot of people talking about: the Third Offset Strategy. It's probably even more accurate to say Third Offset Strategies, because unlike in the past when we were faced with a single monolithic competitor, like the Soviet Union, we're going to be faced with a plethora of different types of competitors, and each of the strategies that we pursue against them might be different.

But they will be -- the whole purpose of the Third Offset Strategy or Strategies is to identify the technologies, identify the operational and organizational constructs, the new operational concepts to fight our future adversaries. Now, unquestionably, a big part of this is going to be identifying, developing and fielding breakthrough technologies, in addition to using the capabilities we have now in a different way. So we just demonstrated firing the Tomahawk land attack cruise missile against a ship, without changing its seeker-head, completely doing it by off-board sensing. Well, now we have 2,000 potential thousand-mile range anti-ship missiles.

It is using the weapons that we have differently, as well as looking for these breakthrough technologies that are going to provide our troops with a competitive advantage. And one of the things that places like the Army War College can do is to think about this in a strategic way, and how we ought to approach looking after these technologies and the technologies we field that will provide us with an enduring advantage.

Now, I am often accused of being too technologically oriented. Well, the only thing I can say is that since World War II, American military strategy and our entire national defense strategy has been built upon an assumption of technological superiority, and the better-trained individual -- individuals, men and women, organized to employ these technologies in an innovative way. I like the way Dwight Eisenhower explained it after World War II. He said, "While some of our allies were compelled to throw up a wall of flesh and blood as their chief defense against the aggressor's onslaught, we were able to use machines and technology to save lives."

Now, during the Cold War, we pursued two broad technological offset strategies to counter Soviet conventional authority. The first one was laid on top of a conscript force. It relied upon nuclear weapons. We did not want to conscript enough people to numerically match 175 Soviet divisions, so we explicitly decided to rely upon tactical nuclear weapons as an offset for numbers. In the 1970s, when the Soviets achieved strategic nuclear parity with the United States and the threat of tactical nuclear warfare was too great, was no longer an effective deterrent, we changed sites and we went after what was then called conventional weapons with near-zero CEP, or conventional error probability -- what everybody knows today as smart guided munitions.

That was on top of an all-volunteer force in which we said we will explicitly choose a smaller, all-volunteer, highly trained professional force using advanced technologies to offset Soviet conventional advantage. But please don't confuse my attention to technology with my inattention to the human domain of combat. I was commissioned in 1974, the year before we introduced the all-volunteer force. So when I arrived in Okinawa in July of 1975, the last conscript had washed out of the U.S. military and we were an all-volunteer force.

Between 1975 and 1981, I can tell you, and anyone who was on active duty at that time can tell you, moving to the all-volunteer force was not a sure thing. Quite frankly, three years in, I wasn't certain it was going to work. And it was because of the people dimension. Sure, we were getting the M1A1 tank. We were buying the F-15. We were buying the F-117 Stealth Fighter. We were doing all sorts of things technologically sound.

But I've got to tell you, I went to sleep at night not knowing if we were going to be able to swing it because the quality of the people that we had between 1975 and 1981 was nowhere near where we needed to be to make the all-volunteer force and the second technological offset strategy work.

So after 40 years, I assume and I am confident in my assumption that we have an enduring advantage in our people, that I will stack this all-volunteer force up against any potential opponent and especially those that are authoritarian in nature, because they will never, ever be able to match the creativity, the initiative, the mission drive that our people have. So I assume that superiority.

But I'm telling you right now our technological superiority is slipping. We see it every day. And that is why I talk about it so much. But please do not think that my time and attention on technology in any way, shape, or form keeps me not focused on making sure we retain the best people that we can possibly get. The fact is we want to achieve an over-match over any adversary from the operational theater level, all the way down to the fighter plane, Navy ship or infantry squad. As General Dempsey has often said, we never, ever want to send our troops into a fair fight.

So it's all about innovation, it's all about staying ahead of potential adversaries. It's all about questioning our comfortable assumptions and asking whether things that have worked in the past for us are going to work in the future. And if we say they won't we have better have the courage to do something about it.

So this is all about trying to find new ways of fighting. It's all about to find new ways of training. It's all about trying to find new organizational constructs. The American way of war that we've grown accustomed to over the past three decades -- and believe me, we have had three decades of relative bounty.

All of the potential regional conventional adversaries we've had to think about were generally far inferior to our own capabilities. But in the same time, just like Hezbollah, our enemies have gone to school on us at least since 1991 Desert Storm. And they have adapted with a vengeance. They spent the past few decades investing heavily in capabilities that counter our own. And you hear a lot about anti-access area denial at the theater level, but they have been investing as heavily has Hezbollah did at the tactical level.

Now as any good student of Clausewitz knows, the fundamental nature of war is an interactive clash of wills. It's a two-sided dual. Any action we take is going to cause a reaction to the enemy, which will cause our reaction to that reaction. Battlefield advantages in the future are going to be very short-lived, because the amount of technology that is going out there right now is unbelievable. And different adversaries will pick technologies in ways that will surprise us. Without question, we have to be very, very adaptable.

As Professor Conrad Crane of the Education and Heritage Center has famously said, there are two ways our enemies will fight us, asymmetrically or stupidly. And we can rest assured, that they will not choose stupidly.

And since our potential adversaries have adapted, we have to do the same. And that's what the Defense Innovation Initiative and the Third Offset Strategy is all about. We want to confront our adversaries with multiple dilemmas and relying on one service or two services or mastering one domain, operational domain, is destined to fail because of this range of threats that we see, because a thinking adversary is always going to develop a counter.

And what don't want to cede any domain. And that last point is important, because I don't want the enemies to think that we are overly focused on one domain or one type of way of fighting that they will be able to block us. So the real essence of the third offset strategy is to find multiple different attacks against opponents across all domains so they can't adapt or they adjust to just one, and they died before they can adapt again.

Now, that's, kind of, at the strategic level. Let me just give you three examples.

The thing that's kicked off the second offset strategy was an ACTD -- an advance capability and technology demonstration called Assault Breaker. The United States Army had adopted active defense. After the 1973 Yom Kippur War, active defense was going to be a guided munitions fight right on the FEBA -- the forward edge of the battle area.

And we were going to try to stop the penetration of Soviet forces by out-missiling them; by using TOWs, Copperheads, and Apaches. Well, the Soviets fought in echelons, and that wasn't going to work. Active defense was a failure. And luckily enough, leaders in the Army recognized it. And they said, "We are going to have to start to go after the second and the third echelon before it reaches the FEBA or we will lose."

And the Assault Breaker technology demonstration was designed to show that sensors, coupled with long-range guided munitions, conventional guided munitions, would be able to break up the assault and therefore make the guided munition exchange at the FLOT, forward line of troops, we were going to win.

And sure enough, the Soviets cranked their models after seeing this demonstration, and they said, "You know what? Conventional weapons with near-zero miss will achieve the tactical effectiveness of tactical nuclear weapons." And the game was over for them. And they could not compete in that domain.

Well, now a whole lot of our enemies have guided munitions also. And they are going to be able to throw guided munition salvos as dense as our own and sometimes over long range. So what we need to be thinking about right now is raid breaker because the competitor who can demonstrate the ability to defeat the guided munitions salvo competition is going to have a unique advantage at the operational level of war.

Now, you're saying: Why are you telling me this? We always think about THAAD and PAC-3 missiles. That's all going to be great. But now what we need to be thinking about is electromagnetic railguns and powder guns. Right now, every Paladin that the Army owns might be a very effective counter-swarm weapon by combining the smart projectiles with our hyper-velocity guns, our electromagnetic railguns, using the exact same rounds, and advance computing. All of the modeling right now is telling us that every single Army artillery piece using powder guns, using these advanced guided munitions, will be able to knock down heavy missile raids.

Now, what that means for us is the electromagnetic railgun is going to provide us deep magazines and high volumes of shots. It's going to change the cost-imposing strategy on its head. Right now, we're firing $14 million missiles to go after a $50,000 missile. It doesn't make sense. But when you have electromagnetic railguns and powder guns, using the same smart projectiles, now you can start to break the raid.

And what Paladin will provide the Joint Force is a mobile raid-breaking capability. We've already demonstrated this on the Navy's five-inch guns. This summer, we're going to demonstrate it on the Paladins. It's something the Army needs to think about. The Army, with its THAAD and its PAC-3s and potentially Paladins in the future will be the mobile raid-breaker for the Joint Force.

Now, a lot of this is talking about A2/AD, because enemies will try to keep us out of theater. But the thing that you all have to realize is in many instances, we will take the first salvo simply because we will not initiate combat. So Raid-Breaker for the Army is as important for the Army as it's important for the Navy and the Air Force.

But once we break into theater, we're going to have to think about AirLand Battle 2.0. We are going to have to think about fighting against enemies which have lots of guided rockets, artillery, mortars and missiles, and are using informationalized warfare to completely disrupt our heavily netted force. So what does AirLand Battle 2.0 look like? I don't know. The Army needs to figure this out.

And they need to be having experiments, like they had on the Louisiana Maneuvers, and then they have to transport it over to the National Training Center, and then they have to inculcate it into the force. Here is what I believe. It is a hypothesis.

Tyler Cowen wrote a book called "Average is Over." He's an avid chess player. What he said was, "It used to be a matter of faith that a machine would never beat a human," because a machine would not have the intuitive cognition. You know, it just wouldn't be able to have the intuitive spark to think through an interactive dual like chess. That proved to be wrong. Now machines consistently beat grandmasters. And what he found out in a thing called three-play chess is the combination of a man and a machine always beats the machine and always beats the man.

I believe that what the Third Offset Strategy will revolve around will be three-play combat in each dimension. And three-play combat will be much different in each dimension, and it will be up for the people who live and fight in that dimension to figure out the rules.

We will have autonomy at rest, our smart systems, being able to go through big data to help at the campaign level and to be able to go through big data at the tactical level. So autonomy at rest and autonomy in motion. And I will tell you right that autonomy in motion on the human domain is the hardest nut to crack. Just getting robots to move over terrain is one of the most difficult things that you can imagine. Much, much more difficult than either in space, in air or on the sea or under the sea.

So how far do we take three-play combat in AirLand Battle 2.0? How does it affect our command and control? Where are we comfortable having autonomous decision-making? Where are you going to have man in the loop? How will you net all of this together to give you a decisive, enduring advantage on the battlefield? This, I think, is the fundamental challenge for organizations like the Army War College to think this through and to give us some ideas.

I talked about the kind of strategy level, this whole idea of having to go against guided munitions, and I talked about AirLand Battle. But it will come all the way down to the squad level, and the squads are going to be operating far more disaggregated than they've had in the past.

When I went to Afghanistan to visit Marine units, I asked General Joe Dunford, "Fighting Joe" Dunford, "What is the record for the disaggregation of a single infantry battalion across the battlefield"? And he told me that the record was a single battalion disaggregating itself into 77 discreet units spread over a wide area. That's astounding to me. A single-infantry battalion disaggregating to 77 different units. That means, in some cases we'll have to go to smaller than squads. But that has a big, big implication for leadership, command and control, especially in an informationalized warfare environment in which the enemy is constantly trying to get into your networks and disrupt your command and control.

So the key to ensuring that these aggregated small units have overmatch by providing support in fires, intelligence and logistics. And if we combine them into well-trained, cohesive combat teams with new advances in robotics and autonomy and unmanned systems, three-play combat at the squad level, we can create super-empowered squads, super-empowered small units with enhanced situational awareness and lethality.

DARPA's Squad X program, among others, is working on a number of ideas right now to increase human and machine collaboration at the lowest tactical level, including ground robots, small micro-drones, and trying to figure out how to push the squad situational awareness and lethality out to a large, large battlespace area.

And this is not as far away as you might think. The Army is -- right now is kind of leading the way in manned and unmanned teaming with the Apache in the shadows, which is going on in the Army's Aviation Restructure Initiative, which we think is exciting and kind of a leading indicator of where we need to go.

Automated driving seemed like the work of fiction not long ago, but there's a race going on between big-tech companies and some of the larger auto makers who are looking to develop self-driving cars. So, in the not-too-distant future, squads are going to operate with robotic support, sapper robots, counter-mine robots, counter-sniper robots. And much of this technology is going to come from the commercial sector.

This is an exciting time for the force. We spend far too much time worrying about sequestration. Now, do I think sequestration is stupid? I absolutely do. Do I think there's a 50/50 chance we might see sequestration? Unfortunately, I would say yeah. Maybe even a little better than 50/50. Because I'm not certain that Congress is going to figure out how to de-trigger it.

There are positive signs. But we spend far too much time worrying about that, and not enough time worrying about this. Because it doesn't matter how much money we have. This problem requires thinking. And we need to tackle it together, and not worry so much about the resources as the intellectual capital that we need to put in the bank to allow our joint force to be so successful in the future.

You know, I tell everybody -- you've heard -- probably many of you have heard me say this. In fact, I've said it so many times, I went to a speech and somebody else said it. You know, I sleep like a baby every night. I wake up crying every two hours.

But the thing that always allows me to go back to bed is, one, the incredible advantage we have in our people. That is the thing that I'm most confident -- I am most confident saying that we have an enduring competitive advantage. We can screw it up. We better not. But that is a place that always says we're going to be able to figure this out. And I know with people like you in this room, and all of the people that you represent -- whether it's in the Army, the Navy, the Air Force, the Marine Corps, the Coast Guard or our allies, we can figure this out, but we have to get after it. And I look forward to doing that with you over the next couple of years.

Thank you.

* * * * * * * * * * *

HERBERT R. (H.R.) McMASTER, JR.

* * * * * * * * * * *

Biography: Major General H. R. McMaster

Commanding General, U.S. Army Maneuver Center of Excellence

Major General H. R. McMaster assumed command of the MCoE and Fort Benning on 13 June 2012. Prior to his arrival at Fort Benning he most recently served as Commander, Combined Joint Inter-Agency Task Force Shafafiyat (Transparency) in Kabul, Afghanistan. Previously he served as Director of Concept Development and Learning at the U.S. Army Training and Doctrine Command. He was commissioned as an officer in the United States Army upon graduation from the United States Military Academy in 1984. He holds a PhD in military history from the University of North Carolina at Chapel Hill.

McMaster's previous command assignments include Eagle Troop, Second Armored Cavalry Regiment in Bamberg, Germany and in Southwest Asia during the 1991 Persian Gulf War; 1st Squadron, 4th Cavalry in Schweinfurt Germany from 1999 to 2002; and 3d Armored Cavalry Regiment at Fort Carson, Colorado and in Iraq from June 2004 to June 2006. Staff assignments include special assistant to Commander, Multinational Force-Iraq from February 2007 to May 2008; director, Commander's Advisory Group at US Central Command from May 2003 to 2004; and squadron executive officer and regimental operations officer in the 11th Armored Cavalry Regiment from July 1997 to July 1999. He also served as an assistant professor of history at the United States Military Academy from 1994 to 1996.

McMaster's military education and training includes the Airborne and Ranger Schools, Armor Officer Basic and Career Courses, the Cavalry Leaders Course, the U.S. Army Command and General Staff College, and a U.S. Army War College fellowship at the Hoover Institution on War, Revolution, and Peace. McMaster has also served as a senior consulting fellow at the International Institute of Strategic Studies in London.

* * * * * * * * * * * *

Made in the USA
San Bernardino, CA
03 September 2018